ADVANCE PRAISE FOR

Women's Work, the Family, & Social Policy

"Looking beyond their borders, in recent decades individual European countries have had to rethink socio-economic norms in light of the supranational project of European integration. Closer to home, these countries must now look into their homes, their offices and their domestic markets to address the growing socio-economic impact of women in the work force. Focussing on the exemplary case of Italy, this excellent collection presents valuable data and insightful analysis of national and supranational dilemmas posed for the workplace, the family, and the economy by the growing and varied presence of women in the workforce." - *Sima Godfrey, Director, Institute of European Studies, University of British Columbia*

"This book includes contributions by leading researchers in Italian academia and the Bank of Italy, specializing in the condition of women at home and in the labour market. The economic contributions give us interesting insights into the link between fertility and labour market participation of women, and between the latter and the employment status of their husbands. The only sociological contribution argues that Italian women have made considerable progress towards equality with men in the legal and economic sphere, but have still some way to go. The abundant comparative material allows the reader to place the Italian case in its European context." - *Professor Alessandro Cigno, University of Firenze, Department of State Studies*

Women's Work, the Family, & Social Policy

STUDIES IN EUROPEAN UNION

Margherita Repetto-Alaia
General Editor

Vol. 2

PETER LANG
New York • Washington, D.C./Baltimore • Bern
Frankfurt am Main • Berlin • Brussels • Vienna • Oxford

Women's Work, the Family, & Social Policy

Focus on Italy in a European Perspective

EDITED BY
Daniela Del Boca
& Margherita Repetto-Alaia

PETER LANG
New York • Washington, D.C./Baltimore • Bern
Frankfurt am Main • Berlin • Brussels • Vienna • Oxford

Library of Congress Cataloging-in-Publication Data

Women's work, the family, and social policy: focus on Italy in a European
perspective / edited by Daniela Del Boca and Margherita Repetto-Alaia.
  p. cm. — (Studies in European union; vol. 2)
Includes bibliographical references.
1. Women—Employment—Italy. 2. Family—Italy.
I. Del Boca, Daniela. II. Repetto-Alaia, Margherita.
HD6154 .W66   331.4'0945—dc21   2001034680
ISBN 0-8204-2564-8
ISSN 1094-6209

Die Deutsche Bibliothek-CIP-Einheitsaufnahme

Women's work, the family, and social policy: focus on Italy in a European
perspective / ed. by: Daniela Del Boca and Margherita Repetto-Alaia.
–New York; Washington, D.C./Baltimore; Bern;
Frankfurt am Main; Berlin; Brussels; Vienna; Oxford: Lang.
(Studies in European union; Vol. 2)
ISBN 0-8204-2564-8

© 2003 Peter Lang Publishing, Inc., New York
275 Seventh Avenue, 28th Floor, New York, NY 10001
www.peterlangusa.com

All rights reserved.
Reprint or reproduction, even partially, in all forms such as microfilm,
xerography, microfiche, microcard, and offset strictly prohibited.

CONTENTS

	Daniela Del Boca and Margherita Repetto-Alaia Editorial Foreword	vii
Chapter 1.	Chiara Saraceno Changes in Italian Families, from the Sixties to the Present	1
Chapter 2.	Daniela Del Boca Labor Market Participation and Fertility of Italian Women: A Comparative Perspective	33
Chapter 3.	Stefania Rossetti, Paola Tanda Human Capital, Gender, and Labor Market Performances	48
Chapter 4.	Daniela Del Boca, Marilena Locatelli, Silvia Pasqua Earnings and Employment of Italian Husbands and Wives in the European Context	65
Chapter 5.	Tindara Addabbo "Atypical" Work in Italy in a Gender Perspective: The Case of Parasubordinates and Part-Timers	83
Chapter 6.	Lia Fubini Women's Unemployment in Italy	109
Chapter 7.	Renata Livraghi Economic Aspects of Families and Generational Employment Patterns in Italy	124

Chapter 8. Andrea Brandolini, Giovanni D'Alessio
Household Structure and Income Inequality in
Italy: A Comparative European Perspective   148

List of Contributors   193

DANIELA DEL BOCA

MARGHERITA REPETTO-ALAIA EDS.

EDITORIAL FOREWORD

The project leading to the publication of this volume originated with an international symposium that took place at Columbia University in New York a decade ago. The symposium was organized by the Italian Cultural Institute in New York and the Italian Academy for Advanced Studies in America at Columbia University, and was hosted at the School for International Affairs of the University. The symposium addressed women's issues, especially those of working women, from the viewpoint of social policy measures which had been enacted during the preceding two decades or had been the object of debate both in the United States and in the European Communities. The symposium, entitled "Women and Social Policy in Comparative Perspective: with Special Attention to the European Communities", included a number of women scholars, researchers, experts, activists, policy makers, elected representatives and heads of agencies from Italy and the United States, from European member countries (Germany, Spain), from the European Commission, and from the European elected institutions. The papers presented were informative and passionate, all conveying that special mix of militant fervor and professional expertise that characterized the previous two decades of the "women's movement" in Europe and in North America.

The presentations covered many issues, exploring women's status from diverse angles such as women in politics, women in management, effectiveness and leadership of women in society, legislation on sexual harassment and crimes against women, equal opportunity for women in education and employment. The latter subject—equal opportunity—received special attention relating to Europe and the United States. The implementing of legislation which had been passed in the previous ten or fifteen years in the United States and in European countries was being very closely scrutinized in both continents. Where the European Communities were concerned, an ad hoc report was read at the Symposium by the head of the special unit established within the Directorate-General of Employment and Social Affairs of the European Commission. While progress in implementing the law was being appraised in different fields and countries, the social approach revealing the dynamics resulting from change taking place in the status of women proved more interesting and most deserving of further investigation. The complex interaction between family and society, which holds at its core woman's role, is destined to react to every minimal shift in the way the role is redesigned as a result of cultural and economic forces in play. Women, work and family, the dilemmas of social policy dealing with the interfacing of all factors, and the impact on the economy at large, fuelled fruitful and passionate debate at the Symposium.

When a decision about materials for the proceedings had to be made, choice favoured a collection of essays tackling socio-economic issues. The idea of putting together a volume comparing Europe and the United States was abandoned, although that had been the initial inspiration behind the symposium. The reason for this was that the papers dealing with the situation in the United States, though indeed stimulating to comparative discussion, were intended to touch on specific aspects—sexual harassment, equal opportunity and positive action, child care—rather than provide ground for understanding the two situations, one in Europe and one in the United States, which differed so much in terms of the nature of the forces at play. Since most of the structured presentations were rooted in the Italian situation, the choice was made in favour of a volume of essays focussing on the Italian situation in a comparative perspective with other European countries. This required calling for additional papers by scholars and experts who had participated in the Symposium or, in some cases, by others who could not be present at that time but would qualify as valuable contributors. In the course of this gathering process, which was made lengthier by changes occurring in the personal and professional lives of some of the key players in the original project, and among them this editor (I have become an adoptive mother twice since then), the attention in dealing with issues regarding women, work and the family has considerably shifted everywhere from the institutional perspective to one based on the dynamics of the economy and of individual and collective behaviour induced by it. Thus the present volume, as described in this same foreword by Daniela Del Boca, co-editor and contributor—and herself a participant in the Symposium held in New York—allows for an analytical view of the interplay between institutional and regulatory policies and strategies put to work by women and families against the backdrop of an economy which has been increasingly dominated by market forces of accelerating globalization hardly imaginable a decade ago.

As chair of the Steering Committee of the International Symposium described early on, it is my task to acknowledge the support provided then by many institutions, human and financial resources and logistical support. Inasmuch as the present volume is in many ways the ultimate result of that endeavour—and especially so regarding the funding set aside for publication—special recognition is due to the two institutions which stood behind the project from the beginning, i.e. the Italian Academy for Advanced Studies in America at Columbia University and its director at the time, Professor Maristella Lorch, and the Italian Cultural Institute in New York and its director then, Dr. Furio Colombo. Other institutions which provided help in different ways, including financial, in making possible both the Symposium and this publication should also be mentioned: the Electric Power Authority (ENEL) of Italy, the Helena Rubinstein Foundation in New York, the Delegation of the Commission of the European Communities (as it was called at the time) in Washington, D.C., the Institute for Research on Women and Gender in New York and its President Mariam K. Chamberlain.

As everyone knows, the European scenery has undergone major changes in the past decade. The process of European integration, especially the process of economic and financial integration, has responded to many challenges that at the time were only looming in the background and that were often quoted with open scepticism by many commentators and opinion makers, especially on the American side of the Atlantic. I believe that the essays in the volume are helpful also in this respect, that they give a real contribution to understanding how far the *social integration* of the Continent has actually progressed by showing a picture where the agents at work are as real as they could be, women, men, children, husbands and wives, families, the "human capital", as one of the essays defines it, with a terminology deserving due consideration for the weight it implicitly carries.

Margherita Repetto-Alaia

The essays comprised in this book revolve around the issues of women's work, the family and social policies in Italy. The analyses presented here focus on the changes of women employment and unemployment, the interactions with family behaviour in productive and reproductive activities in last three decades. The Italian situation is analysed in a comparative approach with particular attention to the European Union.

The authors analyse several important dimensions of women's work, the motivations and consequences of the changes in trends of women's employment, and the interrelationships with the institutions governing the labor market and social system.

Why do women work? What is the impact of increasing education, the pattern of male/female wage differentials on women's attitudes to work and the fertility behavior? How recent Italian social policies have supported women's strategies to conciliate work and children? And finally how has women's labor market participation affected families' income and income distribution?

Chiara Saraceno traces the relationship between women's changing behavior in the labor market and families from the sixties to the nineties. These changes in behaviors and attitudes brought about during the seventies movements which advocated reforms that were aimed to provide protective legislation concerning working women especially in terms of rights of working mothers. However the Italian family is still today left to perform essential roles of compensating for the lack of appropriate social services (especially for children and the elderly) as well as for the lack of transfers to unemployed youth.

Daniela Del Boca explores how characteristics of the rigidities in the labor market, the social service system and the credit market have contributed to the increase of costs of participating in the labor market for mothers and to reducing their employment opportunities. Low female participation, low fertility, and high poverty rates of families with children is in this view the outcome of relatively high child 'costs' which negatively affect women's work probabilities as well as the number of children they can afford to have. Policies should be implemented to help reduce the constraints families face in their allocation choices and to alleviate the burden on family relationships. Tindara Addabbo show that the recent changes in regulations in the labour market, by allowing greater flexibility in the choice of working hours and consequently helping to conciliate market work with family responsibilities, have significantly affected women's propensity to work.

The relationship between institutions (social policies and labor market regulations) and household behavior is particularly important in Italy and other Southern European countries. These countries share several features of the so-called "Southern model" characterized by a strong role played by institutions (especially in labor market regulations) and a very low level of social protection (especially regarding public expenditures for families and children). What are the implications for household decisions and for interdependence among family members?

The low employment rate of married women and the high unemployment rate in Southern European countries seem to provide important indications of a labor market and a social system that do not provide enough flexibility for women to combine work with demanding family activities. Renata Livraghi and Lia Fubini consider patterns of employment and unemployment of Italian women that show an increasing propensity to participate to the labor market and that appear not to reflect the business cycle or short-run difficulties in the family (such as husbands unemployment rate or loss of incomes), but rather a long-run labor market attachment.

But who are the women who have increased their labour supply and why? Important explanations are found in the increasing education rate of women as compared to men and in the relative decline in gender wage differentials in Stefania Rossetti and Paola Tanda's paper, "Human capital and labor market performance of Italian men and women in a European context." While in southern European countries, the labor market performance is positively influenced by the education level, the choice to participate in the case of men is largely independent of the schooling level. A wide family gap appears to exist between the earnings and labor market opportunities of spouses, reflecting the differences in work experience and family responsibilities.

Daniela Del Boca, Silvia Pasqua and Marilena Locatelli analyse the relationship between the employment status and earnings of husbands and wives at the micro-level. Coherently with the strong relationship between education and earnings of the spouses, women's response to husbands' losses of income appear to be very small. Women seem to be driven to work by relative higher earnings and greater opportunities in the labor market, and to react to changes in the household income only in households where their work has long been accepted and viewed positively.

Finally what are the effects of these important changes of family structure on income distribution? Brandolini and D'Alessio examine how changes in the household structure during the last two decades affect the evolution of income distribution in Italy in the context of the European Union. The analysis shows that, while older families enjoy some economic improvement, there is a gradual deterioration of conditions in the case of younger families and larger families. In spite of the efforts of the extended family to compensate for the lack of public support for families with children and for labor market imperfections and rigidities, the households with children seem to fare worse than others.

The book focuses on the Italian situation and proves to be very helpful in shedding light on some features of that society which relate to the interconnection between women's work, the family and the economy. These are features that are often ignored or misinterpreted as to their nature and causes. One good example is the demographic decline, which has singled out Italy among all other industrialized ecountries in the course of the 1980s and 1990s. The complex web of societal responsibilities, economic constraints and individual choices accounting for the "zero growth" does indeed receive some basic explanations in many direct and indirect ways in several parts of this book. While Italy is the touchstone for many of the analyses to unravel, a remarkable body of information is supplied with respect to the other member countries of the European Union. Here too, the grouping and regrouping of these countries according to the issue on hand is often far from the obvious and not always to be anticipated.

It is the hope of the editors and the contributors alike that the volume may attract the interest of scholars, who may feel encouraged to pursue further study and inquiries on the various subjects, and of teachers, especially in the fields of Labor Economics and Economics of the Family, who may find portions of the book to be useful readings for their students.

Daniela Del Boca

CHIARA SARACENO

CHAPTER 1

CHANGES IN ITALIAN FAMILIES, FROM THE SIXTIES TO THE PRESENT

Premise: The fifties as prologue

Changes in the ways families are formed and perceived are the outcome of slow, mostly unintentional and apparently unrelated processes, which collect until they become apparent—and are acknowledged and appraised—as patterned, intentional, social behaviors. Changes in the rate and level of schooling of younger generations, as well as in the gender gap in education, in the labor market, and in the occupational structure, in the availability of consumption goods as well as in domestic technology—all these affect the ways individuals enter families and the ways families organize and perceive themselves, This is not to say that families are just the dependent variable of social change. On the contrary, they mediate and interpret social change in the everyday interaction of their members. And in so doing they change, or re-create, themselves: their relationships, their meanings, their priorities.

This work of mediation and interpretation was particularly called for in postwar Italy: in the twenty years in which not only material, political, civic, and cultural reconstruction took place, but Italian society changed from mostly rural—in which the majority of the population and of families lived off agriculture—to mostly urban and industrialized. Moreover, the fifties and early sixties were a period of mass internal as well as external migrations. Whole kin networks were displaced and had to deal both with adjustment to a totally new, an sometime unfriendly, environment and with the maintenance of family and kin solidarity across great distances. In those years new consumption goods and behavior patterns became available in a wide range of fields, although with a different timing in the various geographical areas and social classes: transportation (e.g., Lambrettas and cars), household appliances (refrigerators, washing machines, gas stoves), and leisure activities (television, imported movies, imported music, imported, ready-made clothes like jeans). These changes implied multiple redefinitions both of individual options and life chances, and of the relationship between individuals and their families—or of the individuals' family roles. Thus, for example, changes both in level of schooling and in the occupational structure caused the tremendous process of intergenerational social mobility, which has not only transformed the Italian social structure in the short span of two generations but has involved the great majority of multigenerational kin networks in the fifties and sixties: in most families, sons and daughters in the fifties and sixties on average studied longer than their parents.[1] And sons achieved a different occupational status from that of their fathers (De Lillo 1988). This change has required a process of mutual adjustment, of redefinition of authority and tradition within the family and across generations, which has been barely studied. Also the new availability of consumption goods, while it changed in many ways some of the features of domesticity (as well as of domestic work), had a twofold, to some degree contradictory, effect on family life and organization. On the one hand, the new consumption style offered new resources and opportunities for the development of family activities; on the other, it promoted non family-centered activities and emphasized consumption by individuals rather than families. These two effects might derive from different resources; but the same resource might have this dual effect, either simultaneously, or over time. A good example is private transportation, which allowed the lucky owner (usually a male head of the family, or a son) to move about more freely and by himself, but which might also be used for developing a new kind of family leisure activity: taking trips together, even if only for a Sunday. Another example is that of television: in the first few years after its introduction it was ambivalently perceived as a means of encouraging people to get out at night, since not many families owned a set; therefore many people—sometime whole families, but often only some members—would go to a bar or to a relative's or friend's home to watch it. But the very success of the first TV programming, particularly of a program such as *Lascia o Raddoppia?*, which drew thousands people in every town and village out of their homes to watch it, reversed this process: soon almost all families owned a TV set, and the new "concern" became that people would not go out any longer, and households would close in among themselves in front of the TV screen.

Simonetta Piccone Stella (1993) has made insightful observations on the underground changes which affected behaviors and relationships first of all among the youth, but indirectly among their parents, in the fifties: making small waves on the apparently smooth surface where continuity and tradition seemed to continue to reign while everything else was changing. The young cohorts of the fifties and early sixties, as a matter of fact, were both accused of being too conservative and down to the earth and with dangerous tastes for transgression.

Certainly the young continued to marry—and at the highest rate ever—and to have children right away. Yet the young entering marriage in the fifties and sixties expected from their family life something different from what their parents had, and particularly so young women: intimacy and domesticity, sexual expression and faithfulness, companionship, even if within a persistent gender division of labor.

But changes did not involve only the younger cohorts. From a certain point of view, one might even say that the cohorts who were already adult at the end of the war were those who took most of the brunt of social change not only at the political level, but in everyday living: becoming, consciously or not, protagonists of an unprecedented learning process and experiment which left untouched almost no dimension of their life: from where and how to live and work, to how to do the washing and cleaning, to what and how to cook, to how to raise one's own children (Saraceno 1991, Siebert 1991).

Thus, if it is true that the social movements which "made" of 1968 a symbolic turning point were to a great degree the expression of a generational conflict, they were not only prepared, as is obvious, by what had been going on for some time. They were, so to speak, prepared by the conscious or unconscious changes in the lives and behaviors of the older cohorts and generations now being confronted by the younger ones. Discontinuity was at last as great in the life course of the adult and older cohorts as it was between cohorts and generations. In Italy this was particularly visible and thorough because changes and discontinuities involved not only personal behaviors and relationships in family and private life, but also politics, ways of working, and so forth.[2]

As a matter of fact, indicators that changes in family behaviors were already occurring before 1968 became statistically visible already by the midsixties, as Barbagli (1990) pointed out, both at the level of marriage and at that of fertility. With regard to the first, the same period which has been defined the "golden age of marriage," given its unprecedented high levels rates of first marriages, witnessed also the beginning of an upward trend in marital separation, which had remained fairly stable for over a century. Separations started to steadily increase, in fact, from 1965 (six years before the introduction of divorce) onwards, involving all marriage cohorts, not only the younger ones. At the same time, couples increasingly asked for a consensus, not judicial (i.e. conflict-based), separation. These two phenomena suggest that the definition of marriage was changing: on the one hand, it was no longer "compulsory" to bear a marriage which had became intolerable, at least within the more educated, urban strata; on the other hand, in order to end a marriage it was no longer necessary to find a guilty (and reciprocally an offended) party. These trends are so clear that one might persuasively argue that the subsequent changes in legislation, with the introduction of divorce in 1970 and the reform of family law in 1975, were as much the consequence of changed behaviors as the cause of further cultural and behavioral changes.

A second area of transformations in the way the meaning of marriage and family was perceived at the individual level and negotiated within couples, households, and kin networks, became statistically visible already in the midsixties is that of fertility, which was already near the substitution rate. Actually, at this level continuity is more clearly detected than discontinuity in Italy. Contrary to what happened in other industrialized countries (and also contrary to many self-perceptions and representations of the time), there was no baby boom; the downward trend initiated by the cohorts born at the beginning of the century was kept up also by the cohorts born in the thirties and forties, which elsewhere were the protagonists of the baby boom in the first half of the sixties (Santini 1997). While the completed fertility was 2.5 children for women born in the twenties, it was between 2.3 and 2 for those born in the forties. Discontinuity and diversity was clearer among regions, since these averages hid such diverse situations as that of Liguria, where women born in the twenties had 1.5 children only, and Sardinia, where by contrast the same cohort bore an average of 4 children. As a matter of fact, in all Center-North regions all cohorts who were of fertility age in the past fifty years never reached the substitution rate. From this point of view, the low fertility of the eighties and nineties in these regions is no news and no radical innovation at all, as it is in Sardinia, Basilicata, and Puglia, which about halved their fertility passing from the cohort born in the twenties to that born in the sixties—that is, in about two generations. But given mass internal migration, the variety of fertility patterns which was much more apparent in the fifties than it is now became an element of cross-cultural confrontation, of resocialization in the migratory process, and of negotiations within the newly formed couples and between them and their kin. These changes occurred either because the individuals came from different cultural and geographic backgrounds or because young second-generation immigrants, and particularly young women among them, developed new ideas and new values concerning family life and motherhood.

Ambivalent emergence of youth as an autonomous life course stage

The cultural changes, of which 1968 was at the same time the consequence and the symbolic beginning, had an impact on different dimensions of family formation and family relations.

First, as was mentioned above, it constituted the framework within which differences of interests, behavior, and cultural outlook between cohorts, and particularly between generations, might find a voice in a society where the principle of authority based on age and status was still very strong, not only in the family but, possibly more so, in the workplace, in politics, and in associations. The strong politicization of the generational conflict in Italy might in part be explained by the fact that, unlike other countries, there had yet developed in Italy neither places, nor behaviors, nor routines by which the youth were acknowledged to have a status, a social identity of their own. Even the fact that their experiences were greatly different from those of their elders at their age was not properly acknowledged as having a specific value and as offering them specific competencies.

Thus, the political climate of the years immediately following 1968 allowed the expression of the younger generation's aspiration to have a life of one's own, outside their parents' home, habits, dependencies. As in other countries, this was voiced as well as practiced more clearly among university students. But, differently from other countries, this aspiration did not find in the university organization structures—housing first of all—which easily allowed it. University in Italy is not organized residentially, in most cases, and it presumes that most of its students live in their parents' homes. Therefore, on the one hand, living outside one's parents' home for students whose family lived in a city where there was a university was an explicit act of transgression (as well as costly); on the other hand, this transgression had both an easier and more normative legitimization for students coming for small towns which had no university nearby: the only ones for whom "going away" to attend the university was part of a long-standing tradition. In any case, "living away from home" was legitimized at least as much in political, conflictual terms ("I slammed the door and went away," was the routine expression) as in terms of growing up and needing autonomy. Although in statistical terms very few young people even in those years lived apart from their parents, or at least went as far as to change their residence before marrying, this conflict-based discourse on autonomy prevailed as the normative one. In this light, it is not surprising that in the subsequent cohorts, when political conflict was no longer the prevalent discourse on the relationship between generations, and when the authority structure of the family had been weakened and transformed both by legislation and by the behaviors and values of the new cohorts (actually, the so-called 1968 generation) entering in the role of parents, the new youth cohorts had neither ready made discourses nor behaviors on which to fall back to voice their desire for autonomy. If there is no conflict, why should one wish to live by himself or herself, particularly in the face of a societal organization which has no provision for the young living alone?

To synthesize, the surplus of motivation offered to intergenerational differentiation and to the demand for youth autonomy by the cultural and political climate of "68" proved in the long run too period- (and cohort-) specific, without allowing a longer-term change in the mode of entrance in adulthood—at least with regard to the choice of whether to live alone or in the parents' home before marrying. Marriage still remains by far the main reason for leaving the parents' home, even in the nineties. Since the beginning of the eighties, however, the marriage rate has steadily decreased, and the age at the first marriage has increased (Righi 1997), reaching 29.3 for men and 26.5 for women,[3] so young people actually stay at home longer in the nineties than in the fifties and sixties. Indeed, the percentage of 25–34 year olds still at home has further increased since the early eighties (De Sandre 1997a): in 1995, 51% of the 25–29 year olds lived in their parents' home, and particularly so in the Center-North, where the percentage was 61% . At the same time, there has been no increase of unmarried cohabitation among the young. The slight increase in the proportion of 25–29 year olds who live alone (4% of women and 6% of men at the 1991 census) may indicate the emerging of a new attitude, particularly in the Center-North, where the proportion is higher.

Of course, staying on in one's parents' home is occurring under different conditions than in the past decades, as it is apparent also through some statistical indicators: there are more students than before among the young living at home, particularly among the daughters. Conversely, the incidence of homemakers among daughters living at home has declined sharply, and it is now about 2–3% (although it is higher in the South). The incidence of those in employment, following the economic trend, first increased and then decreased, particularly among young women. In any case, the profile of the young living at home is somewhat stabilizing, with half of them in employment, one third studying and one third looking for a job.[4] This means that the young, and particularly women, are "using" their parent's home and support to enhance their opportunities for future autonomy through a better level of education or a better job, as well as to allow themselves a standard of living and a style of life which they could not afford on the basis of their own means. Moreover, remaining in one's parents' home does not hinder the development of a life of one's own in terms of leisure, social relationships, and also sexual behavior. Particularly among women, in fact, the trend towards a decrease of the age at the first sexual intercourse initiated with the cohorts born in the forties has continued and has a faster pace among the younger cohorts: 20% of women born in 1942–51 were no longer virgins at 19, compared to 34% of those born in 1953–56 and 47% of those born in 1960–72. Given the delay in marriage, this means also that an increasing proportion, de facto the large majority, of women does not consider marriage as the precondition for having a sexual life (Castiglioni and Della Zuanna, 1997). Many young people, although living at home with their parents, have a life as semicouple or semicohabitation with a partner: during weekends, during their vacations, and so forth (Saraceno 1994).

These changes in turn were possible because of the cultural changes symbolized by the 1968 turning point: individuals, and particularly adolescent and adult children within households, are acknowledged a wider range of individual rights, space, and interests. Apparently in Italy the way to autonomy while young is achieved through the delay of marriage on the one hand, and the support of the family on the other hand:[5] it is autonomy within one's parents' family, rather than outside it. It implies the development not only of adaptive but of negotiating attitudes and skills on the part of all the family members, of the ability to detect nuances, respect privacy, acknowledge internal boundaries, balance dependence with autonomy, and so forth (Cavalli and De Lillo 1993). The family as a social institution and as a crucial resource is strengthened by this development of its launching role for the younger generation (Saraceno 2000), although the content of the generational roles and positions is radically reshaped by the long cohabitation of parents and children who have the full status of adults (in cultural value, not only legal terms.) One might detect ambiguities in this family-based autonomy: on the one hand, the young become financially autonomous increasingly late, not only because of a delayed entrance in the labor market, but because, even when they have their own earnings, they do not have really to live exclusively on them.

Thus they can have a higher standard of living than that they could afford on the basis of their own earnings, but also de facto remain financially dependent children. On the other hand, they remain dependent to a great degree on their mother's family work. The little research which exists in this area shows a remarkable absence of sharing and reciprocity by adult children living at home, although there are class—and even more, gender—differences: in families with modest economic means adult children pay more towards their maintenance while living at home. And daughters not only are likely to take care more of their own housework, but also to help out more with the common chores.

One might conclude that those who were young in 1968, after having rebelled as children, once they became parents have raised a generation of children who at the same time take more for granted their rights as individuals and their rights as children (the latter also for a longer time), while acknowledging their parents' formal authority—be it consensually or conflictually—for a much shorter time.

Changes in family formation: Marriage, separation, divorce

For the cohorts who were directly or involved in the cultural and political upheavals of the late sixties and early eighties while young, marriage continued to be as popular as for those who had immediately preceded them. Change concerned rather the expectations and resources with which they, and particularly women, entered marriage: women were more educated, and an increasing number had had experience of coeducation at least in high school. Young men and women had shared experiences while growing up—in school, in youth associations, in leisure time activities—to a greater degree than any cohort before them. Although most women did not take part actively to the women's movement, the ideas, expectations, and dissatisfactions which spurred it were to some degree shared by many adult young women of the time, as well as by many already well into adulthood, and had the same biographical and social causes: gender relations and the gender division of labor in the family as well as outside it appeared much more resistant to change than intergenerational relations, labor relations, and political organizations. Even the so-called sexual revolution did not eliminate the double standard; at the same time, to be "sexually emancipated" might be perceived as a cultural prescription as coercive as that of virginity at all costs.

Not all women expected or wished for gender equality. But to many women, who were now more educated on average than their mothers and increasingly as educated as their husbands, the full-time homemakers role which they had been the first generation to be raised to look at as a desirable and normative model for adult women of all classes started to appear too narrow. The late fifties and sixties had been the period of the full-fledged housewife; the late sixties and early seventies were those of the returning woman worker: labor-market analysts pointed to what appeared a new and emerging phenomenon in our country: that of women returning to work after the child-raising years. But, as a matter of fact, it was a short-lived phenomenon, due not only to the difficulties mature women found in reentering (or entering for the first time) the labor market, but to an emerging pattern of behavior among younger women. These entered the labor market in greater numbers, particularly in the service sector which was opening up under the dual impact of the expansion of the private tertiary sector and of the developing welfare state; however, they tended not to leave the labor market when they married and had children, but stayed on.[6] This last behavior, not that of the returning worker, stabilized as the new gender model for adult women, for which the expression "dual presence" has been invented. Comparing 1971 and 1991 census data in a region like Piedmont, the size of change is impressive: in 1971 the highest occupation rate of around 30% among women with children was found among those whose children were 15 or older; the lowest was that of women with children under school age. In 1991 the highest rate—around 50%—was found precisely in the latter group.

This new behavior by women, intentionally or often unintentionally, weakened some of the basic assumptions regulating marriage and the gender division of labor: that a full-time homemaker, wife, and mother was necessary for a good house; that a good male provider was one whose wife did not "have to work"; that men might "help out" occasionally around the house, but a good wife would not expect them to do it systematically. All these expectations did not disappear, to be sure.[7] They persist even today. But their legitimacy started to be weakened, or contested, both in private and in public. Other models of behavior and relationship started to compete with them as valued and legitimate ones (e.g. Saraceno 1987). Therefore, marriage, always a social and interactive construction, became more visibly and explicitly a terrain of negotiation both at the level of behaviors and at that of meaning. This change coincided with a change in men's outlook. Men who had became adult in the late sixties and seventies, therefore being directly or indirectly involved in the social movements of the time, in some way developed a critique of the male model represented by their elders, although they did not frame it explicitly in gender terms. In particular, they distanced themselves from a model of fatherhood little involved with the physicality of children's bodies, with the tenderness and fun involved in taking care of little children. They might certainly "skim off the cream" of child care, leaving their puzzled wives the hard work while stealing their total monopoly (e.g. Saraceno 1980); but in so doing they too initiated negotiations around what marriage and the family is about.

While the male and female cohorts entering adulthood in the late sixties and thirties did not refuse marriage, but struggled to change it from within, subsequent cohorts apparently try a different strategy: they negotiate before entering marriage, which they delay until each spouse is somewhat settled. This is particularly clear in the case of women: their time schedule seems to go somewhat as this: first, obtain a degree as high as possible; second, settle in a job or profession which gives either security or self-fulfilling rewards, or both—in any case not to be considered secondary and dispensable with regard to marriage and motherhood; third, marry; and fourth, have a child. Parents, particularly mothers, now even warn their daughters that before marrying they should first settle in an occupation. While this change delays marriage and possibly increases the quota of people who will never marry because, while delaying, they develop a taste for singleness, it renders negotiations around and in marriage more complicated. The number of younger couples is increasing in which the woman's job or career chances must be taken account of both in the division of labor in the family and when taking any important decision, be it about marrying, moving, or having a child. These younger couples, at the same time, are experiencing a degree of insecurity in their work life unknown to the majority of their parents at their age. Therefore, each member of a couple perceives his/her negotiated decisions as at the same time more crucial and as more risky, for each one of them separately as well as for the couple.

Negotiations have no preordained outcomes. At the same time they render explicit possible conflicting expectations, interest, aims, as well as the legitimacy to hold and express them. Particularly among the more educated social strata of the Center-North, and among dual-worker couples, conflict with regard to gender roles[8] and dissatisfaction with one's own marriage were not only more explicitly given voice to but brought about separation (Barbagli 1990): from 1965 to 1985 legal separations increased six-fold, up to eleven-fold in 1994, equal to about 16% of all marriages. The change in the meaning of marriage appeared more dramatic at the cultural level. The referendum promoted in 1972 by the Christian Democrats in order to repeal the law introducing divorce approved in 1970 was lost since the great majority of the population voted no to the repealing, notwithstanding the pervasive effort by the Catholic Church to influence the vote. Although the divorce rate remained fairly low and stable until 1982, when it started to raise (but still remaining quite low compared to other countries),[9] this phenomenon indicates that at the cultural level marriage had become completely secularized: not only was it deemed legitimate and even positive to separate if the marriage did not work out; it was also deemed legitimate to marry again.[10] Remarriage was more acceptable for men, however, than for women: divorced men remarry more often than divorced women; moreover the former tend to remarry with a previously unmarried woman, while the latter remarry more often with a divorced man. This gender difference has started to be reduced in the late eighties, indicating a deepening of the acceptance of divorce, particularly for women (Rettaroli 1997). At the same time, the divorce rate has increased, doubling in the decade 1985-1994: from 4% to 8% (Maggioni 1997). To be sure, the rate of marital instability in Italy is still very low compared to that of other European countries. Even in the cities and regions which exhibit the highest separation and divorce rates in Italy, such as Genoa and Rome, Emilia-Romagna, and Piedmont, these are still lower than those of the Netherlands, France, and Austria—that is of the European countries which have the lowest marital instability rates, excluding the Southern ones (i.e. Spain, Portugal, Greece, in addition to Italy). Yet, while divorce rates seem to be stabilized in those countries, and generally in all countries which exhibit higher divorce rates, in Italy the upward trend is still clear.

At the same time, the pattern of marital instability has somewhat changed over the years. While the marriage cohorts of the middle sixties were the first to exhibit an increasing proclivity to separation irrespective of the length of marriage, the marriage cohorts between 1968 and 1984 interrupted their marriages both at a higher rate and earlier.

By the mid-eighties apparently as a consequence both of behavioral and cultural changes in the older generations and of the changed work and education circumstances of the younger ones, marriage as an institution and as the main marking event of adulthood had shifted meaning and place: people married less and later; marriages were more unstable and shorter-lived, and, as we will see in the next paragraph, were also less fertile. Remarriages by divorced people became more frequent, and so did also civil marriage. This last phenomenon is not only an obvious consequence of the increasing number of marriages in which at least one spouse is divorced, and therefore cannot marry in Church according to Catholic rules. Also the number of first civil marriages is increasing, particularly among the better educated, who live in the large cities of the Center-North (the same who remain longer in their parents' home). Cohabitation without marrying, unlike what happens in other countries, is not emerging either as a pre-marriage experience or as an alternative to marriage. The number and characteristics of unmarried cohabiting couples has remained fairly stable over the past fifteen years. These relationships involve more mature individuals than young ones, and they appear to be entered more due to a temporary impossibility to marry (because one of the partner is involved in a divorce proceeding), or out of disadvantage to marry (in the case of widows and widowers for instance), than out of a value choice (Sabbadini 1997, Zanatta 1997). The quota of young cohabitants is however increasing, together with the length of cohabitation.

Another interesting indicator of the changing meaning of marriage is that concerning the patrimonial regime (Barbagli 1997). The family law finally approved in 1975 had clearly innovated in this field introduced shared property as the normal patrimonial regime within marriage, as against the separated property regime which prevailed before and which privileged husbands in a situation were few women had their own earnings. The new family law was influenced, in this respect by the women's movement and its exposure of the unacknowledged value of family work performed by homemakers for the benefit of their families in general and of their husbands in particular. The shared property regime in some way completed the transition towards a companionate marriage, in which each spouse contributed according to his or her capacity and no contribution was deemed of a higher value than the other. The choice of the separated property regime was, and is, still possible on demand, if both spouses agree. The common property regime was tremendously popular in the first year of application, apparently indicating that it corresponded to common feelings and perceptions. Yet, starting with 1976, a substantial quota (between 7 and 15%) of those who had opted for common property asked to change to separate property, and an increasing quota of the newly wed chose the latter regime: from 1976 to 1991 the quota of those who chose the separate regime went from 1% to 45%, touching 66% in some regions of the Center North (Piedmont and Aosta Valley, Emilia-Romagna). This choice is in fact more common in the Center-North, were the majority of couples opts for the separate, especially among the higher strata, the self-employed, those who are married only on the basis of the civil code, and among dual-worker couples, particularly if the wife has a highly qualified and well-paid profession. While the preference for this regime by the self-employed is readily understandable in financial and administrative terms, the reasons of the growing popularity of this regime among other social groups and, albeit to a different degree, in all strata, are less readily found, particularly in view of the fact that separate property represents an undoubted economic risk for wives in a period of increasing fragilization of marriage. Barbagli points to three factors which may help explain this unforeseen phenomenon: the growing number of wives who earn their own money and therefore the diminishing proportion of couples in which the earning differential between the spouses is great;[11] the fragile statues of marriage itself, which renders young couples and their families wary of any patrimonial settlement which is traditionally associated with long-lasting marriages, and the search for autonomy and freedom from husbands' control on the part of women. This new emphasis on separate property is indicated by still another phenomenon: among dual-worker couples, in the management of the family budget two patterns emerge (Bonato 1997): on the one hand there is the pooling of resources in a "common pot" out of which to pay for the family's expenses; on the other hand, there is a separate management of resources and expenses. The former pattern, while more attuned to a marriage founded on sharing, intimacy, and communion, allows not only redistribution from who earns more to who earns less, but also hiding, censoring, and possible invidious contrasts on who earns how much as well as possible asymmetries de facto. The latter pattern, viceversa, is more attuned to an idea of marriage where each partner has his/her owns space and autonomy, where boundaries remain distinct, negotiations explicit. It is the latter pattern which is growing in the metropolitan areas of the Center-North.

Possibly the "new" family law, in this respect, was already late with regard to not only the changing behavior of women in the labor market, but also to changes in the perception of marriage: the partners increasingly perceive themselves as distinct entities (also because "unity" beforehand was slanted in favor of the husband), particularly because women had access to cultural and material resources to posit themselves as autonomous individuals. They also know that they might separate. The fierce debate which had accompanied the introduction of divorce in Italy and the repealing referendum had the paradoxical effect of magnifying this possibility, notwithstanding the reduced numbers of those who actually did, and do, it. It was a sort of anticipatory socialization which significantly changed the common outlook on marriage.

These changes to some degree deepened regional and class differences: marital instability is higher in the urban contexts of the Center-North,[12] among the higher educated, and among dual-worker couples; also civil first marriages are more frequent in the same areas and social strata. In the South the popularity of marriage is higher and people marry at a younger age, particularly for women who on average marry a year younger than their Northern contemporaries. Marriages last longer; but when they end in separation the process is more often contentious than in the North.

Changes in family formation: Fertility patterns in Center-North and in the South

There are two stereotypes concerning Italian fertility patterns: first, that Italy has long been a country with a very high fertility which somehow suddenly became one with the lowest fertility in the world; and second, that this change is found in the Center-North.

Research taking account both of regional differences and of cohort behavior over a century (Santini 1997) offer us a less clear-cut view of trends and behaviors, while at the same time stressing the little significance of a "national" approach in this field, at least as far as Italy is concerned. As was mentioned in the introductory paragraph, in fact, at least two broad patterns of fertility have been in existence in Italy for many decades, reproduced by each consecutive cohort of women: the fertility of women of the Center-North was well below replacement already in the cohorts born in the twenties, with the exception of Umbria, Marche, Lazio, and Abruzzi, where in any case the fertility rate was not above 2.6 children per woman; in all the regions of the South, by contrast, those same cohorts had an average of 3 or more children. Thus, the high Italian fertility pattern of the first half of the century was exclusively due to the behavior of Southern women. But precisely for this reason, the subsequent low fertility pattern which came to identify Italy is indebted more to changes in behavior of Southern women than of Northern ones. In the words of Santini (1997, 116), "Two Italies emerge: one, which was always characterized by a very low fertility and which in the past twenty years has moved farther from reproduction rates barely sufficient to generational replacement; the other, which is in continuous transition from very high fertility rates to an average number of children only slightly lower than that which was typical of the former during its stability phase."

Although in both "Italies" fertility has dropped, it has dropped more in the second. Yet, the patterns of fertility remain as distinct as ever. In the Center-North the small decline in fertility has developed a pattern by which, particularly among the cohorts who came of age around and after 1968, the only child is most prevalent; women become mothers later because they marry later, and they tend to postpone childbearing until after they have settled in a job and their relationship with their partner, usually a husband, is stabilized. Possibly as an unforeseen consequence of the delay in childbearing, there is also an increasing quota of women who do not have children at all, albeit it is still very reduced and lower than that prevalent in the majority of European countries. In the South, by contrast, the two children family is the norm. At the same time, the quota of childless women is higher than that with only one child, as well as higher than that present in the Center-North. In other words, in the Center-North, the pattern is "a child, and a child only, at all costs"; in the South, if one chooses to have children at all, then she has at least two, and close by. Otherwise she renounces, either by choice or by necessity.

The scarcity of social services and difficult economic conditions may explain only partly the Southern model: women who anticipate engaging in a demanding profession or, in any case, wish to invest in paid work may be discouraged from having children altogether, by the scarcity of services and by the competition in the labor market. Yet, these same elements do not deter women, and couples, who wish to have children from having at least two. These differences in behavior among the two great geographical areas[13] indicate that two long-standing and deeply rooted models of family, not only of women, are at work. They are certainly modified and reshaped as each cohort threads its way and develops its own strategies in the face of the circumstances it encounters. Yet, this reshaping up to now maintains distinct patterns, and there cannot be imputed only to external social and economic circumstances, but also to family cultures and traditions.[14]

Both the reduced size of fertility in the Center-North already in the forties and fifties and the subsequent reduction in all regions in the following decades is particularly striking in the face of the illegality of contraception and of contraceptive information up to 1975 (including obstetricians, gynecologists, and nurses adequately prepared to give relevant information.) Once again, when the law allowing it was finally approved under the pressure of the women's movement, it was more a consequence either of a deeply rooted behavior or of already changed behavior, than a real turning point. It certainly was a turning point in the training of physicians; and it lightened somewhat the constraints imposed on unmarried young women who were more likely to be dependent on the will of the physician to impart the "illegal information." Indirectly the trend in prenuptial pregnancies—which increased after 1968, but decreased in the second half of the seventies—confirms such an effect on this particular group of women. At the symbolic level, it was certainly striking to witness the cultural relocation which accompanied the new visibility of a very old contraceptive device—the condom—which suddenly appeared not only in pharmacies, but soon also in supermarkets and on television as the instrument of safe, regular sex within marriage and for young unmarried couples, after a long history of association with prostitution. A more radical impact, at the practical as well as at the symbolic level, had the law allowing abortion, approved in 1975, again under the pressure of the women's movement. The referendum to repeal it, asked for by the Christian democrats, with the support of the Catholic Church and of all most conservative groups, was not won by a vote much closer than that which had refused the referendum to repeal the law introducing divorce.[15] This closeness indicated that the issue of abortion was much more controversial, but also that freedom of choice in reproductive behavior, as well as medical safety, were two hard won values which the majority did not want to lose, even if it was not willing to openly fight for them.

The reduced fertility rate, its postponement until a more mature age of the parents, and particularly of the mother, at least in the Center-North, its being explicitly negotiated within the couple, but also within the mother's life course strategy, strongly modified both the experience of motherhood and fatherhood, and the experience of being a child and growing up. To grow up as an only child of a working mother became a common experience, no longer an exception, in the Center-North, and having very few siblings (and cousins) was increasingly common in the South. Being cared for by someone else than one's own mother, for at least part of the day, is increasingly part of the curriculum of growing up no longer only for children of well-to-do families (with their nannies) or of rural families (where grandmothers or sisters-in-law might share the care), but for a substantial quota of children both of working and middle classes. Although grandmothers and female kin still make up a large portion of nonmother child care for small children, they are increasingly substituted for, or supplemented, either by baby sitters or by institutional day care. In cities like Bologna, Milan, and Turin, between 20 and 30% of all children under three attend a *nido* (the national average is 5%). Although *nido* attendance is still perceived as less legitimate, in cultural and relational terms, than kindergarten attendance, in the areas where the offer of nidi is higher and perceived as of good quality, sending one's child to a *nido* rather than hiring a baby sitter or relying on a grandmother is perceived as a sign of modernization, investment in early education, as well as a way of tracing boundaries with one's own parents and parents in law (e.g. Bimbi and Castellano 1990). So much so that even full-time homemaker mothers may require as well a space and opportunities for extra family socialization for their little children and for themselves.[16] Conversely, combining motherhood and paid work at a relatively mature age became the normal pattern for an increasing quota of women of the Center-North— now the majority. It became also the ideal norm for the great majority of women in the younger cohorts, also in the South. At the same time, for a large quota of women, and particularly for those who have a job and live in the Center-North, it is normal to have just one child. Besides, an increasing quota of mothers takes long maternity leaves, both compulsory and optional, because the legislation regarding working mothers was improved (in addition to the changed composition of working mothers themselves, who are now better educated and work in better-protected jobs). Thus it is a rare instance that in which a child starts to attend a *nido* at three months, as it was more common twenty years ago. The very recent changes in the labor market, with the emergence of so-called atypical labor contracts, which are in general more temporary and less secure, as well as less social security protected, might cause a reversal of this trend, or a differentiation among mothers, with those with less secure jobs returning to work earlier. It should be pointed out that, notwithstanding the law allows it since 1977, albeit limited to employee husbands of employee mothers, very few fathers take a parental leave when they have a child, indicating that changes in fatherhood do not go as deep as to substantially modify gender arrangements in child care and men's time schedules. Possibly, this resistance to change does not come only from fathers, but from mothers. Precisely because they are going to have only one child, they do not want to lose the opportunity to spend the first few months taking care of it; therefore they are not willing to share the optional leave.[17]

One change in fatherhood which should be mentioned is a consequence of growing separation and divorce as well as of changes in criteria for assigning child custody. Judges, in fact, following the 1975 family law reform, should assign custody neither on the basis of a parent's "guilt" (for breaking the marriage) nor of the children's age, as in the past, but on the basis of the "child's best interest." The consequence is that in over 90% of cases they assign custody to the mother. Although joint custody has been introduced recently as a possibility, it is seldom either asked for by parents or applied by judges. In the face of the growing number of separations, the interplay between a traditional view of gender roles and the persisting stronger legitimization of a mother's desire to obtain custody for her child over a father's desire and juridical practices causes a growing number of fathers and children to live apart.[18] At the same time, a number of these fathers, if and when they remarry, live with the children of some other man. Research indicates that in Italy, as in other countries, after two years from marital separation a quota of about 20% of fathers already has no contact with their children. (Barbagli and Saraceno, 1998) The same quota does not pay for child support (although the two are not linked together). The risks of relinquishing one's own responsibilities as father are higher if either he or his wife has a new companion, as if fatherhood were something which might be more easily expendable, or given over, than motherhood. This is particularly true among fathers (and former couples) who during marriage held a traditional vision of gender roles and of the gender division of labor and responsibilities. The better educated both were more present in their children's lives when married and are more present after separation. In any case, even when the non-cohabiting father is present, he has to develop a way of being a father which cannot easily rest on the fact of cohabitation and on the mother's mediating work. Different patterns and models of fatherhood emerge in practice, if not yet in common knowledge and culture, parallel to new patterns and models of motherhood which may be only very abstractly, and possibly misleadingly, lumped together under the "lone motherhood" heading (see also Saraceno forthcoming b).

Reduced as it may be, in Italy fertility is still a family affair, which occurs within marriage to a degree much higher than in any other European country, with the exception of the other Mediterranean ones, notwithstanding the increase of pre- and extramarital sexual relationships. As formal cohabitation without marriage remains a rare instance, so it is for premarital and extramarital fertility. Yet, this conclusion should be qualified. The turmoil and changes in interpersonal relationships and individual behavior that occurred in 1968–1978 did show up in at least one phenomenon: premarital and extramarital pregnancies, which in that decade increased in all cohorts of women (indicating a period, rather than age, effect) (Castiglioni and Della Zuanna 1997). This increase stopped (in the case of extramarital pregnancies) and partly reverted (in the case of prenuptial pregnancies) in the following years: not because women reverted to abstention from sexual intercourse before or outside marriage, but because they started to use contraception devices more effectively. I would stress that this change in attitude was brought about as much by cultural changes as by the new legal availability of contraception: insofar as having a sexual life outside marriage was becoming a normal, not a deviant practice, also at the individual, psychological level, protecting oneself from becoming pregnant became legitimate and normal among unmarried, particularly young women.[19] It should be observed that something similar occurred also with abortion: while in the first years of its application it was mostly required by young, unmarried women, in the following years, and up to now, it is rather used as a possibly last resort, contraceptive means by married women who already have the number of children they want. Finally, the fact that most children born outside marriage are not only acknowledged by both parents, but subsequently are "legitimized" upon the marriage of the latter, indicate that the great majority of pre- or extramarital pregnancies occur within couples who have some kind of common project together.

In conclusion, following the cultural changes of the late sixties and early seventies, in Italy marriage has certainly been secularized, insofar as it has became reversible, and it is no longer the necessary requirement to enter sexual relations. Yet, it is still the main reason to exit from one's parents' household and the precondition for having a child. From this point of view, its symbolic and social status as a crucial social institution is far from being weakened.

Diversification of family forms and changing life course patterns

Delay in entering marriage, cohabitation with one's parents well into adulthood, separation and divorce with ensuing remarriage as well as "in between" cohabitation—all these phenomena have not only caused a change in the social and cultural meaning of the still-prevalent family form based on marriage. These factors have produced also a diversification of family forms similar, although not as widespread, to those occurring in other countries (Zanatta 1997): one-person households, one-parent families, reconstituted families, cohabitation without marriage—all these become to some degree visible and socially legitimate ways of being and forming a family. In most cases these different forms exist side by side only from a statistical point of view, insofar as they rather represent different stages of the "same" family which may start off as conjugal, pass through an only-parent stage, and become reconstituted upon the new marriage of the remaining parent. But exactly this phenomenon "explodes" both the normative family life cycle and the individuals' life- course patterns through family forms, experiences and membership. At the same time it explodes also boundaries between families and reshapes kin networks. Multi household membership—or commuting between households—in fact is another aspect of some of the phenomena we have mentioned above (see also Saraceno 1994b): young adult children continue to reside with their parents, but *de facto* may spend many months or days a week as students or workers in another town, or may have different living arrangements for workdays and for holidays. Children of separated parents may (actually are expected to) commute more or less systematically between two households, which in turn must be organized around not only this intermittent presence, but also around the (financial and otherwise) obligations it implies.[20] Even the elderly who have remained alone may alternate periods of living by themselves to periods living in a child's household, or, if very frail or ill, periods in some old people's home or rehabilitating institution. And both separated households and reconstituted ones re-arrange their kin network in ways which both strengthen some blood ties and loosen others,[21] while at the same time a parent's new marriage may represent a way of acquiring a total new set of "relatives."

Changes both in family arrangements and obligations and in life-course patterns, however, do not derive simply from intentional behaviors. And intentional behaviors themselves have unforeseen, and often long-term consequences on family and kin arrangements. The reshaping of kin networks as a consequence of marital instability is a case in point. Another is the impact of reduced fertility: intentional in its short-term objective and in the immediate range of the people involved—the conjugal family and its individual members—it has deep consequences both for the experience of children, who have an increasingly reduced range and number of peers within their kinship network, and for the shape of the kinship network itself. The latter is becoming "long and lean," to use Peter Laslett's words. It is easier for a child to have four grandparents and at least one or two grandparents, than to have cousins. The overturned age pyramid is experienced directly in the shape of one's kin network while growing up.

This phenomenon combines with another which is not directly the consequence of intentional choices: the rising life expectancy. Becoming old and living for many years as an old person has become expected and natural. And most people have a long-life stage when they are old and are well and able bodied and are a resource both for their children and grandchildren and for their community. The increasing percentage of couples with no children at home and of individuals living alone is a direct consequence of this lengthening of life in a social context in which the nuclear family as the dominant family form has been stabilized for a while. Thus, there is no "abandonment" or isolation in principle behind the many elderly couples and individuals who live by themselves. Actually research indicates that in Italy the elderly live generally within a (kin) network in which exchanges and mutual supports are frequent and strong (ISTAT 1994). From this point of view, both the stereotype of the poor abandoned elderly and that of the elderly as a social and kinship burden are just that: ill-founded stereotypes. But research indicates also both the existence of strong gender differentials and of situations of vulnerability and risk. Since women both live longer than men and marry men older than themselves, it is more likely that elderly men live within a couple until they die, and are taken care of by their wives when ill or disabled (Facchini 1997).

By contrast, it is more likely that women spend the last part of their lives living alone, and sometime with nobody who can easily take care of them, or having to be displaced in a child's household in order to be taken care of. It is a paradox that women, who very rarely live alone when young or in their middle years, either because they stay at home as young, marry young, or, if they separate, more often than men remain with their children, risk spending their last years alone, or as guests in someone's household.[22] Moreover, the cohorts who are now the oldest, given their marginal or interrupted work history and social security contributory records, on average have lower pensions than men, and therefore fewer means to face health and caring needs. Finally, since family and kin support, in the form of spouses' and children's support, is so crucial for the frail elderly's well-being, the unavailability of such support—due to singleness, childlessness, migration, or other—is likely to leave such frail elderly without resources.

The increasing proportion of elderly in the kin network also increases the risk that a quota of them, for a variable length of time, may need caring support. This is thought of as a problem at the social policy level. Curiously enough it is not thought of as a problem for kinship networks, which on the contrary are called for as the main solution. Yet, this calling forth for family responsibility overlooks a few issues. First, caring for the frail elderly is mostly performed by elderly women, that is, by elderly spouses, or by middle-aged and near-old ones, such as daughters and daughters-in-law. Second, hosting a frail elderly requires multiple displacements: that of the elderly, and that of the hosting household which has to reorganize its space, time schedule, internal and external obligations and alliances, and carefully negotiated balances and compromises. It isn't a no-cost operation for all those involved. Third, caring for an invalid elderly parent may be a very tension-ridden and psychologically overburdening activity which should not be taken as granted lightly and which, on the contrary, would require careful support and monitoring. Fourth, but by no means the least importance, this calling forth of "the family" overlooks the great changes which have occurred within it: in both demography and attitudes. The dual process which underlies the aging of the population actually produces a numeric imbalance previously unknown. Both the absolute number and the ratio of surviving elderly to adult children is growing at an unprecedented rate. It is this unbalance, with the added disarticulation both of spouses' and of kin solidarity due to marital instability, more than the growing women's labor force participation rate or rather than growing individualism and selfishness, which renders this recourse to the family as a solution to the frail elderly's needs too simplistic and abstract.

The unfinished, contradictory process of redefining the family juridically, institutionally

Family changes are not easily traced to one single cause or factor. Yet one cannot deny that women's changing behaviors, perceptions of themselves, and life-course strategies had a great impact on what occurred in, and with regard to, families since the mid-sixties. Actually, these changes in behaviors and attitudes, together with a political climate of the period overall more democratic and attentive to individual rights in turn prompted far-reaching changes in legislation concerning both family and gender roles. During the seventies changes and pieces of legislation were introduced in the Italian law system which had been asked for in some cases since the end of the war, in others (divorce) since the beginning of the Italian state, and in other cases (reform of family law, but also the institution of regional governments and the workers' statute) set forth in the Constitution but never developed or approved.

Family and gender roles were still regulated from the fascist code approved in 1941, which had a very hierarchical view of the family, both in gender and intergenerational terms. Although the republican Constitution had carefully couched the principle of gender equality in terms which somewhat subordinated it to the superior principle of family unity,[23] existing legislation was contrary even to that restricted vision of equality, since the wife's adultery continued to be considered a more serious offense than a husband's, a wife had to follow her husband wherever he decided to set his residence, and so forth. Juridical practice had already started to interpret the existing regulations in a way more favorable to wives (e.g. in the case of residence, with a sentence by the Corte di Cassazione, which sentenced that if a wife did not change her legal residence to follow her husband because of her profession's requirements, this should not be considered as an act of fleeing from "the marital house," and therefore as ground for separation). But the situation remained patchy and controversial. It was only with the social movements of the late sixties that the cultural and political climate became more favorable both to long-present instances and voices which had been somewhat silenced in the postwar years (such as those of the lay republican and liberal tradition) and to the new demands of the new social actors—women among them.

It is worthwhile noticing that not only family relations but gender roles as such were at the center of most legislative reform in the seventies. This was only indirectly true for divorce, although the conservatives, who opposed it, had a somewhat clearer anticipation of its implications for gender roles, as well as for marriage as an institution, than its supporters. The campaign for the repealing referendum, in fact, was conducted by pointing out the risks for men of such an introduction: if marriage could be unmade, then women might no longer be kept under control and obedience, their services might no longer be expected as coming without negotiation and reciprocity. This fear may sound a little paradoxical in a country in which both marital instability and married women's activity and occupation rates were so low, and remained relatively so, compared to other European countries. Moreover, divorce and separation do not always result in a clear women's advantage, in Italy as elsewhere, at least form a financial point of view. Yet, in the new cultural climate of the time, and in the face of the first indicators of changing women's behavior (in labor-force participation, as well as for those remaining in education) the conservatives' fears were founded. In those new conditions, divorce might become a symbolic resource for women in their negotiations with men, as well as in their perceptions of themselves—even if they did not have recourse to it.

If the woman's movement was not directly involved in the campaign for divorce, which it considered at best with ambivalence, its presence had a direct impact on the reform of family law in 1975, when the figure of the family head and rendered completely equal husband and wife 50 years after the approval of the Constitution's principle. This family law reform also had a direct impact on the legalization of contraception and of abortion (the latter within limitations). To be sure, the new family law innovated not only in gender roles, but also in intergenerational relations, designing an overall more democratic family,[24] while at the same time maintaining a wide range of family and kin obligations which also at present differentiate Italy from most European countries. Parents are financially responsible for their children virtually without any age limit, children are responsible for parents, children-in-law for parents-in-law, and siblings for each other. Actually, the new family and kin obligations designed by the new law, as well as by the subsequent practice at the judiciary, but also labor law and social security level are ones in which the marriage tie is weakened, as well as the authority structure. From this point of view the Italian welfare state is much less a so-called breadwinner model than a family-kin model. But this is another story we cannot develop here.[25]

While the new family law radically democratized the conjugal family based on marriage, it left outside any regulation the new family forms which were emerging not only from choices alternative to marriage (such as cohabitation), but also from the consequences of divorce: For example, relationships between parents and between parents and children after separation and divorce are still underregulated (particularly with regard to criteria for child support). Reconstituted families remain somewhat clandestine from the point of view of socially and legally acknowledged norms regulating their internal and external relationships, such as the rights and duties involved in the relationships between stepparents and stepchildren; and so on. Although family forms have greatly differentiated, and an individual can pass through different family forms along his/her life course, the prevalent norm, also at the legal level, tends to consider the family based on (possibly the first) marriage as the only existing form. This in turn has consequences both for children born outside marriage, to whom the law acknowledges only partly the same rights as those born within it (for instance, their being part, legally and relationally, of a kinship network is strongly reduced—see Vincenzi Amato 1997), and for children of separated parents. Not only the entitlement of such children to be adequately supported by the noncohabiting parent but also their rights to have access to such a parent is little supported; if the parent remarries they also are likely to see their entitlement to inheritance, be it in the form of survivor's pension or of property, superceded by the new spouse's competing right, irrespective of their own age and economic condition.

The law which more radically overturned gender roles, however, at least at the symbolic level, was that allowing abortion. To be sure, this law involves more than one symbolic rupture. And possibly that involving gender roles might appear minor, secondary, in the light of that involving the status of the fetus and the so-called "right to life." Yet, in my opinion, its impact on gender roles should not be undervalued and helps us understand also, at least partly, the issues and debates underlying those other dimensions. First, this law allows the identification, and legitimization, of a woman's interest as separate than both that of her companion, even of her husband, in procreation, and that of a perspective child. Woman becomes her own person, in body and destiny. Second, it renders it more dramatically visible than in contraception that a man's desire to become a father must necessarily be subject to the woman's consensus to become a mother. No wonder that one of the most controversial features of the law, denounced somewhat hypocritically as unfair and biased in favor of women, is that which stipulates that the woman, not the couple, even if married, and even if the father is willing to keep and raise the baby by himself, has the ultimate say in the abortion decision. The woman is not just simply a means, an instrument for fatherhood, but the authorizing actor. In other words, with all its limitations, the law says that a woman may not be simply considered a "walking womb"—be it for the sake of a baby to be, or for the sake of a father to be. It is precisely this acknowledgment of the woman's authority and autonomy in reproductive behavior and choice which appears as scandalous and traumatic as the "killing of the fetus."[26]

Also within labor laws important, although not as radical, innovations were developed,. First, the protective legislation concerning working mothers was improved, both in terms of length of leave (with the addition of an optional period) and extended to cover all wage workers; subsequently, in 1977, within the so-called equality law, the right to benefit from the optional leave was extended to fathers, although under the threefold condition that they were themselves wage workers, that they were married to a woman entitled to the leave, and that she renounced it. This last innovation up to now has remained symbolic since very few fathers take advantage of it. Yet it has represented a cultural shift on two grounds: first, fathers are acknowledged in principle to be as good child caregivers as mothers, also in the case of babies; second, the leave is no longer exclusively couched in terms of mothers' and babies' health needs, but also in terms of babies' caring and relational rights. The latter passage has been made clearer in a few Constitutional Court's sentences in which also the right to the compulsory leave has been extended to fathers in the case of a mother's death, absence, or incapacity. Thus, at issue here is not only gender equality, but both a new conception of fatherhood and a new conception of children as having needs and rights of their own. "The family" as a homogeneous unity, de facto regulated by some authority principle and by the interests defined by the actor having such authority (the father-husband) is now progressively acknowledged as a complex, internally diversified community, comprising different individuals with their own interests and rights, which may be composed and balanced only through negotiation and mutual consent. From this point of view, the disentangling of mother and child as an homogeneous entity through a disentangling of women and mothers, has allowed not only the acknowledgment of women's rights within, as well as outside the family, but also of children's rights as individuals.

Adoption and foster-child legislation also points to a new attention for children's needs and rights, with its focus on the child's needs rather than on the prospective parents' ones. Although criticized recently by some for its restrictive view of the adequate family and adequate parents (with its limitation to married couples and to rigidly defined age thresholds), its aim was to avoid children being submitted to adults' strategies which take little account of their needs and their liberty.

It is worthwhile pointing out that the emergence of a focus on individual rights, and not only on rights derived from one's family status, was both acknowledged and denounced as an attack against "the family" by opponents not only of the new legislation concerning family and gender,[27] but also of public social services from child care to family clinics. These services were, in fact, not only asked for by supporters, but criticized by opponents, as catering to individual needs and rights, therefore offering resources for a degree of individual autonomy and existence irrespective of family membership. It is noteworthy that this critique to (public) social services as too focused on individuals rather than on "the family," and more generally the opposition between the value of "individualism" and that of "family solidarity," has gained new popularity in the nineties, also partly within the left. Possibly it is a consequence of the need to offer some cultural legitimization to welfare state cuts, as well as of the new political alliances. But in my view it is also a consequence of the not full understanding, in the seventies and early eighties, of what the new value attached to the individual autonomy of wives and children-who beforehand had almost no social existence outside the family-meant for the conception and organization of the family, and of its gender and intergenerational structures and relations. Within the left it was perceived that the acknowledgment of individual rights might be achieved without substantial changes in family relations, particularly with regard to gender ones. Also the demands of the women's movement were to a great degree perceived as those of an "additional" social subject, to be added to the long list of the oppressed, with no real perception of how these demands interrogated both men's and women's gender roles as well as the conception and organization of the family based on them. Thus, the left was not so much unprepared to face the consequences of what it had, more or less willingly, supported as without the means to understand and elaborate fully the implications of what it supported.[28] The new emphasis on the family in the nineties, from this point of view, within the left, is less a turnabout than it seems: as it was not thought contradictory in the seventies to campaign for (albeit very partial) individuals' rights without questioning deep-rooted assumptions concerning the gender structure of existing family and kin unity and solidarity, today's evoking the family as a panacea to welfare cuts and to a "heartless world" is not considered at odds with the persistent defense of women's individual rights. The parallel, rather than interlocking approach to family and gender issues continues to be prevalent: either families seem to exist outside individuals, or individuals appear to exist without families, women continuing to constitute an "exception."

Actually, the contradiction is exposed more clearly at the level of intergenerational relations: be it evoking "the family" as the solution to the needs of the frail elderly, or waving "family's right to choose how to educate one's children" when supporting the long-standing request by Catholics for financial support to private schools. What disappears from the discourse is the relative autonomy of generations from each other: the young generation as children and the older as frail elderly parents or relatives disappear once again "into the family"—its resources, its power structure, the willingness of some of its members to perform caring work, and so forth.

Once again, although everything started, in 1968, with the explicit staging of intergenerational conflicts, and although apparently everything changed in intergenerational, particularly parent-child relations, these seem to remain even more resistant to change, at least at the level of expected obligations and dependencies, than gender ones. As a matter of fact, they are also the less studied and reflected upon in research, notwithstanding the mass of research on "the young" and notwithstanding using the family (parents) as a scapegoat is the easy and standing topos of any discourse on youth deviance or maladjustment.

Thus, in continuing to maintain a strong degree of "familization," in principle as well as in practice, and in perceiving any degree of "de-familization" as an attack on the family,[29] we are singularly unprepared either to fully grasp the possible risks, in terms of developing an adult competence and outlook, of the long dependency of children on their parents, even (or maybe particularly) in a "democratic" and negotiated home setting; or to face the consequences of the aging of the population as well as of marriage instability for intergenerational relations and the development of resources adequate to the needs of a growing proportion of frail elderly. Demography, in fact, is both an outcome and a cause of changes in individuals' and families' life-course patterns which is still far to be fully taken account of in policy thinking for its consequences on kinship networks, intergenerational and gender relations, and life-course patterns.

Notes

1. The gender gap in schooling in Italy started to close in the seventies, about a decade later than in most industrialized countries. Yet the younger female cohorts of the fifties and sixties improved their level of schooling relative to the older ones, and particularly to their mothers.
2. Two phenomena should be mentioned: first, that in Italy the renewal of workers' struggles in 1969 was as important as the student's movement of 1968 from the point of view of changing social relationships (as well as of intergenerational relationships

within trade unions); second, that the social movements of 1968 and 1969 both confronted directly existing political parties, particularly of the Left, and changed to some degree the political spectrum at the institutional, not only ideological, level.
3. In Italy the age at marriage never fell as much as in other western countries in the postwar years. The lowest was 26.7 for men and 23.4 for women in the seventies, when both very young (below 18) marriages for women and late ones decreased and the average and modal age, came nearer.
4. The incidence of the unemployed is higher, of course, in the South, where, however, the young tend to exit from their parents' home sooner, because they marry younger (see also Piccone Stella 1997).
5. It should be added that even those young who live by themselves as students are mostly supported by their parents. And even those who eventually marry have access to housing through their parents' financial help. Leonini (1997) has also found that an increasing proportion of the transmission of wealth from one generation to the next is done through donations, not inheritance: that is, parents redistribute part of their wealth to their children while they themselves are still alive and their children are still young, as a means of easing the former's entrance into an autonomous life (see also Del Boca 1997).
6. According to a study which uses longitudinal data (Bison, Pisati, and Schizzerotto 1997), the increase both in women's labor force participation since the seventies and in the pattern of continuity in participation, notwithstanding changes in family status (marriage, child-bearing) owes more to the increase in women's education over the succeeding cohorts than to a decrease in gender discrimination. In other words, all—or most—change derives from the fact that more women in the younger cohorts have the qualifications and enter the kind of jobs that also in the past made it more likely for women to remain in the labor force even if married and mothers.
7. Interestingly, young women interviewed in the early seventies would reproach their mothers both for being full-time homemakers and for having a paid job who kept them out of the home for part of the day when they were little: the normative images of "adult women" and "mothers" did no longer fit together seamlessly (see e.g. Pancino, Saraceno, and Schnabl 1978).
8. Recent research continues to document the persistent rigidity of the division of labor in the family on the basis of gender, with women continuing to have by far the greatest share, irrespective of their professional status (see e.g. Palomba and Sabbadini 1994).
9. In order to obtain a divorce, save in the case of long prison sentences and particularly serious crimes, a couple must be legally separated for three years (until 1987, five years). Over 40% of all separations do not end in a divorce (De Rose 1994).
10. This attitude was confirmed also by a national survey a decade later, in 1983 (Palomba 1987), when the majority of the interviewed expressed their favor of divorce (not only separation) in the case of major conflicts and supported the divorce law. In the same survey a substantial percentage (about 30%) expressed a positive opinion about cohabitation without marriage, indicating that the whole marriage complex was involved in a change of meaning.
11. The shared property regime is particularly protective for women in the case of traditional marriages. Yet, it should not be forgotten that a) the percentage of couples

choosing the separate property regime is higher than that of dual workers; and, b) there is a gender differential in wages, with women earning between 80% and 60% of the male wage. The differential is higher in the higher professions.

12. Regional differences do not concern only the rate of marital instability, but also the legal procedures by which it is brought about: while in the Center-North only 10% are judicial, contentious separations, the remaining being consensual ones, in the South between one third and one fourth of all separations are of the judicial type (Maggioni 1997).
13. Of course, this division is very rough, and internal distinctions might be detected, particularly within the Center-North, which is not totally homogeneous. Yet, the diversity of the South from all the other geographical areas is strong enough to allow at least this first distinction.
14. A study by Della Zuanna and Schiavone (1995) points out that family cultures, even in reproductive patterns, do not simply follow the mother-daughter line. Rather, one should take account of complex mediations between the cultures of the two families and kin networks which are linked through marriage, as well as of the prevalence of a matrilateral or viceversa patrilateral kinship pattern within a given social group or geographical area. For a more general overview of attitudes towards motherhood and fatherhood, as well as of fertility behaviors, see the results of the Second Fertility Survey in P. De Sandre (ed.), 1997a.
15. The repealing of the law was not approved not so much because the majority voted no, but because of a substantial quota of blank votes (abstention), particularly in the South: people went to vote, and cast their ballot without choosing either yes or no.
16. The growing attention by local administrations for developing services somewhat alternative to the *nido* may be read as the effort at meeting multiple and, to some degree, conflicting demands: that of developing less costly services, that of providing more flexible and more varied services also for their traditional target, in the light of a growing awareness—among parents, as well as among other caregivers—of the relational and educational needs of little children, and that of providing services not targeted exclusively on children of working mothers.
17. For this reason, following examples of other European countries, the minister of social affairs is preparing a bill by which if fathers take up at least two months of parental leave, the overall parental (optional) leave will be lengthened by two months.
18. It should be mentioned, however, that the number of children involved in a separation is decreasing, not only because marriages are in general less fertile, but because this is particularly so in recent years for marriages which end in a separation.
19. Possibly, at least in the urban contexts of the Center-North, also the development, following the legalization of contraception and abortion, of family clinics which catered to "the woman, the couple, and the family," were a means to develop such an attitude. It should be pointed out that there are great cultural variations in the degree to which sexual freedom is allowed for young, unmarried girls. And, as in other countries, adolescent girls still remain vulnerable to lack of information and of contraceptive skills.
20. It may be interesting to observe that the same "commuting" pattern and dual membership is expected also in the case of foster care, which is increasingly being considered as a possible alternative not only to institutionalization, but to adoption.
21. Since kin relationships are mainly kept up by women, even across blood lines, a

separation may easily bring about a weakening of the ties with the fathers' kin, as grandparents sometimes lament. See also Cioni 1997.
22. There are 161 men living alone for every 100 women living alone among the persons under 34, but 25 for every 100 among the persons over 65.
23. See article 23: " Marriage is regulated on the basis of moral and juridical equality between spouses, within the limitations required by the unity of the family."
24. For a synthetic overview of the main innovation implied in the 1975 family law reform see Vincenzi Amato 1997.
25. On this see Saraceno 1994a, 1997, and 1998.
26. It should be mentioned at least in passing that the much more recent debate on reproductive technologies, while it has shifted once again the terms of the issues concerning reproductive behavior and reproductive rights, is indebted to the abortion debate more than it is acknowledged for: not only more or less extreme developments of pro-choice arguments may be traced in the position which defends women's wish to bear a child "at all cost" and in any circumstance. Also the biologistic, walking-womb argument may be traced in the position of those who defend surrogate mothering and the legitimacy to "divide up" the reproductive process among different actors/bodies. At the same time, some of the reproductive technologies might appear as a new means by which men may regain control on fatherhood by reducing some women, at least, to "pure" child-bearing bodies. I have developed this more extensively in Saraceno 1998.
27. Other legislative changes of the seventies which should be mentioned in this perspective are the change in the system of taxation, which after a pronunciation of the Constitutional Court was changed from a system based on the idea of the family head to that of individual taxation, and the reform by which also a woman's family members survivors might receive a survivor's pension (thus equalizing men and women who pay contributions to social security).
28. I wonder if some responsibility for this, although by no means all, may be of the current of feminism which was prevalent—at least in terms of public opinion visibility—in Italy since the late seventies: the so-called "difference" feminism, which had also an indubitable popularity within the former Communist party itself and its women's commission.
29. After having defined "de-familization" as "the terms and conditions under which people engage in families, and the extent to which they can uphold an acceptable standard of living independently from the (patriarchal) family." McLaughlin and Glendinning's (1994, 65, 66) argue that "the issue is not whether people are completely 'de-familized', but rather the extent to which packages of legal and social provisions have altered the balance of power between men and women, between dependents and nondependent, and hence the terms and conditions under which people engage in familial or caring arrangements."

References

Barbagli M. "La scelta del regime patrimoniale." See M. Barbagli, and C. Saraceno, eds. Bologna: il Mulino,1997,103–112.
Barbagli, M. *Provando e riprovando*. Bologna: il Mulino, 1990.

Barbagli, M., Saraceno C. *Separarsi in Italia.* Bologna: il Mulino, 1998.
Barbagli, M., and C. Saraceno,eds., *Lo stato delle famiglie in Italia.* Bologna: il Mulino, 1997.
Bimbi, F., Castellano, G. *Madri e Padri,* Milano: F.Angeli, 1990.
Bison, I., Pisati, M., and A. Schizzerotto."Disuguaglianze di genere e storie lavorative." In Piccone Stella, S., and C. Saraceno,eds. *Genere. La costruzione sociale del femminile e del maschile.* Bologna: il Mulino, 1996.
Bonato, M. "La coppia e la gestione del denaro." See M. Barbagli and C. Saraceno, eds., 1997, 173-83.
Castiglioni M., and G. Della Zuanna. "L'inizio delle relazioni sessuali." See Barbagli, M., and C. Saraceno, eds., 1997, 76-85.
Cavalli A, and A. De Lillo,eds., *Giovani anni '90. Terzo rapporto Iard sulla condizione giovanile in Italia.* Bologna, il Mulino, 1993.
Cioni, E. "Il sistema di parentela." See M. Barbagli, and. C. Saraceno, eds., 1997, 214-23.
De Lillo, A."La mobilità sociale assoluta,"*Polis*,1, 1988, 19-52.
De Rose, A. *La (in)dissolubilità del matrimonio. I dati più recenti e la ricerca delle determinanti.* Paper presented at the Conference "Mutamenti della famiglia nei paesi occidentali," Bologna, October 6-8, 1994.
De Sandre, P."La formazione delle nuove famiglie." In Barbagli, M., Saraceno, C., eds., 1997, 65-75.
De Sandre, P, ed. *Matrimonio e figli: tra rinvio e rinuncia.* Bologna, il Mulino, 1997b.
Del Boca D. "I trasferimenti di reddito nelle famiglie."In M. Barbagli, and C.Saraceno, eds., 1997, 224-31.
Della Zuanna G.,and C.Schiavone. "Trasmissione intergenerazionale delle scelte di fecondità." *Polis* IX (2 agosto 1995), 241-62.
Facchini,C. "Gli anziani e la solidarietà tra generazioni." In M. Barbagli, and C.Saraceno, eds., 1997, 281-89.
ISTAT. *Indagine Multiscopo sulle famiglie. La condizione degli anziani. Roma,* ISTAT, 1994.
Leonini L. "La trasmissione dell'eredità." In M.Barbagli, and C. Saraceno, eds., 1997, 193-204.
Maggioni G. "Le separazioni e i divorzi." In M. Barbagli, and C. Saraceno, eds., 1997, 232-47.
McLaughlin, E., and C. Glendinning. "Paying for care in Europe: is there a feminist approach?" In Hantrais, L., and S. Mangen,eds. *Family Policy and the Welfare of Women.* Cross-National Research Papers, U.K. University of Loughborough, 1994.
Palomba, R., ed. *Vita di coppia e figli. Le opinioni degli italiani degli anni Ottanta,* Firenze, La nuova Italia: 1987.
Palomba, R., and L. Sabbadini.*Tempi diversi. L'uso del tempo di uomini e donne nell'Italia di oggi.* Roma, ISTAT, Commissione per le parità tra uomini e donne: 1994.

Pancino, C., C. Saraceno, and E.Schnabl. *Essere donna oggi: ricerche sulla formazione dell'identità femminile.*Trento, Unicoop:1978.
Piccone Stella, S. *La prima generazione.* Milano, F. Angeli: 1993.
Piccone Stella, S. "I giovani in famiglia." In Barbagli, M., and C. Saraceno, eds. 1997, 151-62.
Rettaroli, R."Le seconde nozze." In Barbagli, M., and C. Saraceno, eds. 1997, 257-71.
Righi, A. "La nuzialità. In Barbagli, M., and C. Saraceno, eds. 1997, 53-65.
Sabbadini, L.L."Le convivenze 'more-uxorio'." In Barbagli, M., and C. Saraceno, eds. 1997,86-94.
Santini, A."La fecondità."In Barbagli, M., and C. Saraceno, eds. 1997, 113-21.
Saraceno, C., ed. *Il lavoro maldiviso.* Bari, De Donato:1980.
Saraceno, C. *Pluralità e mutamento.* Milano, F. Angeli:1987
Saraceno, C. "The Italian family: paradoxes of privacy." In Ariès, P., and G. Duby, eds. *A History of Private Life*, vol.5. *Riddles of Identity in Modern Times*, Cambridge, MA, Harvard University Press: 1991, 451-502.
Saraceno, C. "The Ambivalent Familism of the Italian Welfare State." *Social Politics*, 1, 1994a.
Saraceno, C. "Commuting between Households: Multiple Memberships, Shifting Boundaries." *Innovation, The European Journal of Social Sciences.* VII (1), 1994b, 51-62.
Saraceno, C. "Le politiche per la famiglia."In Barbagli, M., and C. Saraceno, eds.1997, 301-10.
Saraceno, C. *Mutamenti della famiglia e politiche sociali in Italia*, Bologna, il Mulino: 1998.
Saraceno, C. "Italian Families under Economic Stress. The Impact of Social Policies." *Labour*, XIV (1), March 2000, 161-184.
Saraceno, C. "Verso il 2000. La pluralizzazione dei significati e delle esperienze materne." In D'Amelia, M., ed. *Storia della maternità in Italia*, Bari, Laterza: forthcoming.
Siebert, R. *E' femmina però è bella.* Torino, Rosenberg e Sellier: 1991.
Vincenzi Amato, D., "Il diritto di famiglia." In Barbagli, M., and C. Saraceno, eds., 1997, 37-53.
Zanatta, A.L. *Le nuove famiglie.* Bologna, il Mulino: 1997.

DANIELA DEL BOCA*

CHAPTER 2

LABOR MARKET PARTICIPATION AND FERTILITY OF ITALIAN WOMEN

A Comparative Perspective

Introduction

In almost all industrialized countries a rise in female labor market participation and a decline in birth rates have been observed in the last few decades. The total fertility rate in OECD (Organisation for Economic Cooperation and Development) countries decreased from 2.45 to 1.63, while the average female participation rate increased from 44.1% to 60.8%. However, in Italy (as in other Mediterranean countries such as Spain and Greece), fertility has declined dramatically while increases in participation rates have been modest.

Time series evidence shows that, while in the United States, Sweden, Denmark, and Norway (countries with high female participation) the total fertility rate recovered after 1990, in Italy as in Spain and Greece (countries with low participation) the decline has continued. Fertility rates differ highly between countries characterized by high participation (such as Sweden and Denmark) and countries characterized by low participation (such as Italy, Spain and Greece). Table 1 shows that in Italy (as in Spain and Greece) the fertility rates and the participation rates are both relatively lower than in other countries.

---

*This paper was presented in seminars in Rome, Amsterdam, and Cornell. I am grateful to Chiara Saraceno, Janet Gondrick, and Siv Gustafsson for helpful comments.

We will explore several possible interpretations for this phenomenon. Our proposed explanations involve institutional characteristics of the labor market, the social service system, and the housing market. In regards to the labor market, the wage policies pursued by the unions during the seventies and eighties have served to increase job security and reduce male/female wage differentials. On the other hand, they increase the costs of finding temporary or part-time employment (the type of job options of particular interest to married women). As a consequence, married women who work will tend to have full-time work commitments incompatible with child-care responsibilities, while married women who are not employed will tend to limit fertility due to insufficient family financial resources. Another consequence of the high costs of entry and the low demand for part-time jobs is the high unemployment rate of the youth, which contributes to their economic dependency on the family.

In regards to the social service system, married women have high costs of labor market participation due to the lack of synchronization of public child care, school, and employment hours. These institutions were developed in an era when the wife did not participate in the labor market and instead organized all family activities. They are evolving slowly over time and continue to serve as a disincentive to the labor market participation of wives.

Characteristics of the Italian housing market, most importantly strict limitations on the size and duration of mortgages, have resulted in parents largely assuming responsibility for providing housing for their mature children. A large proportion of young couples purchasing homes rely on family loans or receive the house as a gift or bequest. Italian children live with their families longer than in any other developed country.

The financial burden associated with having children in Italian families is not only larger than in other countries, but also lasts for a longer period of time, creating additional demands on women's time. Several institutional rigidities essentially necessitate high investments in children, increasing

TABLE 1. Labor force participation (LFP) and birth rates 1997

Country	LFP	Birth rates
Italy	.44	1.17
France	.56	1.81
Greece	.36	1.3
Spain	.44	1.2
Great Britain	.65	1.8

Source: OECD (2000) and Eurostat (1998)

their costs and reducing the number of children the Italian family can afford to have.

In light of these considerations we will include other factors in the determination of labor participation and fertility besides traditional individual-specific determinants of prices and income. In this paper, I will provide empirical evidence, on the relationship between institutional characteristics and women's decisions regarding working and having children. In Section 2 we discuss some of the empirical literature on fertility and participation decisions. Section 3 describes several types of market rigidities in Italy—namely, the nature of employment contracts, publicly provided services which impact the cost of children, and the credit market. In Section 4 we report relevant results from empirical analyses and draw some policy implications. Section 5 provides some closing remarks.

The literature

In the last few years there has been an increasing interest in the costs of children. Research based on the equivalence scale methods have reported that the cost of children is higher in Italy than in other countries and has increased from 1987 to 1995 from 25 to 40 per cent of the budget of a childless couple This cost is much higher if the mother works (Joshi 1990, Eckert Jaffe' 1994). Other costs are a reduction in job commitment and working hours without a substantial change in the distribution of household and care work.

These costs, however, do not represent an inescapable price for having a child. These costs are determined by various contextual elements of the labor market social policies. Other research has analyzed the difficulties encountered by the Italian family in dealing with the imperfections and limitations of the labor market and service system.

As is well known, the Italian labor market is one of the most regulated in the OECD. Del Boca (1997) analyzed the relationship between institutional characteristics of the Italian labor market and unemployment experiences of various sub-populations. Trade union policies have increased job security for the male heads of households but limited the possibilities of entry for first job-seekers. The high incidence of long-term unemployment among first-job seekers may have added an additional negative influence on fertility beside the income effect for households in which the husbands are unemployed. The feelings of uncertainty associated with long-term unemployment among first job seekers could also be an important factor in discouraging fertility (Bettio and Villa 1998).

On one hand a high proportion of the youth unemployment rate concerns women, who may feel worried about future job opportunities in presence of children; on the other hand children's unemployment adds financial burden on the family. The Italian family compensates for the job rationing, providing income support for the children during the periods of unemployment and helping actively in their job search (Bank of Italy 1995).

Another characteristic of the Italian labor market which directly impacts married women's choices stems from the limited development of the service sector. Since women are disproportionately represented in service-sector jobs in OECD countries, this factor reduces both the demand and the supply of female labor.

The characteristics of the service sector are also relevant. Del Boca (1993, 2002) analyzed the characteristics of the supply of public child care. These services are typically inexpensive, though capacity, in terms of number of children and hours per child, is extremely limited. This makes the service compatible with mothers who work part-time but not with those who work full-time (which are the only types of jobs available). The analysis of the relationship between child-care costs and labor supply shows that a reduction in child-care costs increases only the probability of mothers' part-time employment. On the other hand, the presence of another adult in the family significantly increases the probability of the mother's working full-time. In some sense, it appears that Italy is stuck in a "low female participation rate" equilibrium in which one of the major reasons for low participation rates is the mismatch between the types of jobs sought by married women with children and the types of jobs offered. It would appear that this imbalance could be addressed by increasing private provision of child care, which would simultaneously increase job opportunities for women and reduce the costs of taking full-time jobs. For a variety of reasons, almost all of which are related to labor market regulation, the state retains a virtual monopoly in the provision of these types of services.

Several limitations also characterize the credit market. The mortgage market is very small, partially because the maximum amount which can be financed is quite limited, as is the duration of the loan. Del Boca and Lusardi (1996) have shown that Italian households in the period 1987–1993 have overcome financial market limitations and the high burden of the mortgage debt repayment by increasing wives' labor supply. Imperfections in the Italian credit market, such as strict limitations on the size and duration of mortgages, have also resulted in parents largely assuming responsibility for providing loans for housing purchases (Guiso and Jappelli 1995, Cigno, Giannelli, and Rosati 1998, Barbagli and Saraceno 1997).

In addition to financial transfers from parents to their adult children, parents also provide support by having their mature children live in their household. Italian children live with their families longer than in any other developed country (Giannelli and Monfardini 1998). The financial burden associated with having children in Italian families is not only larger than in other countries but also lasts for a longer period of time, during which the family supports the adult children in their search for a stable job and as they make human capital investments (a similar pattern seems to emerge for Spanish households).

The availability of comparable data sets have also allowed interesting comparative work. Gornick, Meyers and Ross (1997) who have used the Luxembourg Income study to analyze the effect of child care found a relevant effect of public child care on mothers' employment. The expenditure on social protection in Italy (as well as other southern countries) shows a small devoted to maternity and family functions (7.5% and 10.5% in EU12). Between 1980 to 1996 the share of expenditure dedicated to family and maternity have declined remarkedly (Saraceno 2000). Their results demonstrate a strong association between policy variables and the employment of mothers with younger children. Some studies have analyzed the complementarity between family and the welfare state, defining the Southern model as a family-care model in which the family acts as the explicit partner of social policies. The Southern family still largely operates as a social clearinghouse, mediating difficult relationships between a variegated labor market and equally variegated income maintenance systems (Ferrera 1996, 21). The specific effects on children have been studied by Micklewright and Stewart (1999). It emerges that among the southern European Countries children's poverty rate is among the highest of the European countries.

Institutional rigidities

The characteristics of the Italian labor market

In spite of recent institutional changes, the Italian labor market still remains a highly regulated one. Eurostat (1995) provides a ranking from 0 to 10 measuring the degree of labor market regulations and reports that Italy is the highest (8) relative to Great Britain and the U.S. (0), Germany (5), France (6), and Sweden (4). Strict rules apply about hiring and firing workers and types of employment arrangements. The hiring system and the high minimum wage severely restrict employment opportunities for labor market entrants. In spite of recent changes in the 1990s towards a more flexible system, Italy is still the only European country where job placement is a state monopoly and private employment agencies are banned. As a consequence, an informal network as a source of recruitment has been developed: according to the recent Bank of Italy Survey data in 1998, over 50% of all hiring has been obtained through friends and relatives.

The firing rules are also very strict. Severance payments are very high and redundancy is not explicitly mentioned as a just cause: the penalty for employers in case of "unfair" dismissal is very high (rehire and compensate). Because of the high costs of hiring and firing, employers tend to use overtime instead of hiring new workers when demand increases. When the regulations on overtime were relaxed, the use of overtime increased significantly, partly reflecting the decline of the power of the unions.

Another important aspect of the rigidity of the labor market is the menu of available employment arrangements. While the contract of indefinite duration has been the norm in Europe, during the last fifteen years a number of flexible contractual forms have developed, such as fixed term or part-time work, temporary work, overtime and work-sharing. In Italy the process towards a more flexible system started later and has been much slower, given the strong opposition of unions. The Italian unions have opposed different employment contracts, fearing that potential division of the workers force could reduce the workers' cohesion.

Current regulations still make the employment of two part-time workers more costly than one full-time. Italian women would prefer to work part-time: recent surveys at different points of time and different areas of the country have reported similar results (Del Boca 1993). More than half of women who were not employed at the time of the interview would like to work, but with a flexible or part-time schedule, and a great proportion of the women who already work would prefer to work fewer hours. Table

TABLE 2. Part-time and women employment in service

Country	% Part-time	% Women in service sector
Italy	10.1	56
France	12	59
Spain	7.0	52
Greece	6.1	54
Denmark	22.8	68
Sweden	24.0	69
U.K.	25	62

Source: Eurostat (1998)

TABLE 3. Long-term unemployed youth

Country	Long-term unemployed youth
Italy	63.4
France	23.7
Sweden	8.2
Denmark	9.3
Greece	49.8
Spain	45.7

Source: Eurostat Labour Force Survey (1998)

2 shows the low percentage of part-time work in Italy relative to other European countries. Another important factor associated to women participation rate is the proportion of employment in the service sector (Table 2, column 2).

The highly protective regulations have made female labor more costly relative to male labor, reducing the incentive for employers to hire them. Employers have preferred male workers, both because they are less expensive (they do not receive maternity benefits) and are more likely to work overtime (Del Boca 1998). These regulations have been largely responsible for the high unemployment rates of women and youth, which increase the economic burdens on the family.

The Italian youth unemployment rate, especially the long-term unemployment, is the highest among industrialized countries. Table 3 reports data on long-term youth unemployment.

The evidence related to the unemployment rate by family composition also shows the particular position of Italian and the other Mediterranean countries. Table 4 shows that in Italy the unemployment rate of children is much higher than in non-Mediterranean countries (such as Germany, France, and Great Britain), yet the proportion of unemployed children

TABLE 4. Unemployment rate by family position on total unemployment 1995

Country	Head	Children	Wife	Other
Italy	17.7	60.9	18.0	3.4
Germany	50.0	12.7	19.5	4.8
Greece	22.9	51.5	23.2	3.5
Spain	24.6	51.5	29.5	4.8
France	40.8	23.3	32.2	3.5
Great Britain	45.1	24.9	55.1	24.9

Source: Eurostat 1998

receiving unemployment benefits is very low in Italy (17.7), Greece (5.43) and Spain (18.7), while is much higher in Germany, France, Denmark (35–55%).

The child care system

Another source of rigidity concerns the Italian child care sector, which is largely subsidized but characterized by extreme rigidity in the weekly hours available and frequent interruptions of service. This makes the service compatible with part-time work but not with full-time activities. The school hours are also limited to half-day while in most countries child-care lasts the full day. School hours per week are 27 in Italy, Spain and Greece, while they are 30 in Denmark, 35 France and 33 in the United Kingdom.

In Italy the percentage of children younger than 3 who are in child care is quite small. A remarkable difference also exists among European countries between the availability of child care for children <3 years and children older than 3 (6 per cent and 91 per cent respectively). Table 5 shows that in Italy the percentage of children less than 3 who are in child care is quite small, while child care for children older than 3 is relatively high.

The child care system shows strong geographical differences. The proportion of children between 0 and 3 years of age in public child care is about 30% in some areas of the North and only 1–2% in most Southern areas. Bradshaw et al (1997) ranked several countries, using a index (between 1 for the highest support to 17 for lowest support,) for the income support provided to families with children. Italy is ranked 10.3, Spain 12.8 and Greece 14.3, while Denmark is ranked 7.0, France is ranked 3.7, Sweden 5.3. In the countries where public support for children is the lowest women participation and fertility rates are also the lowest.

TABLE 5. Percentage of children in child care by age

Country	% child care 0–3	% child care 3–6
Italy	6	91
France	23	99
Greece	3	70
Denmark	48	82
Spain	2	84
Sweden	33	72
U.K.	2	60

Source: Eurostat (1999)

TABLE 6. Participation rate of mothers by age of the child

Country	Participation by age of the child		
	<3 yrs.	3–6 yrs.	7–14 yrs.
Italy	50	51	47
France	61	69	63
Greece	47	49	50
Denmark	84	90	90
Spain	40	44	37
U.K.	47	62	76

Source: Eurostat (2000)

Recent research has focused on various social policies affecting mothers' participation in the labor force. Other studies have shown the effects of other social policies such as maternity leave, with mixed findings (Gustaffson and Stafford 1995). These studies have shown, for example, that the availability of child care services affects significantly women's preferences for non market time versus time spent in paid work. Improvements in child care options are associated with increases in labor supply of mothers in most countries (Ermisch, 1989, Gustaffson 1994, 1995, Blau 1991, Connelly 1992, Gornick, Meyers, and Ross 1997).

These results are somewhat problematic given that an important limitation of the Italian labor market concerns the low availability of part-time employment arrangement. Several studies have shown that part-time opportunities have positively affected women's participation (Meulders and Plasman 1994, Rubery and Fagan 1994). Studies focusing on women participation in the Southern Europe have shown that the low percentage of part-time employment explains the low participation of women and the decline in female activity rate after age of marriage and childbirth, which contrasts with the pattern in most Northern EU countries. These conditions have been largely responsible for the high unemployment rates of women and youth. The Italian unemployment rate is the highest among industrialized countries, especially long-term unemployment. Women's unemployment rate is twice as much as men's (14.8 against 7.7, and the long-term unemployment is 60 per cent while men is 55.8 per cent.) (Eurostat 1998).

Table 6 shows that participation rate of mothers with children under 3 is lower than the participation rate of mothers with children between 3 and 6 (and certainly lower than Denmark, Sweden and France).

The rigidity and limitation of the supply of child care seems to be compensated by the family support. The number of children under grandparents' care is 45.7 (per 100 children) in households where the mother works and 16.9% in households where the mother does not work. Among children between 3–5 years of age the proportion of children under grandparents care are still very high: 39.9% when the mother works and 13.6% when the mother does not (Indagine Multiscopo ISTAT 1998).

According to recent studies on children costs based on equivalence scale methods (1990) children costs in Italy are higher than in other advanced countries and have increased in the last few years (Eckert Jaffe 1994). These studies, however, are based on the assumption that the number of children is not a choice variable, which have important implications on the results (Cigno 1996). In Italy, as well as Spain and Greece, the welfare of children has decreased in the last few years in comparison with other countries of the European Union (Mickleright and Stewart 1999).

The data presented in this section seem to point to the effects of various market limitations in Italy (as well as other Southern European countries) that seem to explain higher costs of raising children and therefore explanation of their limited number. The southern European has been defined as a "family care model" (Sipilaan 1996, Ferrera 1996) where the family is entitled to limited supply of social services as well as low direct support.[1]

The credit system

Other sources of rigidities lie in the credit market. The mortgage market is very small, its duration is on average much shorter than elsewhere, and the ratio required of the down payment to the house value is very high. The duration of the mortgage loans is on average 10–15 years while it is 25–30 years in the United States and in the United Kingdom. The downpayment ratio for housing mortgage loans is still around 30–40% while it is around 80–90% in most other advanced countries. These limitations have reduced the options of younger households to buy: the proportion of younger households (under 29 years of age) who owns their house is smaller than in other selected countries. It is only 25% in Italy, while it is between 45 and 50% in other advanced countries (Del Boca and Lusardi 1996).

The Italian family has compensated for the financial market rigidities in various ways, creating alternative informal markets. Guiso and Jappelli (1991, 1995) have shown that intergenerational family transfers lessen borrowing constraints for young cohorts. Transfers contribute to shorten the saving period to buy a house, reducing the intertemporal distortion induced by mortgage market imperfections. Other behavior such as living

TABLE 7. % of children 20–29 living with their parents in 1987 and 1995

Country	1987	1995
Italy	60	71
France	34	33
Spain	49	59
Greece	41	49
Denmark	32	29
Sweden	29	23
U.K.	30	31

Source: Eurostat (1997)

longer with parents is modified in order to overcome liquidity constraints and increase savings. The proportion of children over 20 living with their parents is much higher than in other advanced countries. As we see in Table 7, the data for 1987 and 1995 show that the proportion of 20–29 years old living with their parents is highest in Italy (and high in Greece and Spain) and has increased during the period of observation, while in most other countries it has decreased.

According to other empirical evidence regarding the proportion of children between 20–29 years of age who are employed and the proportion that are economically dependent from their families, Italy is ranked the lowest for the employment rate and highest for the dependency rate (followed by Spain and Greece) (Del Boca 1997). In the next section we discuss empirical results on the relationship between fertility participation and draw some policy implications.

Policy implications

Recent research (Del Boca 1997, 1998) using the Bank of Italy panel data have analyzed the most important factor determining women's participation and fertility of Italian married women for the period 1991–1995. The empirical results show that beside the traditional variables such as income schooling and age, other variables appear to be important. These variables have been used as indicators of the limitations of the labor market (part-time opportunities) of childcare (number of childcare slots available by region) and mortgage (by region).

The traditional variables have an impact that is similar to that reported in other recent literature on fertility and labor force participation using cross section data (Del Boca, 1997, Gustaffson 1995). The wife's age has a negative effect on participation and fertility. Family income has a negative effect on the probability of working and fertility. Wife's schooling has a positive effect on participation and fertility. The positive effect of wife's schooling on fertility can be interpreted as a permanent income effect, given that father's education is not included in the analysis (assortative mating). The number of children has a negative effect on participation.

Other variables have been introduced as an indicator that family support (which is here the amount of family transfers) has a positive effect on the likelihood of fertility and participation in the labor force of wives. Transfer recipients are on average younger and have lower income than households who do not receive transfers. Studies on intergenerational transfers have shown that transfer recipients are also more likely to be denied credit than the rest of the population (50% of transfer recipients have been denied credit from the financial institutions), confirming an important role for the family as a system of household finance (Guiso and Iappelli 1991). The positive effect of transfer on fertility has also an interpretation related to the characteristics of the transfers. Given that most transfers go from the parents to the children, transfers are more likely to increase with the number of children, confirming other empirical results that show that relatives are more likely to transfer money to families with children (Mayer and Engelhardt 1994). We have analyzed the effect of other indicators of potential family support such as the presence of at least one parent of the wife. We believe that this variable can be interpreted as indicating a potential opportunity for childcare in conditions of limited public childcare facilities. Having at least one of the parent still alive has a positive effect on participation and fertility (Del Boca 1998).

Table 8 reports the correlation coefficient between child care, part-time, mortgage, and fertility, and employment rates of women and employment rates of mothers.

Women's employment rate shows high correlation coefficients with

TABLE 8. Correlations between women's and mothers' employment rates, fertility, child care, part-time, and mortgage

Variables	Women's employment	Mothers' employment	Fertility
Child care	.60	.70	.55
Part-time	.47	.55	.43
Mortgage	.47	.44	.41

Source: Bank of Italy Survey 1995

child care, part-time and mortgage availability. The correlation coefficient with childcare and part-time is higher with mother's employment rate. The third column shows the correlation coefficient with the fertility rate: while mortgage rate and childcare is slightly lower, part-time is about the same size.

Conclusions

In this paper we have discussed the relationship between institutional rigidities and the low fertility and participation of women in Italy. We have compared the Italian case to other southern European countries (Spain, Greece) which also have very limited supply of social services and rigidities in the time arrangements. The labor market is characterized by a high unemployment of youth that increase the dependency of children beyond mature age. The credit market for housing is still highly regulated, and the family often has to compensate by offering loans to the adult children as well as co-residence. The proportion of women in the active labor force is low, but the majority of those who are employed work full-time. The fertility rates of these countries are the lowest in Europe.

We have focused on several aspects of the Italian labor market, housing market, and child care system, in order to take into account relevant constraints that Italian households have to face in their labor market and fertility decisions. We report some empirical results, using the Bank of Italy survey in 1995, on the relationship between women's employment, fertility and variables which represent indicators of child care, part-time and mortgage availability. Our results indicate that labor force participation and fertility decisions are both affected by similar forces. The decisions to work and have a child are positively related to the available supply of public childcare and part-time opportunities in the labor market.

Policies which would reduce the financial burden on the Italian family by providing more flexible working hours choices for working mothers, looser restrictions on family loans, an expansion of the child care system could contribute to reducing the financial burden on the Italian family and have a positive effect on both women's employment and fertility.

Notes

1. In most Northern European countries the age of 18–19 marks the end of any legally enforced financial obligation for parents. For example, students are entitled to financial support on their own right and without account of parental income

(Saraceno 1998). In Italy parental financial obligation can continue until the child is self-supporting or indefinitely.

References

Bank of Italy 1995. "Survey of Italian Households Income and Wealth". Rome 1995

Bank of Italy 1998. "Survey of Italian Households Income and Wealth". Rome 1998

Barbagli M., Saraceno C. "La famiglia in Italia". Il Mulino, Bologna 1997.

Bettio, F., Villa, P. "A Mediterranean Perspective on the Break-down of the Relationship between Participation and Fertility". *Cambridge Journal of Economics* 22, 1998: 137–171.

Blau, D. M. *The Economics of Child Care*. Russell Sage, New York 1991.

Bradshaw J., Ditch, J., Holmes, H., Whiteford, P. *Support for the Children: A Comparison of Arrangements for Fifteen Countries*. London: Department of Social Security, 1997.

Cigno, A. *Economics of the Family*. Oxford University Press 1996.

Cigno, A., Giannelli, G., Rosati, F. "Voluntary Transfers among Italian Households", *Structural Change and Economies Dynamics*, Special Issue "The Economics of the Family", 9, 4, 1998: 435–453.

Colombino, U., Del Boca, D. "The Effect of Taxation on Labour Supply in Italy", *Journal of Human Resources*, Vol. 25, 3, 1990.

Connelly, R. "The Effect of Child Care Costs on Married Women's Labor Force Participation", *Review of Economics and Statistics*, 74, 1, 1992: 83–90

Del Boca, D. *Offerta di lavoro e politiche pubbliche*, NIS, Roma 1993.

Del Boca, D. and Lusardi, A. "Credit Constraints and Family Allocation of Time", *Working Paper*. C. V. Starr Center for Applied Economics, New York University 1996.

Del Boca, D. "Intrahousehold Distribution of Resources and Labor Market Participation Decisions", *Economics of the Family and Family Policies*. In Persson, I., Jonung, C., eds., Routledge 1997.

Del Boca, D. "Labor Policies, Economic Flexibility and Women's Work: The Italian Experience", *Women, Work and Labor Markets*. In Drew, E., Emerek, R., eds. Routledge 1998.

Del Boca, D. "The Effect of Child Care on Participation and Fertility", Journal of Population Economics, 14, 2002.

Eckert Jaffe, O. *"Standard of living and families: observation and analysis"*, John Libbey Eurotext 1994.

Ermisch, J. F. "Purchased Child Care, Optimal Family Size and Mother's Employment: Theory and Econometric Analysis", *Journal of Population Economics*, 2, 1989: 79–102.

Eurostat, Labour Force Survey, Brussels 1997

Eurostat, Statistics in Focus, Brussels 1998
Eurostat, Labour Force Survey, Brussels 1998
Eurostat, Labour Force Survey, Brussels 1999
Eurostat, Labour Force Survey, Brussels, 2000
Ferrera, M. "The Southern Model in Social Europe", *Journal of European Social Policy*, 6 (1), 17–37, 1996.
Giannelli, G., Monfardini, E. *The probability of cohabitation of adult children*. Working paper. University of Florence 1998.
Gornick, J.C., Meyers, M.K., Ross, K.E. "Supporting the Employment of Mothers: Policy Variation across Fourteen Welfare States". *Journal of European Social Policy*, 7, 1997: 45–70.
Guiso, L., Jappelli, T. "Intergenerational Transfers and Capital Market Imperfections", *European Economic Review*, 35, 1991: 103–120.
Guiso, L., Jappelli, T. "Intergenerational Transfers, Borrowing Constraints and the Timing of Home Ownership", *Temi di Discussione*. Bank of Italy, Rome 1995.
Gustaffson, S. "Childcare and Types of Welfare States.", D. Sainsbury ed., *Gendering Welfare States*, Thousand Oaks, Sage, Ca., 1994:45–61.
Gustaffson, S., and Stafford, P. "Public Policies and Women's Labor Force Participation." In P. Schultz ed., *Investments in Women's Human Capital*. Yale University Press, 1995.
Hsiao, C. "Benefits and Limitations of Panel Data", *Economic Reviews*, 4, 1985: 121–174.
ISTAT, Indagine Multiscopo, Rome 1998.
Joshi, H. "The Cash Opportunity Cost of Child-Bearing: An Approach to Estimation Using British Data." *Population Studies*, 1, 1990: 41–60.
Martinez-Granado, M., Ruiz-Castillo, J. "The Decisions of Spanish Youth", WP *Universidad Carlos III de Madrid*, 42, 1998.
Mayer, C., Engelhardt, G. "Gifts, Down Payments and Housing Affordability." *W.P. Federal Reserve*, Boston, 5, 1994.
Meulders, D., Plasman, O., Plasman, R. *Atypical Employment in the EC*. Aldershot, Dartmouth 1994.
Micklewright, J, Stewart, K. "Is Child Welfare Converging in the European Union?". UNICEF, Occasional paper, 1999.
OECD, Employment Outlook, Paris 2000
OECD, Employment Outlook, Paris, 2001
Rubery, J., Fagan, C. *New Frontiers in Industrial Relations*, H. Hyman, ed., Blackwell, Oxford 1994.
Saraceno, C., "Italian Families Under Stress", Del Boca, D., and Tanda, P. eds., *Labour*, Special Issue on Household Behavior and Social Policies, 1, 2000.

STEFANIA ROSSETTI

PAOLA TANDA

CHAPTER 3

HUMAN CAPITAL, GENDER, AND LABOR MARKET PERFORMANCES

Introduction

This study takes into consideration the relation between human capital investment and labor market performances, focusing on gender differences within and among European countries. The aim of the paper is also to show that differences in behaviors and performances of men and women can be easily explained if family choices are considered. When analyzing equal opportunities (segregation) in labor market, it is important to consider both the question of access to labor market and (once one is in) that of earnings opportunities

As to the access to labor market problem, first we look at participation of active population. This can be regarded as a choice—individual or familiar—although nonparticipation may hide a problem of "discouragement," stemming from a "constrained" and not a free choice (for example, in presence either of children or of elderly people, it depends on available services). Secondly, we consider the probability of being employed or unemployed.

Both access to labor market and occupational segregation can be related to human capital investment. First of all, education differentials between men and women in European countries are examined. Secondly,

---

The opinions expressed are the authors' and are not necessarily shared by their Institutes. The authors take responsibility for all errors and omissions.

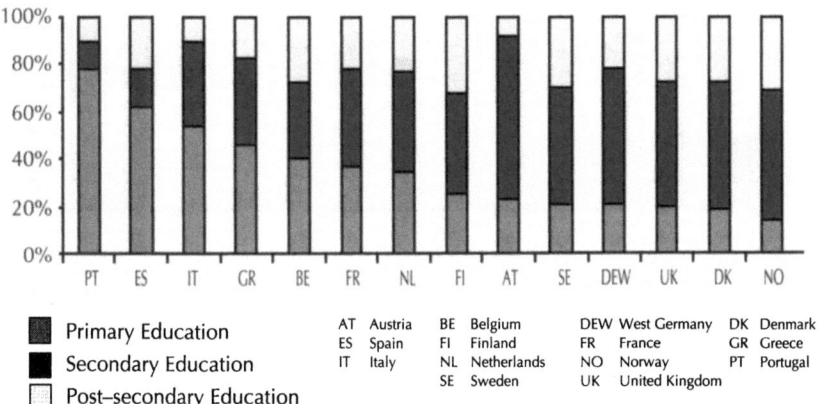

FIGURE 1A Distribution of total population aged 25–29 years by educational attainment (1999)

gender differentials in participation rates, unemployment rates, and employment/population ratios by educational attainment are investigated.

What we expect is that education is a relatively stronger incentive to labor force participation for women rather than for men. Moreover, we know that education improves employment opportunities for both sexes, and it is interesting to understand whether it does so to the same extent. Another issue to consider is whether lower education differentials (that is, good equal opportunities in access to education) also foster a lower segregation in labor market.

An important feature of discrimination against women in the labor market is represented by the difference in earnings opportunities. The existence and the extent of wage differentials between sexes have been

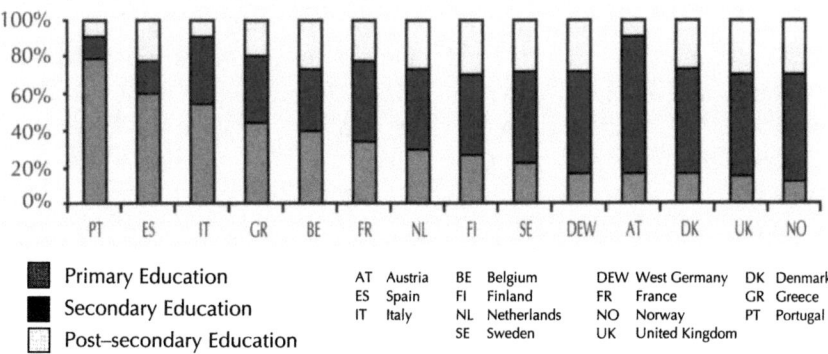

FIGURE 1B Distribution of male population aged 25–29 years by educational attainment (1999)

50   Women's Work, the Family and Social Policy

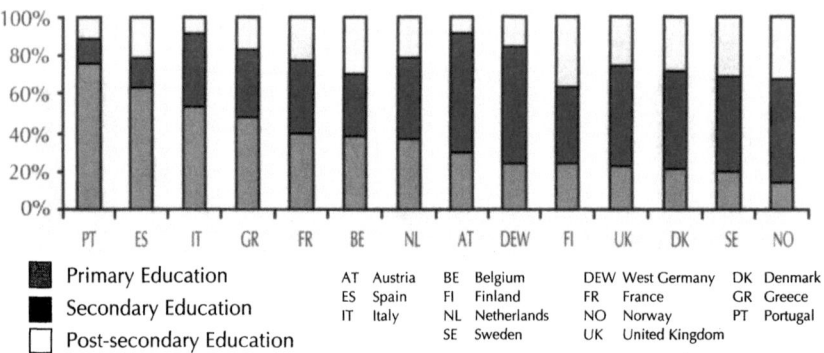

FIGURE 1C Distribution of female population aged 25–29 years by educational attainment (1999)

widely proved for industrialized countries by a large number of studies conducted on microdata. The main drawback of these works is that of being hardly comparable. This paper proposes a synthetic and "aggregate" vision of this subject, trying to analyze some key aspects of the relations among human capital, wages, and sex discrimination. In particular, the hypotheses we test regard the presence of vertical occupational segregation and of wage differential between sexes to account for human capital indicators such as professions. Moreover, in order to make a more exhaustive comparison between men and women in employment, we take into consideration the hours worked that, as for labor force participation choices, can be held as an indicator of the different opportunities for men and women in the job market. With regard to all these issues we try to make out differences in the behavior of the countries considered.

The paper is organized as follows: the first section describes educational attainments reached by the population in the various European countries and defines the scenario behind the reasoning of the successive sections; the second and the third sections first analyze the labor force participation choices in the labor market and then the performances of men and women as expressed by their employment achievements. Finally the fourth section investigates differences in earnings and working hours.

Access to education and gender differences

Figure 1 (a,b,c) shows schooling rates in 1999 for the overall population[1] of 14 European countries by sex and education dividing by the usual three levels classification.² The representation allows us to appreciate disparities both in education levels among countries, and in sex differentials in education. First of all, we can draw a distinction between countries which achieved a good schooling level and countries where the dissemination of education is still in process. More specifically, we observe that Spain and Portugal exhibit the highest share of population in primary education (more than 60% in Spain and nearly 80% in Portugal); Italy follows with a share of 55% in primary education; however in this country the share of upper secondary education is quite considerable (over 30%) and comparable to that of Belgium and France. Then, we find a large group of countries characterized by a relatively large share of people in upper secondary education (Denmark, West Germany, Austria, Sweden, United Kingdom, and Norway). Finally, the Scandinavian countries (Sweden, Norway, Finland, and Denmark) together with Belgium and United Kingdom have about 30% of population with higher education, while the corresponding share is very low (less than 10%) in Italy, Portugal, and Austria.

Referring to the average schooling level of the population,³ that is, a synthetic indicator of the education process, we can draw a ranking of countries (fig. 2). The most educated countries are the Scandinavian ones together with the United Kingdom, followed by the complex of Central Europe countries, while the lowest positions belong to the four Mediterranean countries, with Portugal by far in the worst position.

As far as sex differentials are concerned, it should be noted that on average men exhibit a better educational attainment, although in some countries (Belgium, Portugal, Sweden, Norway, and Finland) the opposite

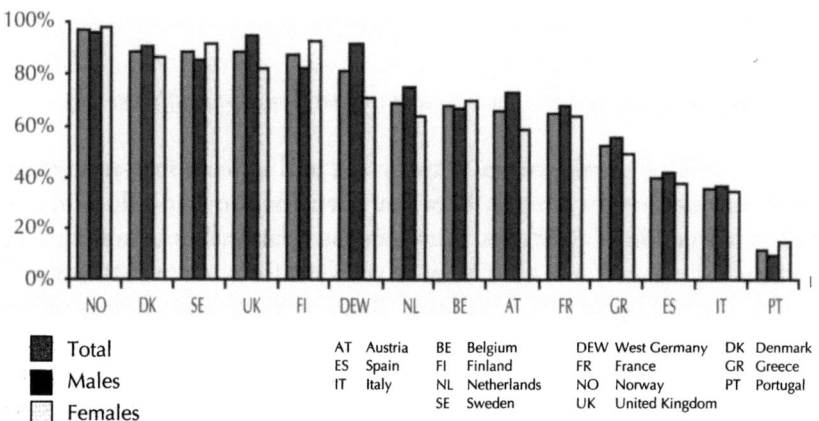

FIGURE 2 Average education level, total and by sex, in some European countries

situation occurs; on the other hand, West Germany, Austria, Netherlands, and the United Kingdom discriminate against women more significantly. In addition, we observe that differences tend to decrease for higher schooling levels. This could be explained by supposing that different cohorts of individuals are taken into consideration for each schooling level. In particular, the population with a primary education should have a larger share of elderly people, reflecting a lower degree of equal opportunities between sexes in access to education, rather than larger schooling differentials. In higher education levels, instead, we have a younger population, for whom a major parity has been realized, reflected by smaller differentials in education.

Looking at single countries, it should be noted that Belgium, Portugal, Sweden, and Finland are the only countries where men exhibit a higher share than women in primary education. In the other countries the share of women is more relevant and in particular in Austria, the United Kingdom, and West Germany. The upper secondary education rate shows an opposite trend: it is higher for women only in West Germany; very similar for both sexes in Belgium, Italy, Portugal, Greece, and Sweden; while in the remaining countries men prevail. The most notable differentials are registered in Austria, followed by Denmark and France. Finally, looking at tertiary education rates, it should be stressed that while in some countries the men's rates are considerably higher (West Germany, Netherlands, and the United Kingdom), in Scandinavian countries (with the only exception of Denmark) and in Portugal, tertiary education is more diffused among women. In the remaining countries the diffusion of tertiary education between sexes is very similar.

Labor market participation

Does education affect men and women participation choices in a different way?

The analysis of participation rates by sex and educational attainments shows a positive correlation between participation and education for both sexes and in all countries. However the relationship between participation and education is clearly more relevant for women than for men, confirming the hypothesis that labor force participation choices of men are determined also by other factors, in particular by their role of breadwinner in the family (fig. 3a and 3b) (Becker 1985; Becker and Tomes 1986). Actually, men's participation rates are very high also for the lowest

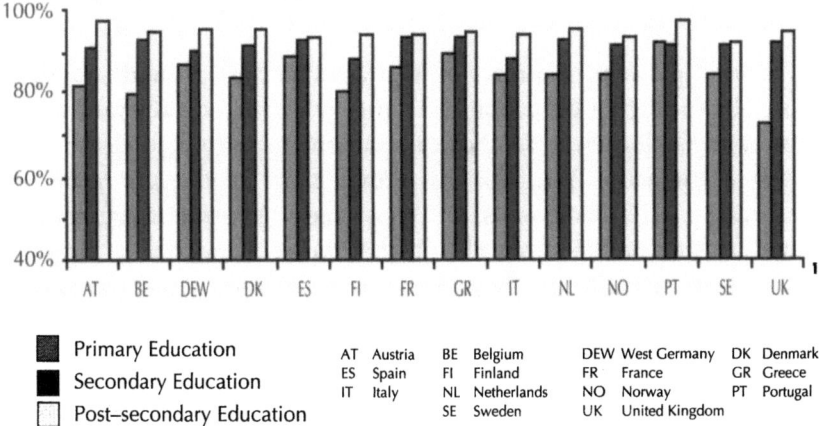

FIGURE 3A Labor force participation rates by educational attainment—males

education level, and there is a gap in participation rates only between primary education and the upper levels, while for women the growth of participation is relevant for upper secondary education with respect to primary and also for tertiary education with respect to upper secondary. As a consequence, sex differentials[4] in participation rates show a declining trend for higher level of education, and are almost zero in countries like Sweden, and Norway.

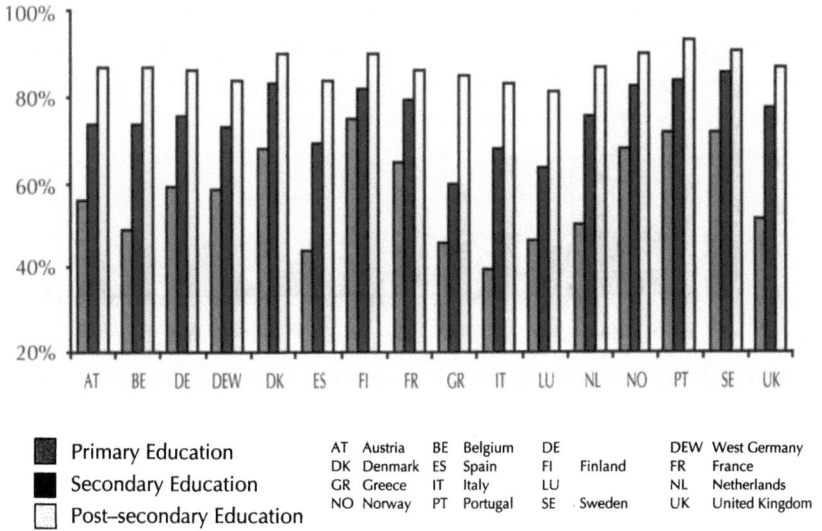

FIGURE 3B Labor force participation rates by educational attainment—females

Which are the main differences among European countries?

In general, participation rates of men are very similar in all countries, espceially for higher education levels (fig. 3a). The most relevant disparities in men's participation choices occur for less educated people. The lowest participation rates for this group, both in absolute terms and with respect to other groups, are registered in Northern countries (in Scandinavian countries, but also in the United Kingdom, in Belgium, and in Netherlands); on the other hand, in Mediterranean countries, with the partial exception of Italy, we find the highest participation rates of less educated men. The opposite situation occurs for women (fig. 3b). The lowest participation rates for primary education are registered in Mediterranean countries (Spain, Italy, and Greece), with values well below 50%, while in Scandinavian countries women labor force participation is high, often around 70%, even for the lower schooling level (fig. 4). It is easy to interpret these differences as the result of different cultural attitudes: on one hand, we have countries where women play a role mainly within the family, and the family itself is a pillar of the society. In order to understand the different organization of the society across countries it should be enough to think that while in countries such as Spain, Italy, Greece, and Belgium about 70% of people aged 25–49 are married, the comparable share falls to about 50% in Scandinavian countries.

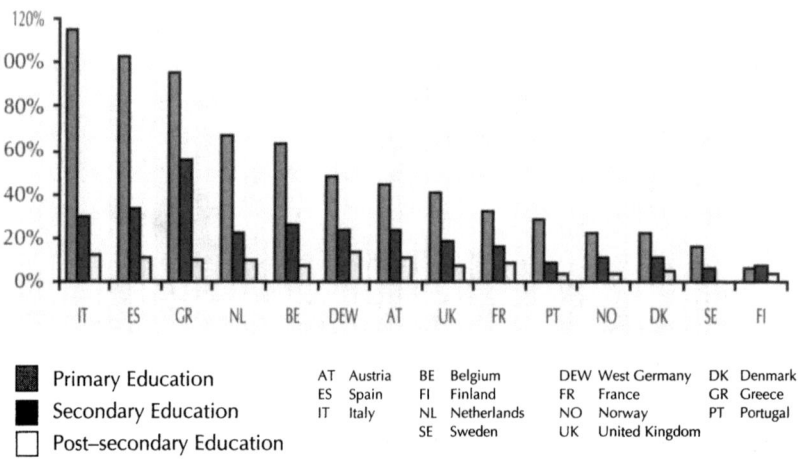

FIGURE 4 Differentials in labor force participation rates—(% values)

Labor market performances: Employment and unemployment

Does education reduce unemployment risk in a different way between men and women?

Unemployment risk decreases as education rises for both sexes and in all countries. However, a higher level of education reduces the probability of unemployment to a notably different extent in the various countries, while within a single country men's and women's behavior is quite similar. In other words, in some countries the impact of education is slight for both sexes (e.g., Spain, Italy, Portugal, Greece, and Sweden), while in other countries unemployment risk is considerably lower for better educated people (Belgium, France, West Germany, and United Kingdom).

An interesting feature is that the "education effect" seems often more relevant for men than for women. This is shown by the analysis of percentage differentials of specific unemployment rates (fig. 5). In fact, in some countries unemployment rate differentials tend to increase for higher levels of education, and often exhibit the largest gaps for upper secondary education (Denmark, France, and Netherlands). In those countries where unemployment differentials for primary education are positive (West Germany, Austria, and the United Kingdom), noting that men's unemployment rates are higher, we observe a reduction of the differential, and sometimes it turns negative—that is, with higher women's unemployment rates.

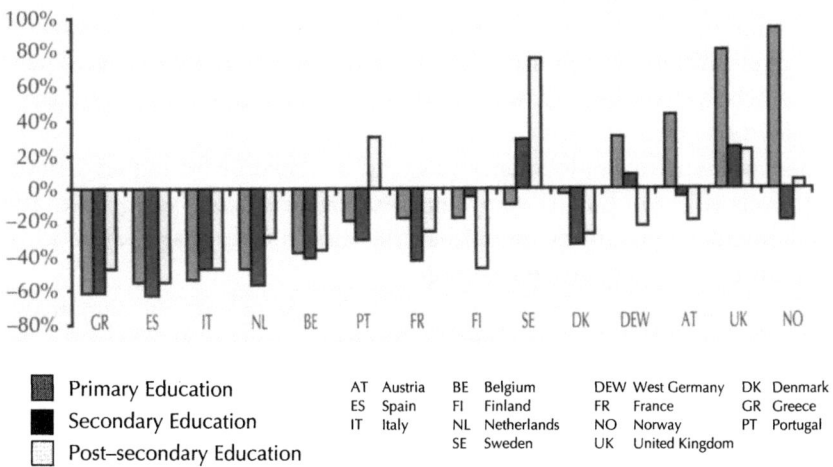

FIGURE 5   Differentials in unemployment rates—(% values)

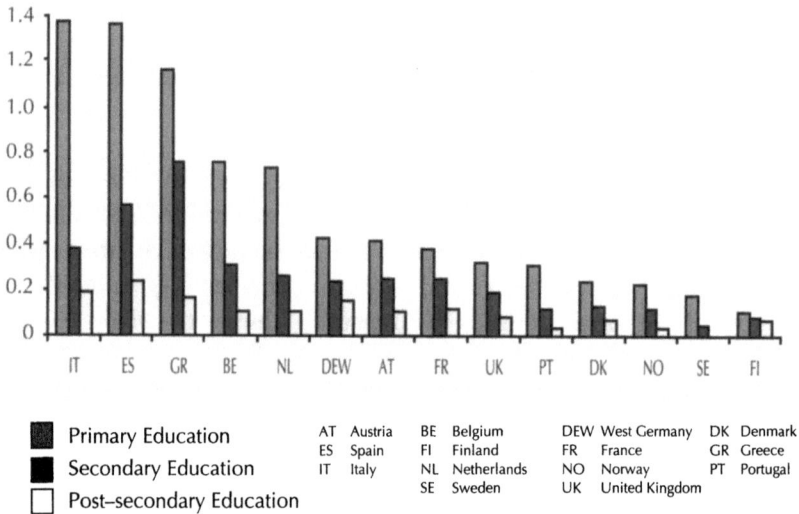

FIGURE 6 Differentials in employment/population ratios—(% values)

This means that, in contrast with the analysis of participation choices, a higher education level does not reduce gender differences.

Does education improve employment opportunities for men and women?

The story told by unemployment rates, however, is partially false. An examination of employment/population ratios (i.e. employment rates) actually gives a different response. The employment rate of less educated people is relatively lower for women than for men, and the gap between employment rates narrows as the education level rises; in other words, males and females employment rates tend to converge for higher schooling levels (fig. 6). This is very apparent for Belgium, Spain, Italy, and Netherlands; it should be noted that the same countries also show a low participation of less educated women.

In general terms, the previous result of the unemployment rates analysis is likely to depend on the fact that in the female component of the active population there is an excess supply of well-educated women.

Do gender differentials in employment rates differ among countries?

In order to account for discrimination towards women both in the family context, represented by the fact that female labor force participation is conditioned by family needs, and discrimination through disparities in employment opportunities, the most adequate indicator seems to be the employment rate. The lowest differentials between male and female employment rates are registered in Scandinavian countries (Finland, Sweden, Norway, and Denmark), while the largest occur in Spain and Italy, immediately followed by Belgium and Netherlands (fig. 6). The satisfactory performances of Scandinavian countries seem to be determined by their ability to give employment opportunities also to less educated women, albeit they are not a significant share of active population, as is the case for Mediterranean countries. From this point of view the case of Portugal is worth noting. In spite of a large presence of women with a low educational attainment, Portugal's employment rate for this group is comparable to those of Scandinavian countries.

Are equal opportunities in education associated with equal employment opportunities in the labor market?

The available evidence shows that the relation between education and employment opportunities is probably weak (OECD, 1998). In fact, on one hand the Scandinavian model shows a substantial parity between sexes in both respects; on the other hand there are countries such as Italy, Spain, and Belgium that, in spite of a good parity in access to education (as the low education differentials show), exhibit considerable differences for both unemployment and employment rates. The most likely explanation is that in these countries the effort of giving equal opportunities to both sexes is partially abated both by the burden of family constraints that significantly influence female labor force participation choices, and by a relevant discrimination on labor market, as confirmed by the greater female risk of unemployment.

Labor market performances: Jobs, earning opportunities, and hours of work

Feminization rates (calculated as share of women employed in total employment by profession and by sector) in 1995 allow us to see whether professions and sectors with a greater female presence coincide with those professions and sectors with lower female wages. In other words we want to verify the existence of gender occupational segregation.

The classification by sectors available distinguishes mainly industry

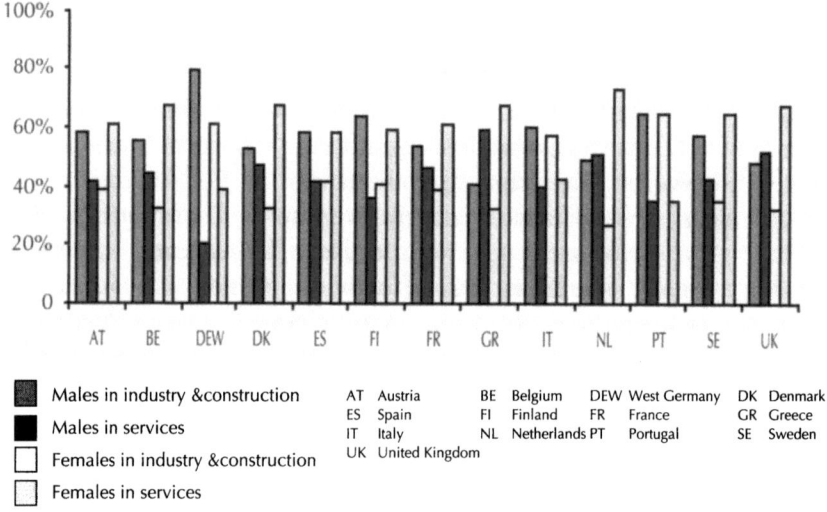

Males in industry & construction
Males in services
Females in industry & construction
Females in services

AT Austria BE Belgium DEW West Germany DK Denmark
ES Spain FI Finland FR France GR Greece
IT Italy NL Netherlands PT Portugal SE Sweden
UK United Kingdom

FIGURE 7 Distribution of employment by sex and by sector

and constructions from services, excluding agriculture and the public sector. Professions, by contrast, are grouped according to the following aggregate one-digit ISCO (International Standard Classification of Occupations) classification: managers and professionals (ISCO 1–2), technicians and associate professionals (ISCO 3), clerks and sales (ISCO 4–5), and manual workers (ISCO 7–9). Calculating the share of male and female employment for each sector and profession, we obtain an indicator of relative scarcity or abundance of male/female presence in a specific sector or profession.

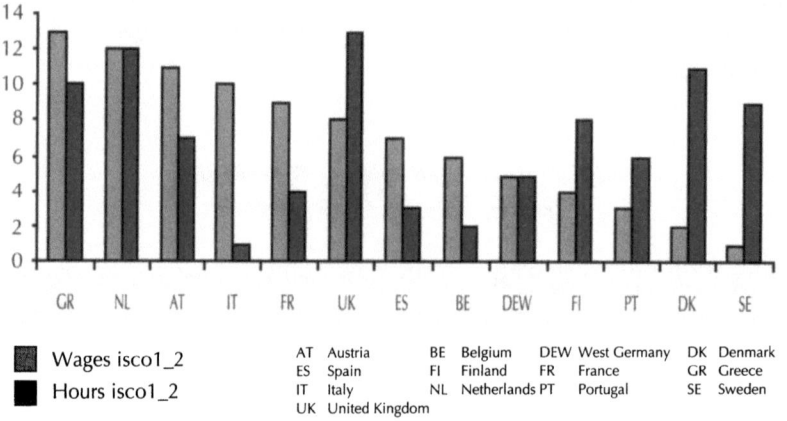

Wages isco1_2
Hours isco1_2

AT Austria BE Belgium DEW West Germany DK Denmark
ES Spain FI Finland FR France GR Greece
IT Italy NL Netherlands PT Portugal SE Sweden
UK United Kingdom

FIGURE 8 Ranking of wage and hourly differentials by profession (isco 1–2)

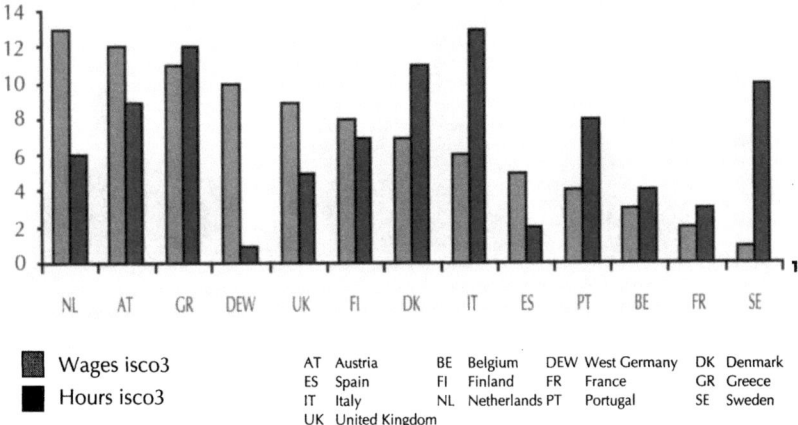

FIGURE 9 Ranking of wage and hourly differentials by profession (isco 3)

In particular, we observe that on average women are more numerous in services, while men prevail in industry (fig. 7). Exceptions are represented by West Germany, and Italy, where women are more present in industry rather than in services. On the other hand the United Kingdom, and the Netherlands have a greater share of men in services with respect to industry.

As to professions, it can be noticed that in general women prevail among clerks and sales (ISCO 4-5), while men are more numerous in manual occupations (ISCO 7-9). Looking at more skilled professions, we note that among managers and professionals (ISCO 1-2) there is a lower share of women in all countries, while among technicians and associate professionals a major presence of women is registered in many countries

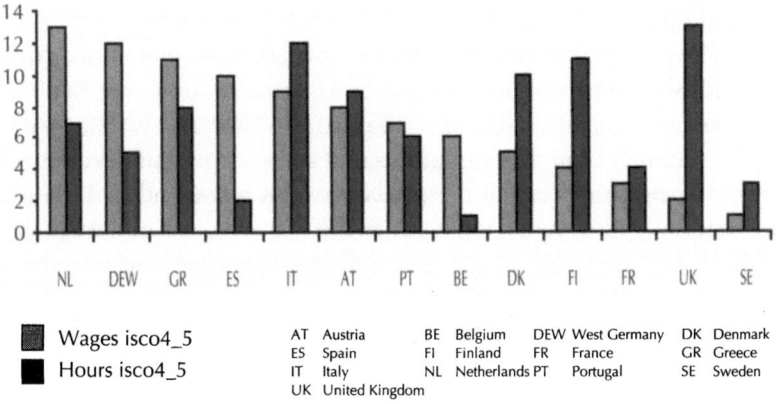

FIGURE 10 Ranking of wage and hourly differentials by profession (isco 4-5)

60   Women's Work, the Family and Social Policy

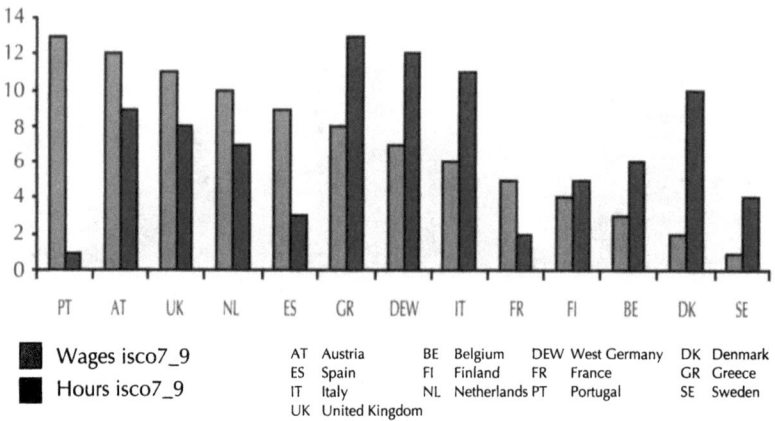

FIGURE 11   Ranking of wage and hourly differentials by profession (isco 7–8)

(Denmark, France, Netherlands, Finland, and Sweden). In addition, occupations where the female presence is scarce, as for the most qualified group (ISCO 1–2), are characterized by higher wages and larger wage differentials between men and women. This result is consistent with the theory of sex discrimination and suggests the existence of vertical occupational segregation problems determined by the presence, either implicit or explicit, of constraints to the access to more qualified occupations (Bettio, 1985, 1990; Del Boca and Fornengo, 1992; Duncan and Duncan, 1985; Gunderson, 1989).

What is the relationship between wage differentials and human capital?

In this paragraph we consider wage differentials among men and women in many European countries, referring to 1995 data. First of all we explore the relationship between human capital endowments, now represented by individuals' professions, and wage differentials (Blau and Kahn, 1992). If we look at human capital as an indicator of social degree of development, we would expect that wage differentials between sexes tend to decrease as human capital endowments increase; in the situation at hand, wage differentials should diminish as professional qualifications rise (Tanda and Bottone, 1996). In practice, the set of considered professions is not sufficiently detailed to allow conclusive evidence of this hypothesis. In the 13 countries considered, and for the classification of professions described above, we observe that on average larger wage differentials occur at each end of the professional spectrum (fig. 8–11). The greatest wage differen-

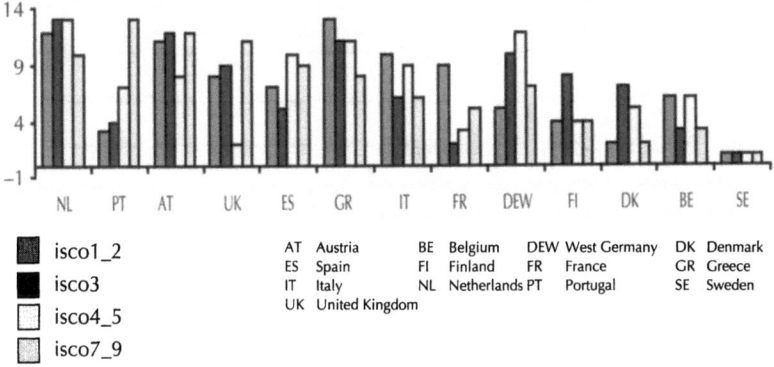

FIGURE 12 Ranking of hourly wage differentials by profession

tials take place in manual occupations, followed by managers and professionals, then by technicians and associate professionals, and finally by clerks and sales. In addition, it should be considered that for greater levels of qualification there are wider differences in individual skills, which may result in more variability in wage negotiation. This situation helps to explain the major wage range that also occurs between sexes in the more qualified professions (fig. 12).

Does human capital influence wage differentials between sexes differently among countries?

In order to explore wage differentials between sexes we have ranked the 13 countries examined according to the amplitude of the wage differential (fig. 13). If we take into consideration the professions, it can be noted that some countries reveal a moderate wage differential for all professions. A significant case is that of Sweden, which has a very low differential for the four groups (fig. 12). Similarly, Denmark, and France have low wage differentials in the various groups except for technicians and manual workers, respectively. Other countries such as Portugal have a large differential for low-skilled professions and small for highly skilled ones. In Italy, Spain, Greece, United Kingdom, and West Germany, we meet the opposite situation: that is, wage differentials between sexes are high for the more qualified groups and tend to be lower for the other groups. These results may also reflect differences in the wage negotiation mechanisms among countries, the degree of development of the economic system, and the level of specialization expressed by each aggregation of occupations investigated by this analysis.

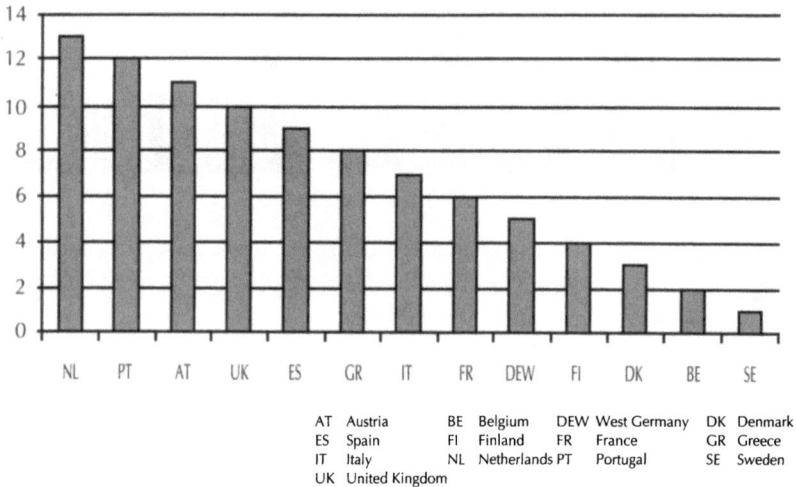

FIGURE 13 Ranking the amplitude of the hourly wages differentials

Are there relevant differentials in hours worked amongst european countries?

Hours of work are considered as a proxy of the time spent in the labor market, including overtime work. Looking at the distribution of hours worked across countries, we do not encounter in general great differences: for men we register a maximum of 42 hours per week in Austria to less than 38 hours in France; for women we have about 41 hours in Austria and 37 hours in France and the United Kingdom. Although in the 13 countries examined we also take into consideration overtime, a considerable difference between men and women in the number of weekly hours worked can be recorded only in a few countries such as Italy, Denmark, Finland, Austria, and the United Kingdom (fig. 8–11). However, it should be noted that some of these countries, like the United Kingdom and Denmark, have a very significant share of women who work part-time, while it is not so in Italy, where the share of part-time work is quite low even among women. In other countries, such as France, Spain, and Portugal, the differential between sexes in hours worked is very small.

Conclusions

This paper has investigated the relationship between human capital and labor market performances of men and women in various European countries. In spite of the limits stemming from the use of aggregate data, the analysis performed helps to stress not only the well-known differences of the main labor market indicators among European countries but also significant differences in the behaviors of men and women which can be attributed to choices of investment in human capital and/or to choices of time allocation within family.

We explored mainly three issues: labor market participation choices; employment opportunities; and the job characteristics of employed people, described by hourly earnings, hours of work, and the type of occupation (also assumed as a human capital indicator).

From the first point of view it has been outlined that in some countries the incentive to labor market participation is positively influenced by the education level for women, while for men the choice to participate is largely independent of the schooling degree. This feature is characteristic of some Mediterranean countries (Italy, Spain, and Greece), which also share a generally low degree of education of the population, and of some countries of Central Europe (Netherlands and Belgium). In these cases it seems that the "filter" of role division within family significantly influences women's participation choices, allowing them to enter the labor market only if the perspective of good earnings, associated with higher human capital, make it convenient. Moreover, it is interesting to note that in these countries, with the partial exception of Netherlands, men and women enjoy very similar levels of education, thus linking this effect to a satisfactory achievement of equal opportunities between sexes.

As to employment opportunities, opposite results can be achieved whether one takes into consideration only active population, then taking for granted the outcome of participation choices, or not. Actually, on the one hand the analysis of unemployment rates shows that investment in education is often relatively more profitable for men; on the other hand, the analysis of employment rates clearly signals the existence of a payoff linked to investment in education that is much more significant for women.

As to the differences in the job characteristics of already employed people, in spite of considerable improvements in the average schooling degree—confirmed by a low differential of education levels between sexes in the examined countries—and in labor market participation of women, there still exist in many countries problems of occupational segregation and wage differentials between sexes.

Our result should be regarded solely as a first step towards comparative research on relationships among human capital investment, labor market, and family context, paying attention to differences between sexes. The suggestions we have just outlined need further insight by means of an analysis on microdata that would make it possible to focus attention on individual behavior.

Notes

1. All data used in this paragraph and in paragraphs 2 and 3 refer to population aged 25-59.
2. We refer to the International Standard Classification of Education (ISCED), using the following standard aggregation: pre-primary, primary and lower secondary education (io-2); upper secondary education (i3); total tertiary education (i5-7).
3. This indicator has been calculated assigning the value 1, 2 and 3 respectively to the three levels of education considered (see note 2), then averaging the three values weighted with the share of population in each level of education.
4. Differentials between sexes are always calculated as percentage differences between the value of a variable for men and the analogous value for women.

References

Becker, G. S., Human Capital Effort and the Sexual Division of Labor, Journal of Labor Economics, 3, 1985.

Becker, G. S. and N. Tomes, Human Capital and The Fall and Rise of Families, Journal of Labor Economics, 4: 1-39, 1986.

Bettio, F., The secular decrease of sex-linked wage differentials: A case of non competition, Economia & Lavoro, 3, 1985.

Bettio, F., Segregazione e discriminazione sul mercato del lavoro: letteratura straniera e Italiana a confronto, Economia & Lavoro, 4, 1990.

Blau, F., Kahn, L.M., The Gender Earnings Gap: Learning from International Comparisons, American Economic Review, 82, 1992.

Del Boca D., Fornengo, G., La segregazione occupazionale, Politiche del lavoro, 19, 1992.

Duncan, O., Duncan B., A Methodological Analysis of Segregation Indexes, American Sociological Review, 20, 1985.

Gunderson, M., Male-Female Wage Differentials and Policy Responses, Journal of Economic Literature, 27, 1989.

Mincer J., Schooling, Experience and Earnings, National Bureau of Economic Research (NBER), New York, 1974.

Mincer, J., Polacheck, S., Family Investment in Human Capital: Earnings of Women, Journal of Political Economy, vol. 82, part II, 1974: 76-108.

OECD, Human Capital Investment. An International Comparison, 1998.

Tanda, P., Bottone, G., Children and Gender-Wage Differentials, Labour, 3, 1996.

DANIELA DEL BOCA

MARILENA LOCATELLI

SILVIA PASQUA

CHAPTER 4

EARNINGS AND EMPLOYMENT OF ITALIAN HUSBANDS AND WIVES IN THE EUROPEAN CONTEXT

Section 1. Introduction

The composition of the work force by sex in all OCDE countries has changed significantly over the past thirty years as more and more women have turned to paid employment.

The situation in Italy is illustrated in Table 1. Male participation rate decreased by over 15% between 1965 and 1997, while women's participation rose by 11.4%.

These changes affected the average household structure. Thus, in the period under consideration, the proportion of dual-earner families rose from 40% to 50%, while single-earner families declined from 52% to 40%, resulting in a significant change in income distribution both across families and within families.

Figures 1 and 2 show for the years 1973 to 1998 the same pattern of increase in female activity rates and decline in male activity rates in all European countries. Balls (1994) has remarked that important reasons come from changes in labor demand. Men, in fact, are mostly employed in manufacturing, the sector hardest hit in recent years due to the restructuring

TABLE 1. Participation in work force rates in Italy 1965–1997

Year	Male	Female
1965	88.6	32.7
1979	82.6	38.7
1983	80.7	40.2
1993	74.7	43.7
1997	73.5	44.1

Source: OCDE, Labor Force Statistics

required by technological changes. Women, however, are mainly employed in the service sector, which is growing in all countries and which is better sheltered from the stronger international competition. A comparison between participation rates by age in 1977 and 1997 (Figures 3–6) shows that in 1997 women's participation in the labor market was higher than in 1977 for all cohorts, but it remained lower then men's participation. In Italy, men's and women's participation by age is increasingly shaping up in a similar fashion. The increase of the participation in the age range 25–49 has also created more similarities with the rest of Europe.

In this paper we want to focus on the explanations and consequences of these trends using Italian data. Section 2 presents an overview of the literature which explores the motivations of the increasing participation of women. In Section 3, by employing the Bank of Italy Survey of Households' Income and Wealth for the year 1995, we analyze the relationship between education and employment characteristics of husbands and wives in order to understand if wives are working because they need to compensate in the short run for the loss of income of their husbands, or because they have a long-run *taste for work*. We also analyze the presence of *assortative mating*, that is, whether wives and husbands, rather than marrying randomly, share the same characteristics in terms of education and employment status. Moreover, we take into account that factors related to women's propensity to work appear to be more important determinants of the decision to participate in the labor market than factors related to the husbands' unemployment status and income level. In section 4 we analyze the impact of women's work on household income distribution. In *assortative mating*, disproportionately more educated women married to highly educated/high income men are in the labor market, and therefore women's work has a disequalizing impact on household income distribution. On the contrary, if women participating in the labor market belong mainly to low-income households, their work may have an equalizing impact.

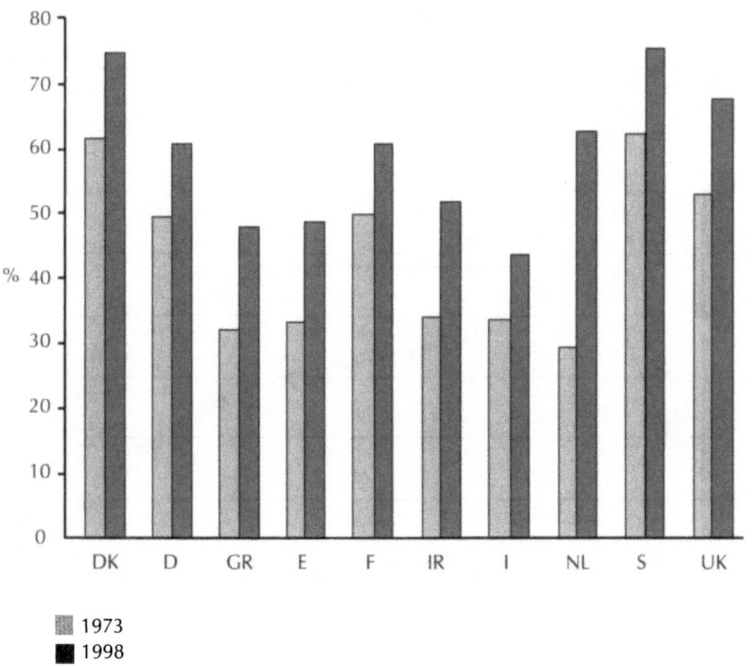

FIGURE 1 Women's Participation Rates in Work Force of Selected European Countries *Source: OECD, Employment Outlook (1999)*

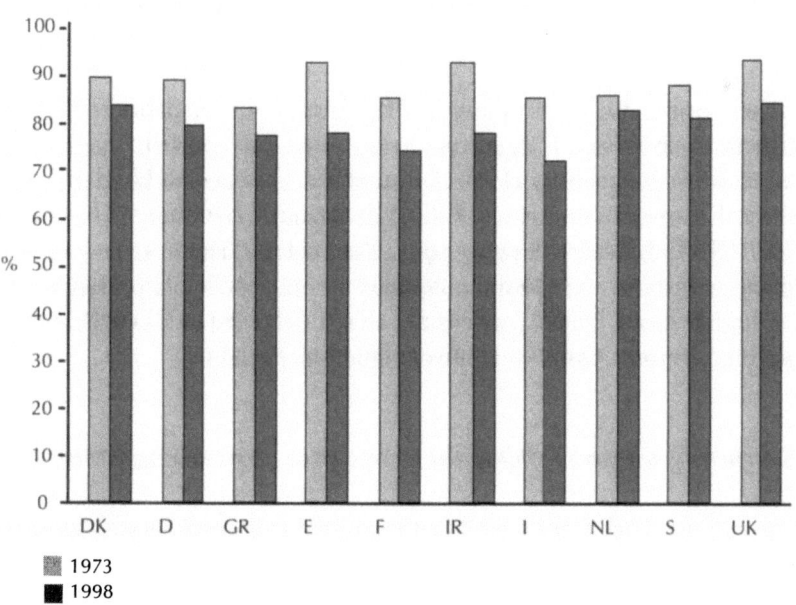

FIGURE 2 Men's Participation Rates in Work Force of Selected European Countries *Source: OECD, Employment Outlook (1999)*

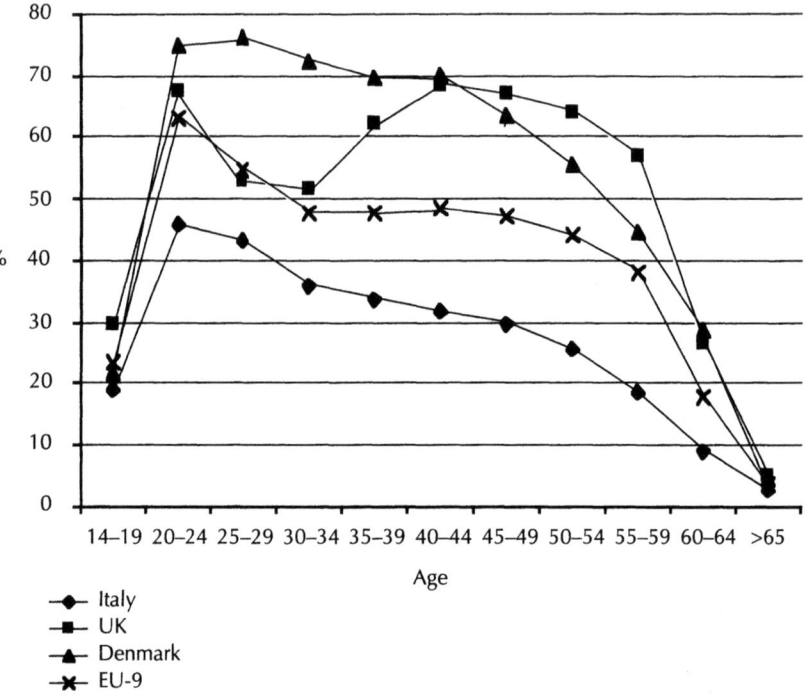

FIGURE 3 Women's Participation Rates by Age (1977) *Source: EUROSTAT, Indagine sulle forze lavoro (1978)*

If we consider European data, in fact, female participation is high in northern countries and it decreases as we move to southern Europe. At the same time, inequality is lower in northern Europe and higher in the southern European countries. Using European Community Household Panel (ECHP) data for the year 1995, Pasqua (2001) shows that women's earnings contribute less to total inequality where the female participation rate is higher (see Figure 7, where I_2 is half of the squared coefficient of variation). Section 5 contains some concluding remarks.

Section 2. Is women's employment a response to men's unemployment?

Changes in the work force have been examined from various standpoints. One subject that has attracted attention, in order to understand motivations and consequences, is the relationship between the growth of employment of married women and the decline in male employment.

The growth of employment of married women may be due to the un-

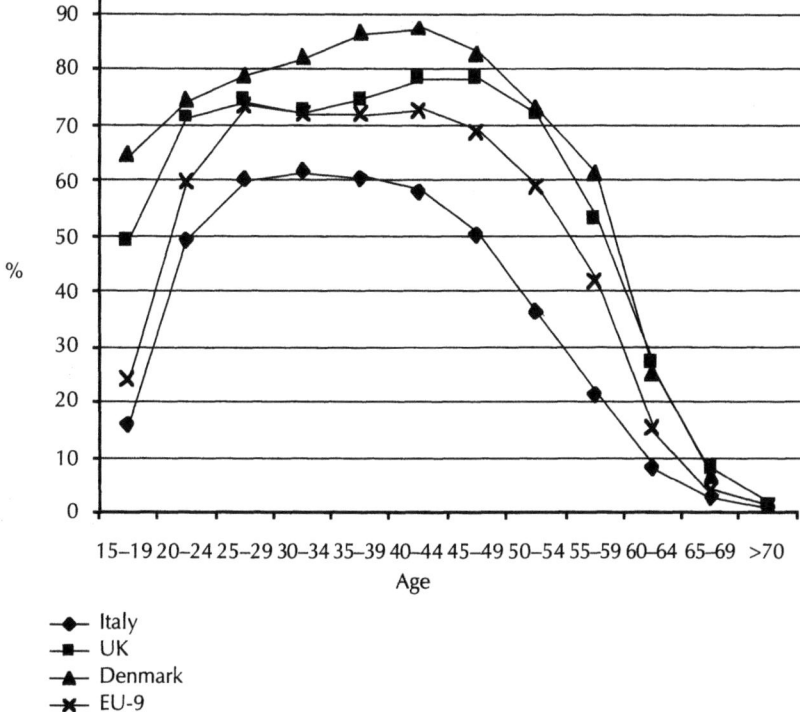

FIGURE 4 Women's Participation Rates by Age (1997) *Source: EUROSTAT, Indagine sulle forze lavoro (1998)*

employment status of the husband, but this situation seems to have two different effects on wife's labor supply: the *added worker effect* increases wife labor supply in order to maintain the same level of income and the same household living standard, while the *discouraged worker effect* reduces the wife's labor supply because woman believes that it is more difficult to find a job when the husband cannot find an occupation. The empirical studies analyzing the relationship between husband's employment status and wife's participation in the labor market have produced mixed results about the prevailing effect.

Macroeconomic data seem to suggest that the increased participation of women is a response to the decline in male employment and wages. On the microeconomic scale, however, this is not the case, since the decline in male employment and wages is greater in lower-income families, whereas the increase in female participation is greater in higher-income families (Davies, Elias, and Penn, 1992). Some earlier studies analyzing U.S. and U.K. data during the seventies and early eighties found a positive relationship between husbands' unemployment and the labor force participation

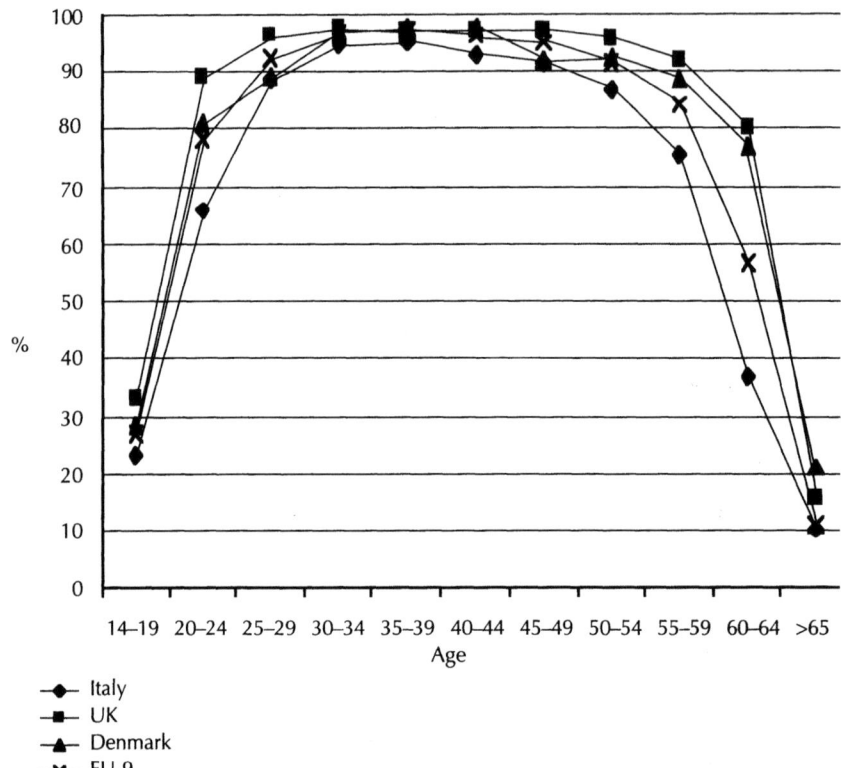

FIGURE 5 Men's Participation Rates by Age (1977) *Source: EUROSTAT, Indagine sulle forze lavoro (1978)*

of married women (Lundberg, 1985). More recently other analyses focusing on other European countries showed that the wives of unemployed men in Britain and France were less likely to be engaged in paid work than the wives of employed men (Davies, Elias, and Penn, 1992; Layard, Barton, and Zabalza, 1980; Barrere-Maurisson, Battagliola, and Daune-Richard, 1985). Other studies focusing on German data did not find a clear impact of the husband's unemployment on labor force status of the wife (Giannelli and Micklewright, 1995). Their results indicated, in fact, that the prevalence of one effect over the other depended on individual characteristics of husbands and wives, the area of the household's residency, and the presence of unemployment benefits.

The comparative data for various countries from the Luxembourg Income Study reported in the same paper of Giannelli and Micklewright (1995) have shown that in the 1980s participation in employment for wives of unemployed men was significantly lower than for wives of work-

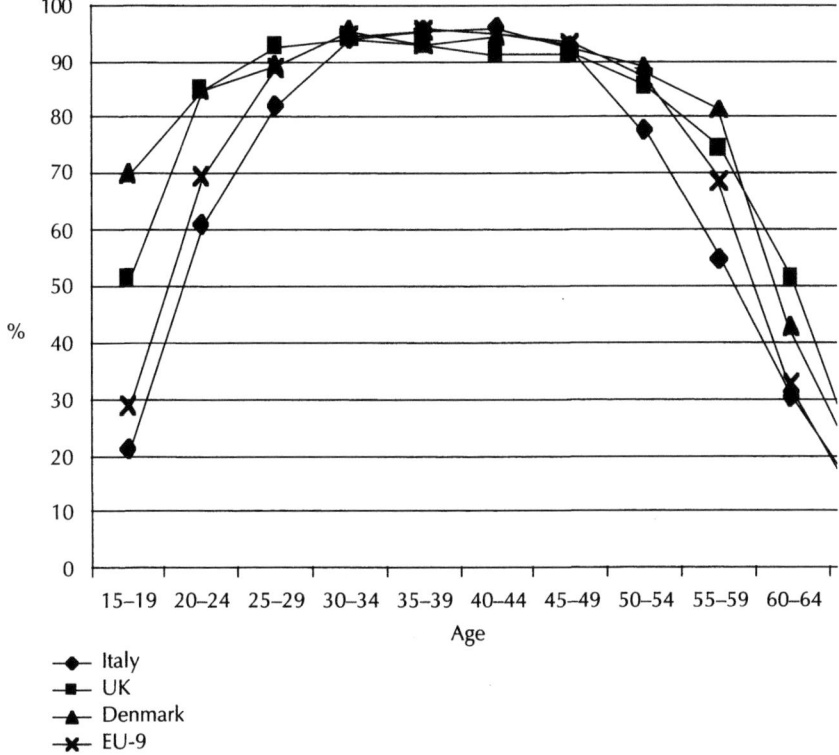

FIGURE 6 Men's Participation Rates by Age (1997) Source: EUROSTAT, Indagine sulle forze lavoro, 1998

ing men. Among all countries considered, Italy was the only exception: the participation rate of wives of working men was 37.3% while the participation rate of wives of unemployed men was 41.2%.

If we examine the cross-tabulation of employment status of husbands and wives using a different dataset and for a different year—the 1995 Bank of Italy data—we find that, differently from Giannelli and Micklewright's reported data, more than 85% of husbands of working women were employed, and only 4% were unemployed or first-job-seekers (Table 2). The same data show that the participation rate of wives of working men was 46% while the participation rate of wives of unemployed men was 31.2%.

In a previous work (Del Boca, Locatelli, and Pasqua, 2000) we have analyzed how variables related to attitudes towards working (such as working status of mothers and mothers-in-law) and environmental opportunities (such as availability of child care) are more important in explaining the decision to work than variables related to economic constraints (such as husband's income, and male unemployment rate). Empirical evidence

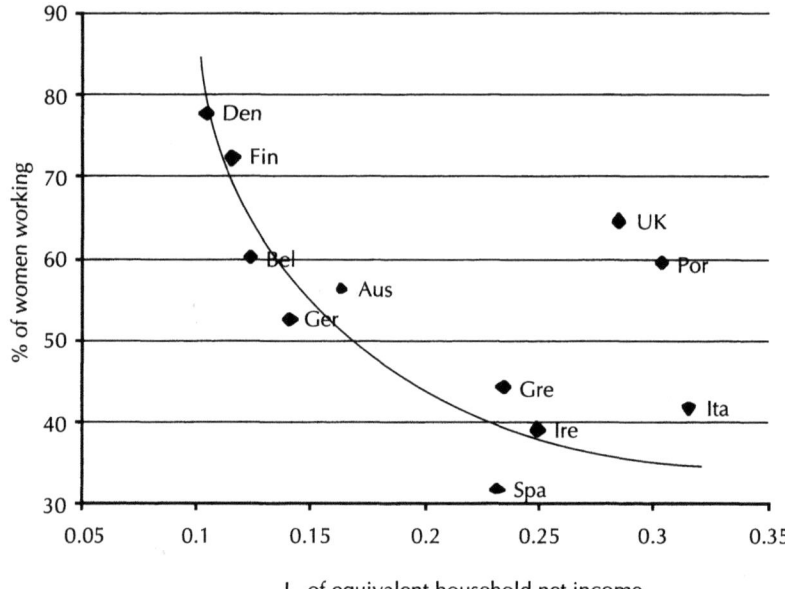

FIGURE 7 Women's Work and Inequality in Income Distribution in Europe (1995) *Source: ECHP dataset, Pasqua (2001)*

showed that women's employment decisions are affected by the employment decisions of their mothers and mothers-in-law, and this implies the importance of family background effects.

In order to explain the increase in women's participation to the labor market in households where the husband is employed, it is important to take into account the fact that people do not get married randomly, but as the result of a process known as *positive assortative mating*: men with higher education and incomes tend to marry women with higher education and incomes. If a positive *assortative mating* effect exists, this means that better-educated women, with better opportunities in the labor market, get

TABLE 2. Occupational position of husbands of working women

	%	% Cum.
Employed	85.85	85.85
Unemployed/First job seekers	3.99	89.84
Pensioners	10.00	99.84
Others	0.15	100.00
Total	100.00	

Source: Our elaborations of 1995 Bank of Italy data

married to better-educated men, who are generally employed and earn relatively high incomes. On the contrary, lower-educated women get married to lower-educated men, characterized by lower incomes and a higher probability of unemployment (Jacobsen and Rayack 1996). Recent empirical analyzes have shown that in about 50%–60% of dual-earner couples both spouses have the same level of education, whereas the similarity is much less with respect to their earnings (Winkler, 1998; Davies, Peronaci, and Joshi, 1998; Rossetti and Tanda, 2000). As a consequence of *assortative mating* we observe a simultaneous increase in the number of families in which both spouses work and in the number of households where nobody works (Gregg and Wadsworth 1996). The conclusion that can be drawn is that the growth in female employment is due more to greater job opportunities (for higher-educated women) than to economic constraints (for less-educated women) to make up for the loss of job or low wage of their spouses (Juhn and Murphy 1997).

Section 3. Marital sorting: Education, employment and earnings of husbands and wives

In this section we want to consider the relationship between education and employment status of married men and women and to test the presence of *assortative mating*. To explore this relationship and other related aspects, we use the Bank of Italy Survey of Households' Income and Wealth for the year 1995. From the dataset, a subsample of married couples in which the woman is below age 60 has been selected in order to consider only persons of working age.

TABLE 3. Level of education of married people

	Working men %	Working women %	Non-working women %
None	1.95	1.61	7.70
Primary schooling	20.04	15.62	42.37
Middle schooling	33.31	26.26	31.66
Vocational diploma (3-year course)	5.98	6.95	3.56
Secondary schooling	28.47	34.67	13.24
University diploma	0.56	0.93	0.11
University degree	9.38	13.80	1.36
Postgraduate qualification	0.31	0.16	—
Total	100.00	100.00	100.00

Source: Our elaborations of 1995 Bank of Italy data

TABLE 4. Occupations of wives per quintile of their husbands' total income

Occupational position of wives	Quintile of husband earnings				
	1st	2nd	3rd	4th	5th
Employed	4.61%	5.46%	6.21%	7.69%	8.84%
Unemployed	0.46%	0.51%	0.65%	0.46%	0.25%
Pensioners	6.39%	4.73%	3.25%	2.61%	3.44%
Housewives	8.42%	9.17%	9.80%	9.15%	7.53%
Others	0.05%	0.07%	0.03%	0.02%	0.14%

Source: Our elaborations of 1995 Bank of Italy data

From Table 3 we can conclude that working women are on average better educated than working men. In 34.67% of the cases women have had secondary education, as opposed to 28.47% of men. In 13.80% of cases women hold an university degree, as opposed to 9.38% of men.

If it is true that better-educated women tend to marry men with higher levels of education and higher incomes, they probably have also less need to work. It would appear that more women in high-income households work than in low-income ones, thus confirming that women's work is not a response to difficult economic situations or to husbands' unemployment, but that other factors affect women's decision to work.

Table 4 shows female working status in terms of the husband's income brackets. The cross-tabulation indicates that a greater percentage of employed wives belong to families where the husband has a high income. These data point to the absence of any close relation between situations of economic distress and the employment of married women.

A related result is presented in the 1997 report published by Italy's National Statistics Office (ISTAT) devoted to "areas of economic distress of the households," showing how the percentage of unemployed adult children is higher (66%) in families where only one spouse works than in those where both parents are present and work. The data also suggest that

TABLE 5. Education levels of the working spouses—couples in which both spouses work

Wives	Husbands		
	< secondary schooling	secondary schooling	> secondary schooling
< Secondary schooling	38.7%	9.0%	0.2%
Secondary schooling	10.2%	0.3%	5.3%
> Secondary schooling	1.0%	5.3%	9.9%

Source: Our elaborations of 1995 Bank of Italy data

more job opportunities are available to women with high levels of education, whereas relatively uneducated women have fewer opportunities and/or the costs of participating in the labor market (in terms of services and possibility of part-time employment) are too high.[1]

In dual-earner families, we examine the relationship between the human capital of husbands and wives to test *assortative mating*. In Table 5 the level of education of husbands and wives are cross-related at each of three educational levels. The sum of the percentages in the matching boxes illustrates the strong concordance between the education of the two spouses: they have the same level of education in 68.9% of the couples, while in 83.4% of cases husband has as much or more education than his wife. These results confirm the findings reported by Rossetti and Tanda (2000), according to which the *assortative mating* phenomenon is quite strong among Italian couples, when educational levels alone are considered. Winkler (1998) examined U.S. data and showed that in 50% of the dual-earner couples in the sample, husbands and wives had the same level of education.

Since education is a very relevant factor of economic outcomes, husbands and wives' wages are also highly correlated, but not as much as educational levels, thus indicating the importance of factors related to labor market and family constraints (Del Boca, Locatelli, and Pasqua, 2000; Rossetti and Tanda, 2000). In fact, even if working women are better educated than employed men, their contribution to household labor income is still lower than men's contribution: in 1995 husbands' contribution averages 55.5% while wives' contribution account for an average 40.3%.[2]

TABLE 6. Descriptive statistics of dual-earner couples in which the wife earns more than the husband

	Husband	Wife
Employment status		
Blue collar	27.87	18.12
White collar	18.82	35.89
Teacher	6.62	19.51
High-skilled white collar	5.23	5.92
Manager	1.39	1.74
Self-employed	40.07	18.82
Education		
<secondary school	44.60	30.67
secondary school	40.77	48.08
>secondary school	14.63	21.25

Source: Our elaborations of 1995 Bank of Italy data

However, the analysis of factors affecting household risk of poverty shows that women's work is an important determinant of the probability of exit poverty (Addabbo, 2000).

However, in a significant proportion of dual earner couples (17.5%) wives earn more than their husbands, while Winkler (1998) found a higher percentage (20–25%) in the U.S. More than 50% of these households live in the Northern regions. As we can see from Table 6, in these couples women are generally better educated than men and have a higher employment status.

Section 4. The effect of women's work on household income distribution

As already mentioned, the change in the sex composition of the work force has altered the distribution of income among Italian families. There has been a move, in fact, away from families with only one income, usually

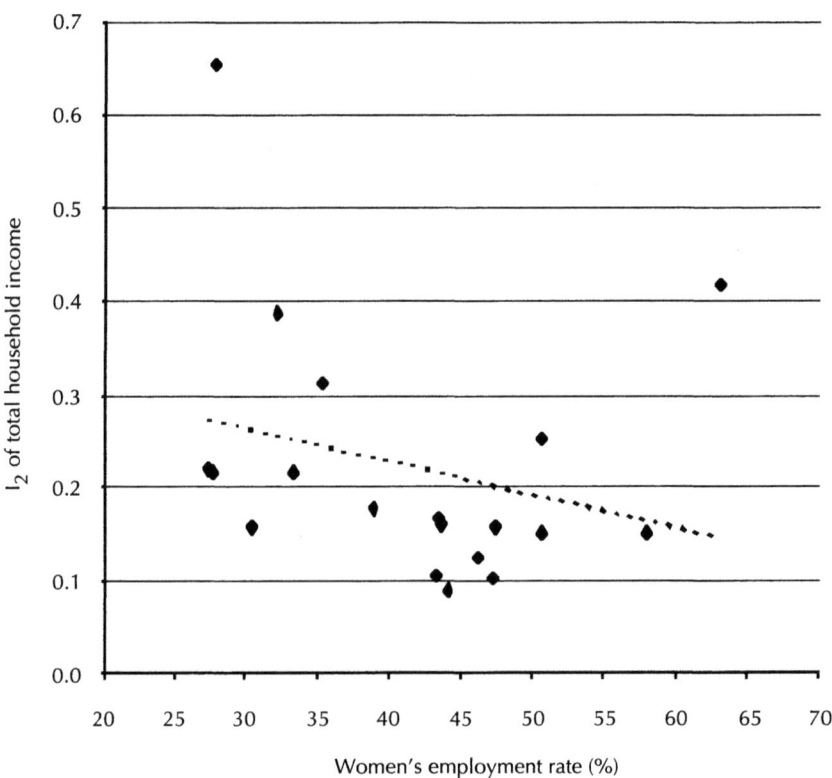

FIGURE 8 Inequality and Women's Employment Rate in Italian Regions (1995)
Source: Our elaborations of 1995 Bank of Italy data

that of the head of the household, to families with two or more incomes. In spite of the shared characteristics, a significant difference exists between husbands' and wives' earnings, indicating labor market and family constraints. Among the latter are the presence of children, a greater propensity to part-time jobs, and more frequent interruptions of work experience due to family responsibilities. Structural family constraints, such as the lack of flexible and adequate public provisions of child care, are likely to be other important factors (Del Boca, 2001; Del Boca, Locatelli, and Pasqua, 2000; Chiuri, 2000).

In a companion paper, we analyzed the effect of women's labor income on household income distribution in Italy in the period 1977–1998 and found that without wives' earnings inequality would have been higher (Del Boca and Pasqua, 2001). In this paper, for the year 1995, we want to consider not only the effect of wives' earnings on income distribution, but we also compare the inequality level in the subgroups of dual-earner and single-earner households. In Figure 8 female employment rate and inequality in household income distribution are considered in the same diagram. We can observe that inequality tends to be higher in the regions where the percentage of working women is lower. Clearly, this indicates a causal relationship between women's work and inequality.

To better understand the effect of women's work on income distribution we have to decompose total inequality (measured by I_2, half of the squared coefficient of variation) by household type and by sources of income. First we split our sample of married couples in which the wife is below age 60 into four mutually exclusive groups: *dual-earner* (DE) households, *man breadwinner* (MB) and *woman breadwinner* (WB) families, and *other type of households* (OH). If we consider K subgroups of population, I_2 can be decomposed as the sum of *within-group* and *between-group* inequalities. Within-group inequality is the weighted sum of inequalities within each subgroup, where the weights are given by the population share and the ratio between the mean income of the group and the mean income of the whole sample. Between-group inequality is the inequality that remains if we give to each person the average income of his/her group, that is, if we eliminate within-group inequality (Blackorby, Donaldson, and Auersperg 1981; Shorrocks 1984; Jenkins 1995).

Table 7 shows the result of this analysis. In the first part of the table, I_2 for each subgroup is presented. Dual-earner (DE) households (that represent 36.9% of population and 46.2% in term of income share) are characterized by a relatively low inequality in total household income distribution, while the MB group (representing 41.5% of population and only 34.9% in terms of population share) has the highest within-group

TABLE 7. Decomposition of inequality by type of household

I_2 total	0.232
I_2	
Dual earner (DE)	0.149
Man breadwinner (MB)	0.334
Woman breadwinner (WB)	0.136
Other households (OH)	0.186
Population share (%)	
Dual earner	36.9
Man breadwinner	41.6
Woman breadwinner	5.2
Other households	16.3
Income share (%)	
Dual earner	46.2
Man breadwinner	34.9
Woman breadwinner	5.3
Other households	13.6
Within-group inequality	0.213
Between-group inequality	0.019

Source: Our elaborations of 1995 Bank of Italy data

inequality. Moreover, we find the lowest level of inequality in households in which only the woman works (WB). Within-group inequality seems to dominate between-group inequality.

This first result seems to indicate that women's work has an equalizing effect on household income distribution, even though women are more likely to be working in households where the husband has already a high income.

In order to isolate the effect of women's earnings on total inequality, we can also decompose I_2 by sources of income. Let's consider S sources of household income. I_2 for total income can be decomposed as the sum of absolute factor contributions of each source to overall inequality (C_s). This depends on the covariance between component s and total income (χ_s), on s's factor share in total income, and on the squared coefficient of variation for source s (Shorrocks 1982; Jenkins 1995). When $C_s>0$, source s has a disequalizing impact; when $C_s<0$, source s has an equalizing impact. We can also define $c_s=C_s/I_2$ as the proportional factor contribution to total inequality.

Therefore, each source contribution to total inequality depends on three factors: the level of inequality that characterizes the distribution of the source, the relative factor share, and the correlation between the source and total income.

In this analysis three sources of income are considered: men's earnings, women's earnings, and the residual category "other sources" that includes both labor income of other family members (children, parents, etc.) and non labor income (capital income, social benefits, pensions, etc.) of the spouses and other household members.

In the first part of Table 8 we present inequality measures, factor shares, and correlation between the different sources of income and total income. In the second part we summarize the proportion of households

TABLE 8. Decomposition of inequality by sources of income

I_2 total	0.232
I_2 *factors*	
Husband's earnings	0.538
Wife's earnings	1.063
Other sources	0.656
% contribution to total household income (χ_s)	
Husband's earnings	43.3
Wife's earnings	15.9
Other sources	40.8
Correlation between sources of income (ρ_s)	
Husband total	0.660
Wife total	0.425
Other total	0.612
% of I_2 (c_s^*100) due to	
Husband's earnings	43.5
Wife's earnings	14.5
Other sources	42.0
% with non zero values of	
Husband's earnings	78.4
Wife's earnings	42.8
Other sources	88.0
I_2 *for non zero values of*	
Husband's earnings	0.315
Wife's earnings	0.158
Other sources	0.518

Source: Our elaborations of 1995 Bank of Italy data

in which each source of income is present and, for every source, the inequality level for the subgroups of those with positive values. In fact, inequality for one source can be high because of the presence of many zeros (as in Betson and var der Gaag 1984; and in Cancian, Danziger, and Gottschall 1992). This is particularly relevant for women's earnings where the proportion of working women is low. It is therefore important to isolate the "effect of participation" from the effect of inequality in the distribution of earnings. As we can see from Table 8, in Italy men's earnings and other sources of income explain the greatest portion of total inequality. The high value of I_2 for women's earnings is due mainly to the low percentage of recipients (42.8%). And in fact, women's earnings among working are distributed more equally than working men's earnings, but the low proportion of working women and the low correlation between women's earnings and total household income explain why they do not help in reducing total inequality (and in fact C_s for women's earnings is positive).

Section 5. Conclusions

In this research we analyzed motivations and effects of women's increasing participation to the labor market. The increase of women's employment rate and the consequent increase in dual-earner families altered the distribution of income among households.

We find strong evidence of *assortative mating*—that is, wives and husbands do not marry randomly but share the same characteristics in terms of education and employment status. Moreover, the data show that the employment rate is higher for more educated women that belong to households with higher incomes. This may induce one to foresee that women's work produces a polarization in family income distribution.

However, when we decompose total inequality by type of household and by sources of income we do not find that strong disequalizing impact. On one hand, dual-earner households are characterized by a lower *within-group* inequality than *man breadwinner* ones. On the other hand, the decomposition of inequality by sources of income shows the effect of women's earnings to be negligible. The largest proportion of inequality seems to be explained by husbands' labor income and by the presence of other sources of income. The minor contribution of women's earnings to total inequality is mainly due to the low participation rate, and in fact the high value of the inequality measure for women is explained by the presence of many zeros in the distribution. Given that inequality among working women is lower than inequality among working men, we would expect that an increase in female participation rate would have the effect of reducing inequality (as in the European context).

Notes

1. ISTAT (1997), *Rapporto sulla situazione del Paese*, Table 6.20 (page 640)
2. The remaining 4.2% is supplied by other members of the household.

References

Addabbo T. (2000), "Poverty Dynamics: Analysis of Household Incomes in Italy", *Labour*, Vol. 14, No.1, 119-144.

Balls T. (1994), "No More Jobs for the Boys", *Unemployment in Europe*, various authors, Academic Press.

Barrere-Maurisson M., Battagliola F., and Daune-Richard A. (1985), "The Course of Women's Career and Family Life", Robert B., Finnegan R. and Gallie D., eds., *New Approaches to Economic Life*, Manchester University Press, 431-458.

Betson, David and van-der-Gaag Jacques (1984), "Working Married Women and the Distribution of Income", *Journal of Human Resources*, vol. 19, 532-43.

Blackorby C., Donaldson D., and Auersperg M. (1981), "A New Procedure for the Measurement of Inequality Within and Between Population Subgroups", *Canadian Journal of Economics*, vol. 14, 665-685.

Cancian M., Danziger S., and Gottschall P. (1992), "Working Wives and Family Income Inequality Among Married Couples", Danziger S. and Gottschall P.,(eds.), *Uneven Ties—Rising Inequality in America*, NY, Russel Sage Foundation, 195-221.

Chiuri M.C. (2000), "Quality and Demand of Child Care and Female Labour Supply in Italy", *Labour*, Vol. 14, No. 1, 97-118.

Davies H., Peronaci R., and Joshi H. (1998), "Gender Gap and Partnership", W. P. Birbeck College, University of London.

Davies R., Elias P., and Penn R. (1992), "The Relationship between an Husband Unemployment and his Wife Participation", *Oxford Bulletin of Economics and Statistics*, vol. 54, n.2, 145-171.

Del Boca D. (2001), "The Effect of Child Care on Participation and Fertility", *Journal of Population Economics*, forthcoming.

Del Boca D., Locatelli M., and Pasqua S. (2000) "Employment Decision of Married Women: Evidence and Explanations", *Labour*, Vol.14, No. 1, 35-52.

Del Boca D. and Pasqua S. (2001), "Employment Patterns of Husbands and Wives and Family Income Distribution", Working Paper CHILD.

Dilnot A. and Kell M. (1987), "Male Unemployment and Women Work", *Fiscal Studies*, vol. 8, 1-16.

EUROSTAT (1978), *Indagine sulle forze lavoro*.
EUROSTAT (1998), *Indagine sulle forze lavoro*.
Garcia J. (1991), "A Participation Model with non-convex Budget Sets: the Case of the Wives of the Unemployed in Great Britain", *Applied Economics*, Vol. 23, 1401-1416.
Giannelli G. and Micklewright J. (1995), "Why do Women Married to Unemployed Men Have Low Participation Rates", *Oxford Bulletin of Economics and Statistics*, vol. 57, n.4, 471-486.
Goldin C. (1994), "The U-shaped Female Labour Force Function in Economic Development an Economic History", NBER Working Paper n.4707.
Greenhalg C. (1980), "Participation and Hours of Work of Married Women in Great Britain", *Oxford Economic Papers*, Vol. 32, 296-318.
Gregg P. and Wadsworth J. (1996), "It Takes Two: Concentration of Employment in Families in OECD Countries", CEPR W.P. 304.
Gronau R. (1982), "Inequality of Family Income: Do Wives' Earnings Matter?", *Population and Development Review*, n.8, 134-138.
Italian State Statistics Office (1997), *Rapporto annuale sulla situazione del paese*, Rome.
Jacobsen J. P. and W. L. Rayak (1996) "Do Men Whose Wives Work Really Earn Less?", *American Economic Review*, vol. 86, no.2, 268-273.
Jenkins S. (1995), "Accounting for Inequality Trends: Decomposition Analyses for the UK, 1971-86", *Economica*, vol. 62, 29-63.
Juhn C. and K. Murphy (1997), "Wage Inequality and Family Labour Supply", *Journal of Labour Economics*, Vol.15, n.1, 72-97.
Layard, R. Barton, M, and Zabalza A. (1980) "Married Women Participation and Hours", *Economica*, vol. 47, 51-72.
Lundberg S. (1985), "The Added Worker Effect", *Journal of Labor Economics*, n.3, 11-37.
Neumark D. and Postlewhite A. (1995), "Relative Income Concerns and the Rise in Married Women's Employment", NBER Working paper.
OECD (1999), *Employment Outlook*, Paris.
Pasqua S. (2001), "Women's Work and Income Inequality in European Countries", *mimeo*.
Rossetti S. and Tanda P. (2000), "Human Capital, Wages and Family Interactions", *Labour*, Vol. 14, 1, 5-34.
Shorrocks A. F. (1982), "Inequality Decomposition by Factor Components", *Econometrica*, vol. 50, 193-211.
Shorrocks A. F. (1984), "Inequality Decomposition by Population Subgroups", *Econometrica*, vol. 52, 1369-1385.
Winkler A. (1998), "Earnings of Husbands and Wives in Dual-earner Families", *Monthly Labor Review*, vol.121, 4, 42-48.

TINDARA ADDABBO

CHAPTER 5

"ATYPICAL" WORK IN ITALY IN A GENDER PERSPECTIVE

The Case of Parasubordinates and Part-Timers

Premise

In the last decade there has been a significant increase in the diffusion of atypical labor contracts (part-time, interim, pseudo-self-employment, fixed-term contracts, etc.) in Europe. For instance, according to Labor Force Survey data, from 1994 to 1999 women took almost two-thirds of the new jobs created in Europe, and 70% of the new jobs created for women in the same period in Europe were in part-time positions. Temporary work has also been increasing, and in 1999 over a third of new jobs created in Europe were temporary and over 13% of people employed in 1999 work in temporary jobs. The percentage of men working in fixed-term jobs increased from 9% at the beginning of the 1990s to 12.5% in 1999, while the percentage of women employed in fixed term contracts increased from 12% to 14% in the same period.[1]

Addressing the implications and characteristics of atypical work also raises the question of its visibility: actually, individual data on some types of atypical work are not available in national household surveys and must be collected by carrying out *ad hoc* surveys. Moreover, inconsistencies often arise between survey and administrative sources of data on atypical work diffusion.

Together with the increase in the incidence of atypical work on the new jobs created, there has been greater attention to the roles played both by the institutions, in enhancing the creation of atypical jobs, and by the law of demand and supply, on the increase in different forms of atypical jobs, and to the implications of the different types of atypical jobs in terms of:

- access to training;
- access to social security;
- low skill;
- career prospects;
- earnings;
- ability to improve the reconciliation between paid work and family life;
- increase in occupational segregation.

The effectiveness of atypical work to act as a bridge towards more stable and better paid employment and its role in improving the reconciliation between paid and unpaid working activities must be compared with the risk that atypical work could increase occupational segregation by trapping atypical workers in low-paid positions with lower career opportunities, higher job insecurity, risk of social exclusion, and risk of reinforcing the traditional gender distribution of total work (with men providing the larger share of paid work and women in secondary labor market employment still bearing the main burden of domestic and care work).

Moreover, as long as atypical work becomes increasingly widespread one must also discuss the implications of its diffusion on the standard of living and also address the point of its sustainability over the life cycle, depending on the degree of its precariousness and its duration. This paper deals with the diffusion of atypical work in Italy.

Introduction

The degree of flexibility in the Italian labor market has sensibly increased. New forms of labor contracts have been introduced and now represent such an important share of the new hiring that in some cases it is incorrect to continue defining them as atypical work. From 1992 to January 2000, individuals employed in atypical positions increased by 45.2%, whereas total employment increased only by 0.7%. This increase brought the ratio of atypical workers to the total number of employees from 10.6% to 15.2% (ISTAT 2000, 253). From 1997 to January 2000, 82% of the increase in employment has been generated by new atypical jobs.[2] In this study, attention is focused on two forms of *atypical* work: parasubordinate

TABLE 1.a. Flexible work in Italy 1992, 1999

Type of work	1992 Absolute value	1992 Incidence	1999 Absolute value	1999 Incidence	change 1998-1999[a] Absolute value	%
Part-time	1,167,000	5.4	1,631,000	7.9	125,000	+8.3
Fixed-term contract	1,163,000	5.4	1,447,000	7.0	214,000	+17.3
Training contract[b]	255,715	1.2	263,978	1.3	-17,967	-6.4
Apprentice[b]	505,680	2.4	423,664	2.1	30,526	+7.8
Interim workers	not available	—	75,524	0.4	23,212	+44.4
Parasubordinate[c]	not available	—	1,676,281	8.1	257,985	+18.2
Employed	21,457,000	100	20,618,000	100	261,000	+1.3

Source: Table 3 Censis 2000

a. 2nd quarter 1999 vs 2nd quarter 1998

b. contracts in 1998 with respect to employment in 1998

c. 30/9/1999 with respect to 31/10/1998 INPS

and part-time work. The latter includes jobs characterized by *traditional* or ruled flexibility (together with temporary jobs, training contracts, and apprentices), while the parasubordinate work belongs to the new type of unregulated flexibility, which has appreciably increased its weight on total employment. According to the National Social Security Institute *INPS* data elaborated by Censis 2000 from October 1998 to October 1999, parasubordinate work increased 18%, being now 8.1%, a figure similar to the ratio of part-time to total employment.[3] Moreover, part-time and parasubordinate work often includes jobs which can encourage women's participation in paid employment.

The gender-specific examples of different forms of atypical work with respect to total employment show that the incidence of parasubordinate work on total male employment (6.9%) more than offsets the incidence of

TABLE 1.b. Flexible work incidence by gender on employment in Italy in 1998

Type of work	Men	Women	Total
Part-time	3.4	14.0	7.3
Fixed-term contract	5.3	8.2	6.4
Training contract	1.3	1.2	1.3
Apprentice	2.0	2.3	2.1
Interim workers	n.a.	n.a.	0.3
Parasubordinate	6.9	9.3	7.8

Source: Table 1 Altieri (2000). Ires elaborations on INPS, Assointerim and ISTAT data. INPS data refer to 1999, the other to 1998.

part-time on total male employment (3.4%). On the other hand, though the incidence of parasubordinate work on women's employment (9.3%) is higher than its incidence on men's employment, the incidence of part-time to total women's employment is even higher (14%, see Table 1.b).

Part-time work

The contribution of part-time employment to the overall increase of women's employment in Italy from 1987 to 1997 is 23%, against the European Union average of 32%.[4] By contrast, men's part-time employment contribution to overall employment change is only 8%. Notwithstanding its increase, in 1999 part-time employment as a percentage of total employment in Italy is 7.9%, still relatively low as compared to other European countries.[5] The share of married women working part-time on total married women's employment in Italy in 1993 was 12%, whereas in the United Kingdom the share of married women working part-time was 53% (European Commission 1995a).

The low diffusion of part-time work in Italy has been related to institutional and labor demand factors; the trade unions' opposition to part-time, the initial rigidities involved by the first law regulating the application of part-time,[6] the scant favor of firms who preferred other forms of work to achieve flexibility (like informal and irregular jobs, overtime, new forms of atypical jobs like youth training contracts or contracts of continuous collaboration, which will be analyzed more in depth in the second part of this essay); the relatively low demand for part-time work in the public sector (as compared to other countries); and the relatively small size of most firms[7]. All these alternative ways of achieving employment flexibility have played a role in the low incidence of part-time on total employment in Italy.[8]

Since 1984 incentives for firms to use part-time work have increased,[9] and the increase of part-time employment is one of the targets expressed in the Italian government's 1999 National Action Plan for Employment:

> One of the major Government goals is to succeed in increasing part-time employment (GL 17). In the period going from 1999 to 2003, the Government aims at increasing part-time employment also as a share of total employment, so that in this respect Italy approaches the European average (16.9%). As a matter of fact, part-time work may further the growth of the participation and employment of those groups that, to date, are insufficiently present in the market. Through recent incentive measures in favor

of part-time, the Government estimates it will be able, in 1999, to add at least 100,000 units to total employment. By the end of 1999, this would cause part-time work to have an incidence on total employment ranging around 8% (as compared to 7.3% in 1998). (1999 National Action Plan for Employment).

From January 1998 to January 1999 the number of part-timers in Italy increased by 13.8%. Also,

> the propensity of the unemployed to accept part-time work has increased from 19% in 1993 to 24% in 1998 (in the South, the willingness of youths and women to accept part-time work increased by nearly one third in the last three years) (1999 NAP).

Part-time workers in Italy are mainly employed in the service sector. They work on average a relatively high number of hours.[10] Part-time work is increasing in some sectors like trading and services to firms. According to a survey by *Cfmt -Athena*, the share of part-time in overall employment passed from 35.7% in 1996 to 36.5% in 1998 in the large distribution sector, from 0.7% to 2.9% in the retail sector, and from 35.3% to 41.9% in the services to firms sector. This percentage should increase given that, according to the *Cfmt-Athena* survey, almost 67% of the firms interviewed intend to extend their use of part-timers.[11] Part-time work is increasing also in the public sector. From 1994 to 1998 the number of men employed as part-timers in the public sector increased from 3,700 workers to 10,500 workers, whereas women employed part-time passed from 9,000 in 1994 to 49,000 in 1998; however the incidence of part-time work in the Public Sector in Italy is still very low (2%) (ISTAT 2000, 481). According to a survey conducted by ISTAT in 1999 on part-timers employed in the public sector (ISTAT 2000), these are mainly women, and, when the reason for being in a part-time position has been specified, women turn out to have chosen this type of work for family or personal reasons, whereas men mainly state that they are working part-time in order to hold another job (ISTAT 2000, 481). An increase in the use of part-time in the Public Sector is expected in the future, given that, according to the 2000 Budget Law, half of the new hiring in the Public Services must be part-time or flexible jobs.

Though the incidence of part-time jobs in total employment in Italy is still relatively low with respect to other industrialized countries, its share in new entrants is higher, especially in large firms, where, according to data reported in NAP-1999, 20% of new entrants in large firms are part-timers.[12]

TABLE 2. Employment and part-time rates

Countries 1999	Employment rate	Part-time
Denmark	76.5	20.8
Netherlands	70.9	39.4
Sweden	70.6	23.8
U.K.	70.4	24.8
Austria	68.2	16.8
Portugal	67.4	11.0
Finland	67.4	12.2
Germany	64.8	19.0
Ireland	62.5	16.7
Luxembourg	61.6	10.7
France	60.4	17.2
Belgium	58.9	15.7
Greece	55.6	6.0
Italy	52.5	7.9
Spain	52.3	8.3
European Union	62.1	17.6

Source: Eurostat 1999 Labor Force Surveys

One should be aware of the risks associated with this type of contract—that is, wage discrimination and lack of career. In fact, in countries where part-time is more widespread than in Italy one can find evidence of wage differentials against part-timers;[13] but where it is possible to check for educational status, one can find evidence of a lower wage differential between part-timers and full-timers for people with college or university degree (OECD, 1999). The risk of persistence in part-time jobs is high, as found by Ferber and Waldfogel (1996) and Blank (1989) using U.S.A. data, and by Tam (1997) using United Kingdom data.[14] Giannelli (1997), using the German Socioeconomic Panel, finds a different behavior for German married women according to their nationality and education level; the transition to full-time from part-time job is more common for foreigners, who are also more likely to be found in lower-qualified positions. The extent to which part-time is a bridge towards full-time employment or a trap has been investigated for Scandinavian countries by Natti (1995) showing a higher degree of precariousness for part-timers in the Finnish rather than in the Swedish and Norwegian labor markets.[15] OECD (1999) data also show a lower investment in training for part-timers by employers, and lower career-related training for part-timers with respect to full-timers. Given the impact of past work-experience and training on wages, this gap in training can reproduce the static wage differential over time, significantly reducing also over time the growth in wages and future employability for part-timers.

TABLE 3. Temporary jobs proportion by type of employment and gender in 1997

	Temporary jobs 1997 percentage within			
	Full-time		Part-time	
	Men	Women	Men	Women
France	10	11	48	22
Germany	11	15	24	7
Ireland	4	6	61	33
Italy	6	7	56	27
the Netherlands	5	10	28	17
United Kingdom	5	6	25	11

Source: Eurostat, LFS OECD, 1999 Table 1.9, 28

A recent microeconometric analysis by Borzaga (1997) on a sample of women living in a northern Italian town with a proportion of part-time relatively higher than in the rest of Italy, finds that the higher the part-time probability, the lower the professional level of the position.[16] This result is shared by other industrialized countries, too, where part-timers also show a higher percentage of temporary work than full-timers and have a lower job-tenure (Table 3 below and OECD 1999).[17]

A significant share of part-time employment continues to be made up

TABLE 4. Under and overemployed by type of work and gender, 1994

	All		Men		Women	
Countries	work P-T prefer F-T	work F-T prefer P-T	work P-T prefer F-T	work F-T prefer P-T	work P-T prefer F-T	work F-T prefer P-T
Belgium	27	17	31	9	25	36
Denmark	14	13	69	7	8	21
Germany	15	7	52	5	12	10
Greece	25	8	33	8	25	9
France	41	17	69	11	35	28
Ireland	38	10	78	8	30	12
Italy	43	26	83	22	42	32
Netherlands	8	16	25	13	7	23
Portugal	62	5	100	7	40	2
Spain	36	10	36	8	37	14
United Kingdom	29	5	72	3	22	9
Unweighted mean	31	12	59	9	26	18

Source: European Commission 1995b; OECD 1999 Table 1.13, 33

of workers who would prefer working full-time. The share of underemployed is significantly higher in Italy with respect to other countries both for men and for women, with 83% of men working part-time preferring to work full-time.

The most frequent reason given by women who work part-time is related to the family; in this connection OECD (1994) states:

> Time-budget studies show that women living in households with more than one person spend twice or three times more time on 'reproductive work' than their male counterparts, whether children are present or not. This division of labor shapes the integration of women into the paid economy. Typical male paid work patterns—full-time continuous employment across the life cycle—impose an external constraint on families' time budgets; women provide the flexibility. Although most women define their decision to work part-time as 'voluntary,' the decision is based on the household division of labor (OECD 1994, 90).

The uneven distribution of total working time within the Italian couple[18] must therefore be related to the reason that women give to their working part-time, and to married women's hidden part-time labor supply. However, as Borzaga's (1997) research on a sample of women living in Trento has shown, overemployed women and unemployed women wishing to work part-time would prefer to work on a short full-time basis, from 30 to 32 hours a week. One should take into account that new part-time jobs may create underemployment and may attract potential part-timers who were discouraged in looking for a job by the low provision of part-time work (therefore the reduction in unemployment from the increase of part-time jobs may be uncertain). The impact of part-time working on the household division of labor must be monitored, since, in a situation of unequal sharing of working time like the Italian one, the diffusion of part-time working may increase inequality.[19]

Co-ordinated and continuing collaborators

Amongst the different forms of new labor contracts, workers who are involved in coordinated and continuing forms of cooperation with firms (*collaborators*) can be considered the most atypical ones since their characteristics lie between self-employment and dependent employment. The collaborator must not be employed in a firm, and she may have jobs with more than one principal.

The statistical visibility of this group of workers can be linked with the retirement pensions reform, which in 1995 established (Art.2 comma 26) that these workers must open a social security position by paying a 10% contribution[20] to the National Social Security Institute (INPS).[21] People who join this fund have come to be called "10% people".[22] Workers enrolled in this fund can be divided into three main groups:[23]

- coordinated and continuing collaborators are collaborators who perform an activity without being employed by a firm in a coordinated and continuing way without employing organized means. This group comprises administrators, syndics and firm auditors, newspaper collaborators, members of exam commissions, and home sales personnel; they have no VAT code and pay 13% social security contribution.
- professionals are those who habitually perform a profession or an art, with a prevalence of self-employed work. They are VAT-registered and are enrolled in a professional register.
- professionals/collaborators are professional workers who also belong to other social security groups and are VAT-registered (mainly administrators, and syndics and firm auditors).

Amongst those groups, the prevailing one is the first (coordinated and continuing collaborators). These groups of collaborators are characterized by different levels of earnings and employment conditions. The IRES survey on collaborators found that of those collaborators who are VAT-registered, 60% have registered voluntarily, the others being obliged by their commissioning clients to do so (Altieri and Oteri 2000, 105). In some cases this requirement conceals subordinate work. Many collaborators resist this requirement because having a VAT code is costly (higher fiscal and administrative costs are involved). The incidence of administrators in collaborations has recently decreased, while the presence of women amongst collaborators has increased.[24]

The regional distribution of these workers reveals that their presence is greater in the most developed regions of the country, with almost 60% of collaborators concentrated in the northern regions of Italy (Lombardia,[25] Emilia-Romagna, and Veneto are the first three regions as far as the regional distribution of collaborators in 1999 is concerned, Table 5).[26] From 1997 to 1999 the incidence of this type of contract increased in all Italian regions, and its incidence at national level increased from 4.1% to 8.3%, with an incidence around 10% in six regions (Table 7). Unlike part-time work, which was initially not well accepted by firms and requires incentives for greater use by them, collaboration contracts have

TABLE 5. Collaborators by regions from 1997 to 1999

Cont. co-ordinated work	31/12/97 A.V.	%	31/10/98 A.V.	%	30/09/99 A.V.	%
Piemonte	89,749	8.3	114,688	8.1	132,424	7.9
Valle d'Aosta	3,372	0.3	4,607	0.3	5,334	0.3
Lombardia	261,414	24.3	336,795	23.7	385,194	23.0
Liguria	31,548	2.9	41,307	2.9	48,816	2.9
Trentino A.A.	28,633	2.7	34,899	2.5	41,500	2.5
Veneto	115,164	10.7	142,331	10.0	164,512	9.8
Friuli V.G.	31,990	3.0	41,417	2.9	48,205	2.9
Emilia Romagna	118,897	11.0	142,442	10.0	167,182	10.0
North	680,767	63.2	860,486	60.7	993,167	59.2
Toscana	94,230	8.7	115,949	8.2	132,828	7.9
Umbria	16,825	1.6	21,703	1.5	26,215	1.6
Marche	31,155	2.9	39,081	2.8	45,545	2.7
Lazio	103,324	9.6	135,481	9.6	160,909	9.6
Centre	245,444	22.8	312,214	22.0	365,497	21.8
Abruzzo	15,480	1.4	21,311	1.5	26,033	1.6
Molise	3,204	0.3	4,706	0.3	5,776	0.3
Campania	33,801	3.1	56,642	4.0	73,630	4.4
Puglia	30,835	2.9	51,021	3.6	65,763	3.9
Basilicata	4,336	0.4	17,312	1.2	8,996	0.5
Calabria	10,988	1.0	7,050	0.5	22,844	1.4
Sicilia	30,478	2.8	57,305	4.0	74,982	4.5
Sardegna	21,859	2.0	30,249	2.1	39,593	2.4
South	150,981	14.0	245,596	17.3	317,617	18.9
Italy	1,077,192	100	1,418,296	100	1,676,281	100

Source: Our elaborations on NIdiL[27] on INPS data

been extensively used in new hiring, since collaboration allows an appreciable reduction in the labor cost (in terms both of social contributions and of pay) and provides a more flexible way of using labor resources.[28]

Disaggregating INPS data by collaborators' town of residence, one finds that they are more widespread in the towns that are regional capitals and in their provinces because of the greater presence of the service sector where collaboration contracts are more widespread.[29]

Turning to the age distribution of the different positions included among the collaborators (pure collaborators, collaborators-professionals, and professionals) one can see how among pure collaborators (who are also more numerous) women tend to be more concentrated than men in younger age groups, while men are well represented also in the older age group. This age distribution denotes a higher degree of precariousness and a different nature of this type of contract for women, who are more likely to be found in the younger age groups; older men are probably collaborators after retirement (like retired construction managers or apartment block administrators) (Table 8).[30] However, it has been noted that there are also cases of employees who, when close to the end of their working career, quit their job to become collaborators; this shift may conceal pseudo-parasubordinate work, and firms prefer this type of position since its social security labor costs are lower than the costs attached to the employee position.[31]

What are the employment conditions of this new type of workers? In order to answer this question, different research centers have had to carry out surveys on samples of collaborators, given the difficulty of distinguishing them in ISTAT labor force survey data or in other household cross-section analyses that do not consider this type of contract separately.

Though initially this type of work seems mainly a way for young people

TABLE 6. Collaborators by gender and regions 30/09/1999

Regions	Men			Women		
	Employed	Collab.	Incidence %	Employed	Collab.	Incidence %
Piemonte	1,015,000	76,772	7.56	662,000	55,652	8.41
Valle d'Aosta	30,000	3,103	10.34	21,000	2,231	10.62
Lombardia	2,277,000	222,821	9.79	1,474,000	162,373	11.02
Liguria	357,000	28,337	7.94	223,000	20,479	9.18
Trentino Alto Adige	240,000	26,942	11.23	160,000	14,558	9.1
Veneto	1,145,000	102,639	8.96	705,000	61,873	8.78
Friuli-Venezia Giulia	284,000	27,917	9.83	183,000	20,288	11.09
Emilia-Romagna	987,000	102,982	10.43	709,000	64,200	9.06
Toscana	816,000	81,013	9.93	533,000	51,815	9.72
Umbria	183,000	15,087	8.24	115,000	11,128	9.68
Marche	337,000	27,792	8.25	224,000	17,753	7.93
Lazio	1,173,000	84,016	7.16	658,000	76,893	11.69
Abruzzo	278,000	14,168	5.1	156,000	11,865	7.61
Molise	68,000	2,996	4.41	36,000	2,780	7.72
Campania	1,069,000	33,910	3.17	457,000	39,720	8.69
Puglia	807,000	29,889	3.7	327,000	35,874	10.97
Basilicata	117,000	4,049	3.46	55,000	4,947	8.99
Calabria	363,000	10,555	2.91	155,000	12,289	7.93
Sicilia	947,000	29,916	3.16	356,000	45,066	12.66
Sardegna	339,000	20,302	5.99	155,000	19,291	12.45
Italy	12,832,000	945,206	7.37	7,364,000	731,075	9.93

Source: Our elaborations on NIdiL on INPS data

TABLE 7. Collaborators by regions, incidence on total employment 1997 and 1999

	1997			1999		
	Employed	Collab.	Incidence %	Employed	Collab.	Incidence %
Piemonte	1,704,000	71,010	4.2	1,677,000	132,424	7.9
Valle d'Aosta	51,000	2,593	5.1	52,000	5,334	10.26
Lombardia	3,672,000	203,061	5.5	3,752,000	385,194	10.27
Liguria	579,000	21,758	3.8	580,000	48,816	8.42
Trentino Alto Adige	396,000	22,980	5.8	400,000	41,500	10.38
Veneto	1,825,000	89,066	4.9	1,850,000	164,512	8.89
Friuli-Venezia Giulia	468,000	25,530	5.5	467,000	48,205	10.32
Emilia-Romagna	1,690,000	94,055	5.6	1,696,000	167,182	9.86
Toscana	1,360,000	77,052	5.7	1,349,000	132,828	9.85
Umbria	298,000	12,186	4.1	298,000	26,215	8.8
Marche	571,000	24,409	4.3	560,000	45,545	8.13
Lazio	1,815,000	76,034	4.2	1,831,000	160,909	8.79
Abruzzo	450,000	11,353	2.5	434,000	26,033	6.0
Molise	105,000	2,460	2.3	104,000	5,776	5.55
Campania	1,483,000	21,614	1.5	1,526,000	73,630	4.83
Puglia	1,145,000	20,956	1.8	1,135,000	65,763	5.79
Basilicata	172,000	2,730	1.6	172,000	8,996	5.23
Calabria	529,000	7,121	1.3	518,000	22,844	4.41
Sicilia	1,283,000	20,884	1.6	1,303,000	74,982	5.75
Sardegna	489,000	16,040	3.3	494,000	39,593	8.01
Italy	20,088,000	822,892	4.1	20,197,000	1,676,281	8.3

Source: Our elaborations on NIdiL on INPS data

(*) incidence: collabor./employed

to enter the labor market in new and atypical professions, it soon became evident that this group was very heterogenous.[32] Actually, the surveys on samples of collaborators conducted both at national and regional level (Censis 1997 on 200 workers, Ires on 234 workers (Altieri and Oteri 2000), and Isfol on 206 collaborators in Emilia Romagna in 1998 (Dall'Agata and Grazioli 1999) show that this group of workers includes both traditional professions (like administrators, revisors, sellers, intermediaries) and less traditional professions (training and communication experts, Internet masters, researchers) with a different degree of precariousness.[33]

The heterogeneity in the type of work is also reflected in a distribution of earnings characterized by a large variance and high discontinuity. This can be found in the Censis (1997) analysis, where out of a sample of 200 collaborators in 1997, 39% of the interviewees have net (of VAT and INPS) monthly earnings higher than 2 million lire, while 29.6% earn less than 1 million lire a month (Table 9). The lowest paid collaborators are women (47% of them earn less than 1 million per month as against 13%

TABLE 8. Collaborators, professionals by gender and age groups, January 2000

Age	Men	%	Women	%	Total	%
A. Collaborators						
less than 25	47,492	5.5	93,506	12.9	140,998	8.9
25-30	105,862	12.3	145,432	20.1	251,294	15.8
31-35	121,497	14.1	134,038	18.5	255,535	16.1
36-40	112,415	13.0	100,677	13.9	213,092	13.4
41-45	98,168	11.4	74,183	10.3	172,351	10.9
46-50	88,065	10.2	56,486	7.8	144,551	9.1
51-55	90,937	10.5	50,056	6.9	140,993	8.9
56-60	82,661	9.6	35,431	4.9	118,092	7.4
61-65	68,988	8.0	21,200	2.9	90,188	5.7
more than 65	47,244	5.5	12,089	1.7	59,333	3.7
Total	863,329	100	723,098	100	1,586,427	100
B. Professional						
less than 25	622	2.2	742	4.4	1,364	3.0
25-30	3,436	12.2	3,538	20.9	6,974	15.4
31-35	5,618	19.9	4,394	25.9	10,012	22.2
36-40	4,621	16.4	2,964	17.5	7,585	16.8
41-45	3,611	12.8	1,834	10.8	5,445	12.1
46-50	2,875	10.2	1,230	7.3	4,105	9.1
51-55	2,680	9.5	1,038	6.1	3,718	8.2
56-60	2,272	8.0	726	4.3	2,998	6.6
61-65	1,891	6.7	341	2.0	2,232	4.9
more than 65	621	2.2	132	0.8	753	1.7
Total	28,247	100	16,939	100	45,186	100
C. Collaborator-professional						
less than 25	3,341	2.7	2,943	5.1	6,284	3.5
25-30	13,293	10.7	10,260	17.9	23,553	13.0
31-35	20,925	16.8	13,475	23.5	34,400	19.0
36-40	20,322	16.4	10,843	18.9	31,165	17.2
41-45	17,051	13.7	7,300	12.8	24,351	13.4
46-50	14,655	11.8	4,668	8.2	19,323	10.6
51-55	13,000	10.5	3,686	6.4	16,686	9.2
56-60	9,884	8.0	2,341	4.1	12,225	6.7
61-65	7,739	6.2	1,188	2.1	8,927	4.9
more than 65	4,019	3.2	517	0.9	4,536	2.5
Total	124,229	100	57,221	100	181,450	100
D. Total						
less than 25	51,455	5.1	97,191	12.2	148,646	8.2
25-30	122,591	12.1	159,230	20.0	281,821	15.5
31-35	148,040	14.6	151,907	19.1	299,947	16.5
36-40	137,358	13.5	114,484	14.4	251,842	13.9

(continued)

TABLE 8. (continued)

Age	Men	%	Women	%	Total	%
41-45	118,830	11.7	83,317	10.5	202,147	11.1
46-50	105,595	10.4	62,384	7.8	167,979	9.3
51-55	106,617	10.5	54,780	6.9	161,397	8.9
56-60	94,817	9.3	38,498	4.8	133,315	7.4
61-65	78,618	7.7	22,729	2.9	101,347	5.6
more than 65	51,884	5.1	12,738	1.6	64,622	3.6
Total	1,015,805	100	797,258	100	1,813,063	100

Source: Our elaborations on INPS data

of male collaborators, Table 9) more concentrated in the South of Italy (where 65% earn less than 1 million lire per month, Table 10), younger (52%, Table 11) and with a lower level of education (Table 12). Altieri and Oteri (2000), using the Ires survey on collaborators, find that 70% of them earn less than 2 million lire per month (48% from 1 to less than 2 million per month); consistent with Censis survey, they also find that women collaborators earn on average less than men and that for two thirds of the sample collaboration work is the only source of income. Moreover, Altieri and Oteri find that collaboration earnings are less than the minimum wage fixed by contracts for dependent workers in the same profession. Only about 50% of collaborators in the Ires survey are regularly paid. Using 1992 fiscal records, Ricci (1997, 200–201) finds that 70% of collaborators have per capita annual incomes lower than 20 million.

The Censis 1997 analysis also enables earnings to be considered by type of contract. Coordinated and continuing collaborators earn on average less than professionals, and, among the former, having more than one employer increases the probability of earning less than 1 million lire (Table 13).

The lower earnings of women collaborators are consistent with the more frequent answer to a specific question in Censis survey on the reason

TABLE 9. Earnings of collaborators by gender

Earnings by gender	Men %	Women %	Total %
up to 1,000,000 lire per month	12.9	47	29.6
from 1,000,001 to 1,500,000	10.9	21.4	16.1
from 1,500,001 to 2,000,000	16.8	13.3	15.1
from 2,000,001 to 3,000,000	21.8	12.2	17.1
more than 3,000,000	37.6	6.1	22.1
Total	100	100	100

Source: Censis 1997, 62

TABLE 10. Earnings of collaborators by region

	Macro regions		
Earnings by region	North %	Centre %	South %
up to 1,000,000 lire per month	4.1	19.6	65.3
from 1,000,001 to 1,500,000	18.9	23.3	7.2
from 1,500,001 to 2,000,000	18.9	19.6	7.2
from 2,000,001 to 3,000,000	23.0	16.1	11.6
more than 3,000,000	35.1	21.4	8.7
Total	100	100	100

Source: Censis 1997, 62

behind this type of work: 40% of women collaborators answer that they work as collaborators since they could not find any valid alternative; on the other hand, only 26.5% of men chose this answer as against 45% who stated that this was the type of job they preferred (against 18% of women). It should be noted that men are overrepresented with respect to women in professional positions that are also higher paid than purely collaborator positions.[34] Women's employment conditions are also reflected in the higher percentage of collaborators who are unsatisfied by this type of work that Censis (1997, 50) found among women. Only 32.6% of women would like to keep their contract as collaborators, whereas for men the collaborators who would not like to change their work amount to 53%. The degree of job satisfaction is lower amongst collaborators than amongst professionals, and for collaborators job satisfaction is lower the higher the number of principals (Censis 1997, 51). The fear that this type of contract could have low career prospects, and fear of its precariousness, are shared by most pure collaborators in the Isfel survey (Dall'Agata and Graziosi 1999, 172). Given the preferences expressed by an important share of collaborators in the different surveys, one should take into account that there is

TABLE 11. Earnings of collaborators by age

	Age			
Earnings by age	19-29 (%)	30-39 (%)	40-49 (%)	> 49 (%)
up to 1,000,000 lire per month	52.0	22.9	25.0	16.7
from 1,000,001 to 1,500,000	29.2	19.7	8.3	3.3
from 1,500,001 to 2,000,000	14.6	13.1	21.7	6.7
from 2,000,001 to 3,000,000		21.3	21.7	26.7
more than 3,000,000	4.2	23.0	23.3	46.6
Total	100	100	100	100

Source: Censis 1997, 62

TABLE 12. Earnings of collaborators by education level

Earnings by education level	Education		
	up to 8 (%)	high school (%)	degree (%)
up to 1,000,000 lire per month	51.6	29.6	17.2
from 1,000,001 to 1,500,000	12.1	23.1	5.2
from 1,500,001 to 2,000,000	12.1	17.6	12.1
from 2,000,001 to 3,000,000	12.1	16.7	20.7
more than 3,000,000	12.1	13.0	44.8
Total	100	100	100

Source: Censis 1997, 62

also a preference towards subordinate work expressed by parasubordinate workers. Accornero 2000, 22 based on Ires survey and Censis 1997, 49 find that among women collaborators 41% prefer a permanent position.

For many young collaborators, continuation of this type of work contract is possible thanks to the possibility of staying with one's family of origin. The need for continuous training has also been clearly expressed by the collaborators interviewed (Dall'Agata, and Grazioli 1999).

Co-ordinated and continuing collaborators have expressed in sample surveys the need to be represented, thirty-six % of collaborators have only one principal and 43.7% with more than one principal according to the *Censis* 1997 survey; according to the latter, 76% of collaborators whose earnings are lower than 1 million per month expressed a high preference for having union representatives (Censis 1997), and their degree of dissatisfaction is higher than other groups as far as earnings and social protection are concerned (Accornero 2000 based on Ires research). The following associations for these new types of workers have recently been created by the leading Italian trade unions: NIDIL (*Nuove Identità di*

TABLE 13. Earnings of collaborators by type of contracts

Earnings by number of employer and type of contract	Coordinated and continuing collaboration— one employer (%)	Coordinated and continuing collaboration—more than one employer (%)	Professionals (%)
up to 1,000,000 lire per month	27.5	39.4	8.3
from 1,000,001 to 1,500,000	19	12.7	16.7
from 1,500,001 to 2,000,000	12.1	14.1	18.8
from 2,000,001 to 3,000,000	15.5	15.5	27.1
more than 3,000,000	25.9	18.3	29.1
Total	100	100	100

Source: Censis 1997, 63

Lavoro, new work identities) by CIGL, ALAI (*Associazioni lavori atipici e interinali,* Atypical and interim workers association) by CISL, and CPO (*Coordinamento per l'occupazione,* co-ordination for employment) by UIL. Researchers interviewing collaborators are struck by the lack of social identity of these workers; Dall'Agata and Grazioli (1999,186) also stress the imperfect knowledge about the characteristics of their contract shown by the collaborators and the difficulties they face in formulating projects for the future.[35]

The need to pass a law on parasubordinate work is shared by the Italian government, which has given expression to it in the 1999 National Action Plan for employment:

> The Government intends to join forces with Parliament for the passage of a body of rules, which has already passed the Senate and is being reviewed by the Chamber of Deputies, aimed at guaranteeing a minimum protection with respect to regular contract payments, continuing education, health and safety, and trade-union rights to those parasubordinate workers who, although formally bound by self-employment schemes, have a relationship of continuing collaboration with a single principal. The core of this protection is a mechanism of administrative certification of the employment relationships that aims at reducing contentious procedures in the matter of qualification of employment relationships, as well as increasing the level of certainty of enterprises which have recourse to labor outside the schemes of dependent employment (1999 NAP).

This projected legislation (named after its first proponent, the Smuraglia Law) has still to be approved and there is a lively debate on whether it introduces too many rules, thus reducing the flexibility of collaborations, and on who must be protected by the law (some collaborators, like retired persons or professionals, are already protected).[36]

Conclusions

This study focuses on two different types of flexible work: part-time work which belongs to the traditional flexibility which was defined by law in 1984 and has lately been encouraged (though the incentives introduced by the "Pacchetto Treu" have been belatedly implemented and their incentive effect cannot yet be detected) and parasubordinate work. The latter atypical work belongs to the new type of flexible work and has yet to be regulated by Italian law. Its degree of flexibility and its lower social security costs have certainly contributed to its spread in the 1990s.

Currently, the incidence of parasubordinate work on total employment is similar to the incidence of part-time on total employment.[37] A gender analysis shows that the incidence of parasubordinate work on total men's employment more than offsets the incidence of part-time, whereas for employed women part-time continues to be more widespread than parasubordinate work.

This analysis, based on previous research, shows that both types of jobs may increase women's participation in paid employment (by supplying working time which is more compatible with women's time constraints, which stem from a still rigid division of work inside the Italian family) at the risk of confining them in unstable and lower paid jobs (though this risk is reduced for better educated women) with low career prospects.[38] The surveys on part-timers and parasubordinate workers show that in both types of jobs there is evidence of disequilibrium, with many workers wishing to change their position (especially as far as their earning conditions and, for collaborators, the issue of discontinuous payment, are concerned) or hours of work.

The closer attention to parasubordinate work through the analysis of available descriptive statistics on the composition of this group of workers and by means of *ad hoc* surveys recently conducted by different research centers in Italy allows one to see how heterogenous is this type of new flexible work: amongst collaborators one can find both highly paid professional workers with many clients as well as workers at the beginning of their career with discontinuous and poorly paid jobs, or workers who were close to the end of their working life and are now under this type of contract merely because they cost less to their firms. Between these two extremes there is a continuum of positions characterized by different economic, social, and demographic characteristics as well as by a different degree of precariousness and job satisfaction.[39]

There is room for a law on parasubordinate work and for the creation of representative bodies.[40] The former is currently under discussion in the Italian Parliament, but the debate seems to be vitiated by the difficulties of impose a structure on a form of work that developed from its very flexibility. For, unlike part-time work, which was initially not well accepted by firms and requires incentives for wider use, collaboration contracts have been extensively used in new hiring since they allow firms a sensible decrease in labor costs (in terms both of social contributions and of pay) and a more flexible way to use labour resources.[41] Trade unions have created new associations to assist these types of workers.

There is undoubtedly room for further research on samples both of collaborators and part-timers, and it would be advisable to identify in the national household surveys currently being conducted the collaborators (enrolled in the 13% INPS fund) included in the employment classification. This would allow one to study the interaction of part-timers and collaborators with the family structure, personal characteristics, and local labor market. For instance, the relatively high presence of collaborators amongst young people and their types of collaboration contracts must definitely interact with their high probability of staying longer in their family of origin and with their postponing marriage and fertility decisions. There are implications also for consumption and savings: collaborators' earnings are often discontinuous and very unstable, and liquidity constraints may well be binding for this type of worker, given the lower diffusion of credit to them.[42]

It is necessary to follow these workers by means of longitudinal surveys in order to detect those amongst them most likely to be trapped by a job that may be low paid, unstable, or both.

The effect of incentives on part-time work introduced in 2000 must be monitored, as well as the development of the Smuraglia Law project on collaborators; the risk, acknowledged by many commentators and social actors, is that of introducing too many norms in the description of the collaboration contract and significantly reducing those labor cost incentives that have encouraged the use of collaboration work by firms in the last decade.[43]

The studies surveyed here report a different degree of time-use satisfaction by flexible workers. The changing working time schedule of the new more flexible part-time contracts and the usually high time intensive work of collaborators are not necessarily well synchronised with the time schedule of schools and services. If the goal is a more balanced gender distribution of total work, it is necessary to monitor how the diffusion of these new types of work changes the distribution of time inside the family.[44]

Notes

1. Data from European Commission, Employment in Europe 2000.
2. Istat (2000) from Italian Quarterly labour force survey data.
3. Censis (2000) critically compares the two types of flexible jobs and their weight in the Italian labor market. Part-time work has increased from 1998 to 1999 by 8.3% while parasubordinate increased from 1998 to 1999 by 18%. (Censis, 2000 Table 3). Altieri and Carrieri (2000, 163) prefer to use the definition of paraindependent work rather than atypical, also in view of the increasing weight of this form of contract in new hiring.
4. OECD (1999) Table 1.A.1, source of data European Labour Force Survey. Part-time employment is defined as work with usual weekly hours less than 30.

5. See OECD (1999) Table 1.A.4 for a cross-countries comparison based on European Labour Force Surveys, and Frey and Livraghi (1998).
6. Law 863/1984 regulated the application of part-time work. It defined part-time as a normal labor contract with a number of hours smaller than that established in collective agreements; the written contract could not be modified and the use of overtime was forbidden (this obligation was removed only in January 2000 when part-time contracts were made more flexible). Giannelli (1997) and Villa (1997) comment on the elements of rigidity contained in this law which contributed to increase the cost of part-time for firms, thus preventing its increase in the first decade of its application. However these elements of rigidity and the lack of incentives to the firm to use part-time have been partially removed by further acts by the Italian Government and budget laws, as Giannelli (1997) and Villa (1997) acknowledge, and as will be discussed below.
7. The smaller the size of the firm, the higher the probability that it will have difficulty adapting to the new organization of the workforce implied by the introduction of part-time (Villa 1997). In order to encourage small to medium firms to use part-time, the Salvi and Amato 12/4/2000 Decree has increased the percentage of part-time to total employment up to which the reduction in social contributions can be applied (firms with less than 250 employees can employ up to 20% of their workers as part-timers and enjoy incentives, the percentage decreasing to 10% for firms with 251–1000 employees and to 2% for larger firms).
8. For analyses on the low diffusion of part-time in Italy see Addabbo (1997), Bentivogli and Sestito (1997), European Commission (1999, Ch.3), Giannelli (1997), Porro (2000a), and Villa (1997). See also OECD (1994) for an overview of the different factors affecting the development of part-time work. On the role played by independent work rather than by part-time in Italy to achieve flexibility, see also Barbieri (1999).
9. For instance D.L. no. 180/1996 and Law 451/1994 have changed the INAIL insurance premium from per capita to a hourly basis. Contribution-related incentives to use part-time labor were also introduced in Law 196/1997. However the delay in the introduction of the D.L. implementing Law 196 on part-time has postponed the impact of these incentives on the increase in part-time (ISTAT 2000, 259). More recently, D.L. 61 20/2/2000 established contribution allowances for firms hiring part-timers in new permanent jobs, implementing the EU 97/81 directive. It also introduces more elastic clauses for part-time work by removing the prohibition on supplementary hours of work and by leaving to bargaining the definition of the maximum number of additional hours of work in a year. Having refused to turn to part-time cannot be used, according to this Decree, as a fair reason for dismissal. Full-time and part-time workers should also enjoy the same work conditions (like holidays, maternity leave, hourly wages). Many incentives established by law did not have the funds to finance them: only very recently (Salvi and Amato 12/4/2000 Decree) have 600 billion lire been earmarked (200 billion for three years) for part-time with the target of creating 100,000 new jobs by 2002, and, in case the application for funds exceeds the limit, precedence will be given to part-time hiring of young unemployed persons, or to hiring of women with children or having disabled individuals in the family.
10. ISFOL (1998).
11. This percentage shrinks to 50% in the case of interviewed firms in the large

distribution sector. The results of Cmft-Athena survey have been shown by Chierchia (2000).

12. Recent new contracts encourage the use of part-time, like the new contract signed in April 2000 for textile workers which also establishes the right of workers to require part-time for family or health reasons.

13. Gornick and Jacobs (1996) find evidence of wage differentials against women working part-time in the United Kingdom, United States of America, Canada and Australia, while Ferber and Waldfogel's (1996) analysis on non standard employment in the United States of America finds that part-time work is related both to overtime work and to lower wage growth both for men and for women. See also OECD (1994).

14. The risk that part-time is a trap is higher for involuntary part-time workers (Ferber and Waldfogel 1996) and for part-timers who work shorter hours, Tam also finds a high degree of dissatisfaction by overqualified or young part-timers on their career prospects (Tam 1997).

15. See also OECD (1994,1999) for evidence on other industrialized countries.

16. A higher presence of part-timers amongst unskilled workers in Milan has also been found by Porro (2000a).

17. The need to improve the contractual status of part-time and of other non standard employment while increasing its application is reflected in the Council of Europe 15/12/1997 Directive.

18. The unequal distribution by gender within Italian households is shown by Addabbo's (1999) analysis based on ISTAT time budget data; a comparison with other countries can be found in United Nations Development Program (1995) and in Goldschmidt and Pagnossin-Aligisakis (1996).

19. This monitoring can be conducted more easily now that more frequent time budget surveys have been established by Law also in Italy. Art.16 in the Law 22/2/2000 on parental leave establishes that every five years the National Statistical Institute must run time budget surveys enabling gender analysis on the distribution of time in the Italian households.

20. 2/3 of the contribution must be paid by the principal and 1/3 by the worker.

21. It has been noted that the social contribution required from collaborators could ensure only a low level of retirement pensions (Altieri and Carrieri 2000, Porro 2000a). The welfare implications of this as well as policy measures to reduce inequality are discussed by Porro (2000a and 2000b) and by Marelli (2000). The government decided to increase the amount of the social security contribution gradually to 19%.

22. In 1973 the law on individual labor disputes was extended by the Act 533/1973 to cover agents, commercial representatives, and other work relationships that could be defined as continuous, coordinated, personal work, even if without subordination. This type of work has been defined by labour jurists as *parasubordinate*. Only in 1995 with the Dini Reform were workers in this position granted social security after a 10% contribution to the national social security Institute (INPS) and began to be called '10% people.' Recently research on this type of workers has been published with the title 'Il popolo del 10%' (Altieri and Carrieri 2000). They should now be named the 13% people, since the last Budget Law raised the social security contribution to 13% as from January 2000.

23. On the definition and characteristics of these different groups see also ISFOL

(1998), Carcano, Botticelli, Ghiraldi, and Jorio (1998), Censis (1999), Altieri, Carrieri (2000) and Porro (2000a).
24. Censis (1999), Altieri and Carrieri (2000).
25. See Porro (2000a) for an interesting analysis on the characteristics of parasubordinate work in Lombardia with respect to Italy and on other forms of atypical works.
26. However, one should note that the entry in the INPS fund is made with reference to the region of residence; work can be performed also in regions other than the region of residence (this point has been raised by Carcano et al. 1998). A similar regional distribution has been found by Ricci (1996, 352-353) using fiscal records for 1991. One should recall that before the requirement to pay a social contribution, collaborators could be identified from fiscal records since DPR 917/86 did include this type of work as taxable income. INPS data (collected after the 10% social contribution was made obligatory) give a picture of collaboration work which is comparable with the fiscal records data used by Ricci (1996).
27. NIdiL, Nuove Identita' di Lavoro (New Labor Typologies) is a sub-sector of the Cgil trade union, created in 1998 to represent atypical workers. See http://www.cgil.it/nidil.
28. Altieri and Carrieri (2000) and Dall'Agata and Grazioli (1999). The latter, by interviewing a sample of firms, find that the possibility of increasing flexibility in the use of labor resources is seen as an advantage to firms more than the reduction of costs in the use of collaboration contracts.
29. ISFOL (1998).
30. This distribution by age and gender of collaborators makes Censis (1999, 14) state that collaborations are for men more close to self-employment than for women who, especially in the south of Italy, tend to use this contract as a way of entering the labor market.
31. Social contributions are around 50% for dependent workers and less than 10% (as far as the contribution paid by the firm is concerned) for collaborators. The risk of pseudo-parasubordinate work has been discussed amongst others by Carcano et al. (1998), Accornero (2000), and INPS president M. Paci in the newspaper *Corriere della Sera* 20/11/1999.
32. On the different characteristics of collaborators see Accornero (2000), Altieri and Oteri (2000), Dall'Agata C. and Grazioli (1999), ISFOL (1998) and Porro (2000a). Accornero (2000) discusses the advantages and disadvantages for collaborators of having only one principal.
33. Given the heterogeneity of collaborators and the expectation that women would be more exposed than men to the risk of lower wages and less qualified positions, in 1998 the Ministry of Equal Opportunities in Italy set up a flexibility monitoring unit to monitor the gender-related effects of the measures promoting a flexible access to the labor market in Italy (NAP 1999). In May 1998, a decree by the Ministry of Labor extended maternity benefits to self-employed female workers and to women having an employment relationship of co-ordinated and continuing collaboration, lacking any other social security coverage.
34. See Censis (1997, 63, Table 10 for reasons given by interviewees for this type of work), and Censis (1997, 39) for the distribution of collaborators and professionals by gender.
35. This is correlated with their discontinuous earnings profile, which also makes it

difficult for collaborators to have access to the credit market, to buy a house, and to have access at a reduced price to public services. Recently Emilia Romagna (one of the Italian regions where collaboration work is most widespread) has approved an Act (Act 168/2000) which also provides collaborators credit for buying equipment both directly, by opening a public fund, and indirectly by encouraging activities which can provide credit to these subjects. This possibility reflects the difficulties of collaborators in having access to normal credit markets. On the problem of identity in new forms of independent work, see also Bologna (1997).

36. For a critical assessment of this project see Accornero (2000, 25–27) and Carrieri and Leonardi (2000, 130–135).
37. However, one should note that INPS data do not report collaborators who ceased to be such, and this is bound to overestimate the number of collaborators.
38. A mix of part-time schedule and collaboration has been found in the Ires research for those collaborators with a very low degree of independence (like telephone operators, interviewers) (Altieri and Oteri 2000, 112). The groups of collaborators defined as executive who work with a very low degree of independence are also characterized by chaotic career patterns, higher probability of experiencing unemployment spells and low upward mobility in their career. (Altieri and Carrieri 2000, 162).
39. For instance, among the elderly there are both collaborators who are close to pseudo-subordinates and workers who decided to use their longer work experience with more than one firm. See also Barbieri (1999) on the polarization in independent work in Italy.
40. Some steps towards the latter point are already under way: in June 2000 collaborators will be summoned to elect their representative on the National Social Security Institute (INPS) board.
41. Altieri and Carrieri (2000) and Dall'Agata and Grazioli (1999). The latter, by interviewing a sample of firms, find that the possibility of increasing flexibility in the use of labor resources is seen as an advantage to firms more than the reduction of costs in the use of collaboration contracts. The incentives in terms of low labor costs for the firms have been stressed also by Ricci (1997) who claims that the reasons for the increase in this new type of work must be sought more at the microeconomic than at the macroeconomic level.
42. This also calls for public policies to increase the available credits to collaborators. This problem has been addressed by the Emilia-Romagna region, which has recently introduced a special fund also for financing collaborators (see above). See also Barbieri (1999) on the social costs connected with the increase of new forms of independent work.
43. Ricci (1996 and 1997) (by using fiscal records) stresses how collaboration work also increased during adverse periods of the business cycle.
44. Analyses conducted in countries where part-time work is more widespread have shown that the diffusion of part-time has not led to a balanced redistribution of family responsibilities (European Commission 1999, 3) microeconometric analysis on unpaid work in Italy (based on 1989 ISTAT time budget survey) finds an increase of unpaid work for women working part-time (Addabbo and Caiumi, 1999).

References

Accornero, A. (2000) Introduzione, Altieri G., Carrieri M., *Il popolo del 10%*, Donzelli, Roma.
Addabbo, T. (1997) 'Part-time work in Italy', H.P. Blossfeld, C.Hakim, eds., *Between Equalization and Marginalization. Women Working Part-time in Europe and the United States of America*, Ch. 5, Oxford University Press, Oxford.
Addabbo, T. (1999) 'Il lavoro non pagato in Italia in una prospettiva di genere', A.Picchio, ed. *Lavoro non pagato e condizioni di vita*, Research Report, CNEL, Roma, 15 December 1999, Ch. 1.
Addabbo, T., Caiumi, A. (1999), 'Stima del reddito esteso e ineguaglianza di genere', A.Picchio, ed., *Lavoro non pagato e condizioni di vita*, Research Report, CNEL, Roma, 15 December 1999, Ch. 3.
Altieri, G. (2000), 'Le nuove forme di lavoro post-fordista: il caso italiano', Altieri G., Carrieri M., eds., *Il popolo del 10%*, Donzelli, Roma, Ch. 1, pp. 29-61.
Altieri G., and Carrieri M., eds. (2000), *Il popolo del 10%*, Donzelli, Roma.
Altieri G., Oteri, C. (2000), 'Atipici, ma quanto?', Altieri G., and Carrieri M., eds., *Il popolo del 10%*, Donzelli, Roma, pp. 62-115.
Barbieri P. (1999), 'Liberi di rischiare. Vecchi e nuovi lavoratori autonomi', *Stato e Mercato* (56), pp. 281-308.
Bentivogli, C., Sestito, P. (1997), 'L'orario di lavoro, fra la tendenza storica e l'incertezza della prospettiva', Ciocca, P., ed., *Disoccupazione di fine secolo. Studi e Proposte per l'Europa*, Bollati Boringhieri, Torino, 1997, Ch. 6, pp. 284-335.
Blank, R.M. (1989), 'The role of part-time work in women's labor market choices over time', *American Economic Review*, 79 (2): pp. 295-299.
Bologna, S. (1997), 'Dieci tesi per la definizione di uno statuto del lavoro autonomo', Bologna S., Fumagalli A., eds., *Il lavoro autonomo di seconda generazione*, Ch. 1, pp. 13-42, Feltrinelli, Milano, 1997.
Borzaga, C. (1997), 'Part-time o short full-time? Un'analisi su microdati dell'offerta di lavoro femminile', *Lavoro e relazioni industriali* (1), pp. 27-65.
Carcano, M., Botticelli, R., Ghiraldi, L., Jorio, F. (1998), *La flessibilità del lavoro: da eccezione a regola?*, CGIL, Camera del lavoro territoriale di Parma.
Carrieri, M. Leonardi, S. (2000), 'I problemi della regolazione sociale', Altieri G., Carrieri M., eds. *Il popolo del 10%*, Donzelli, Roma, 2000, pp. 116-151.
Censis (1997), 'Secondo rapporto Censis sul Patronato in Italia', *Assistenza Sociale* (4).
Censis (1999), 'Audizione informale sui lavori atipici alla Camera dei Deputati, Commissione lavoro pubblico e privato', Censis, Materiali di documentazione.
Censis (2000), *Rapporto sulla situazione sociale del paese 1999*, Collana Censis/Rapporti, Franco Angeli, Milano.
Chierchia, V. (2000), 'Commercio, decolla il Part-time', Il Sole 24 Ore, 21/01/2000, *Il Sole 24 Ore on line*.
Dall'Agata, C., Grazioli, P. (1999), *Senza tetto né legge*, Franco Angeli, Milano, 1999.
European Commission (1995a), *Labour force survey. Results 1993*. Population and

Social Condition Series, accounts and surveys, Theme 3, Brussels, Office for Official Publications of the European Communities.
European Commission (1995b), *European Economy, Reports and Studies No.3*, Brussels.
European Commission (1999), *Transformation of labour and future of labour law in Europe*, Employment and Social Affairs, Final Report, Luxembourg, Office for Official Publications of the European Communities.
Eurostat 1999 Labor Force Survey
Ferber, M., Waldfogel, J. (1996), *"Contingent" work: blessing and/or curse*, Radcliffe Public Policy Institute.
Frey, L., Livraghi, R., eds. (1998), 'Contratti atipici e tempo di lavoro', *Quaderni di Economia del lavoro*, 62, Franco Angeli, Milano.
Gallino, L. (1998), *Se tre milioni vi sembran pochi*, Einaudi, Torino, 1998.
Giannelli, G.C. (1997), 'Offerta di lavoro e orario part-time : alcune indicazioni in merito alle politiche per la flessibilità', Borzaga, C., Brunello, G. eds. (1997), *L'impatto delle politiche attive del lavoro in Italia*, Napoli, ESI.
Goldschmidt, L., E. Pagnossin-Aligisakis (1996), 'Measures of Unrecorded Economic Activities in Fourteen Countries', UNDP (1996), Background papers, Human Development Report, New York 1995.
Gornick, J., Jacobs, J. (1996), 'A cross-national analysis of the wages of part-time workers: evidence from the United States, the United Kingdom, Canada and Australia', *Work, employment and society*, March 1996, pp. 1-27.
Isfol (1998), *Il lavoro in Italia: profili, percorsi, politiche*, Franco Angeli, Milano 1998.
ISTAT (2000) *Rapporto Annuale. La situazione del Paese nel 1999*, Roma, ISTAT.
Kosters (1995), 'Part-time pay', *Journal of Labor Research, Symposium on Part-time employment and employees*, XVI.
Marelli, E. (2000) 'Istituzioni e politiche del lavoro: le tendenze in Italia ed in Europa', Marelli, E., Porro, G., eds., *Il lavoro tra flessibilità e innovazione. Le tendenze del mercato del lavoro in Lombardia*, Ch. 9, Franco Angeli, Milano, forthcoming.
Ministero del Lavoro e della Previdenza Sociale (1999), National Action Plan for Employment (*Piano Nazionale per l'occupazione*) Italy, May 1999.
Nardone, T. (1995), Part-time employment: reasons, demographics and trends, *Journal of Labor Research, Symposium on Part-time employment and employees*, XVI, 3, pp. 275-92.
National Action Plan for Employment (*Piano nazionale per l'occupazione*) 1999, see Ministero del Lavoro e della Previdenza Sociale, above.
Natti, J. (1995), 'Part-time work in the Nordic countries: a trap for women?', *Labour* 9(2) pp. 343-357.
OECD (1994), *Women & Structural Change. New perspectives*, Paris, OECD.
OECD (1999) *Employment outlook*, Paris, OECD, June.
Porro, G. (2000a), 'I lavori atipici in Lombardia: confronti con l'Italia ed altri paesi', Marelli, Porro, eds., *Il lavoro tra flessibilita' e innovazione. Le tendenze del mercato del lavoro in Lombardia*, Franco Angeli, Milano, forthcoming.
Porro, G. (2000b), 'Politiche per l'occupazione ed il lavoro in Lombardia', Mar-

elli and Porro (eds), *Il lavoro tra flessibilità e innovazione. Le tendenze del mercato del lavoro in Lombardia*, Ch.10, Franco Angeli, Milano, forthcoming.

Ricci, L. (1996), 'Tra lavoro dipendente e lavoro autonomo: il caso delle collaborazioni coordinate e continuative', Rossi, N., ed., *Competizione e giustizia sociale. Terzo Rapporto Cnel sulla distribuzione e redistribuzione del reddito in Italia*, Il Mulino, Bologna, 1996, pp. 343-360.

Ricci, L. (1997), 'Il lavoro che cambia', Bologna, S. and Fumagalli, A.,eds. (1997) *Il lavoro autonomo di seconda generazione*, Feltrinelli, Milano 1997, Ch. 6, pp. 193-20.

Tam, M. (1997), *Part-time Employment: a bridge or a trap?*, Avebury, Aldershot 1997.

United Nations Development Programme (1995), *Human Development Report*, New York: Oxford University Press.

Villa, P. (1997), *1997 Report Italy*, European Commission Network of Experts 'Gender & Employment'.

LIA FUBINI

CHAPTER 6

WOMEN'S UNEMPLOYMENT IN ITALY

Unemployment: Some stylized facts

After twenty years of full employment, beginning in the early 1970s most European countries have started suffering a rising and persistent unemployment. In the 15 countries now belonging to the European Union (hereafter EU), the rate of unemployment amounted to a negligible 2.2% in the decade 1961-70 (much lower than in the United States). It doubled in the following decade and then doubled again between 1981 and 1990, reaching approximately 10% in the period 1991-1999.

This phenomenon is peculiar to the European situation. In fact, in the United States unemployment fluctuated considerably, rising and declining according to economic cycles, while Japanese unemployment remained at a very low level till the recent crisis (when, at the end of 1999, it reached a peak of 4.9%). By contrast, in Europe rates of unemployment tended to increase whenever a recession occurred, but they remained stable or declined only slightly during cycles of economic expansions. The cause of persistent unemployment can be found in the interaction between a series of adverse supply and demand shocks and the labor market institutions as well as in the restrictive fiscal and monetary policies which have been carried on in most European countries.[1]

Altogether, the European labor market has performed very poorly over the past thirty years (Table 2). Clearly there are significant differences between individual countries: for example, Luxembourg, the Netherlands, Austria, and Portugal succeeded in maintaining relatively low rates

TABLE 1. Average annual rate of unemployment

	1961–70	1971–80	1981–90	1991–99
European Union	2.2	4.0	9.0	10.2
Italy	4.8	6.1	8.8	11.0
United States	4.7	6.4	7.1	5.7
Japan	1.2	18	2.5	3.0

Source: Eurostat

of unemployment, while other countries like Ireland and Denmark, brought down the figures significantly over the past decade. However, the rate of unemployment is still high in most of the largest EU countries (more than 10% in France, Italy, and Spain, almost 9 percent in Germany). The European labor market has been characterized by a deep demographic imbalance and a high incidence of long-term unemployment. The percentage of individuals unemployed for 12 months and over is 50.1% in the EU against 8.0% in the U.S. This situation has contributed to the marginalization of social categories such as youngsters, women and unskilled workers. For instance, 25 million more men than women are employed in the EU as a whole and women run a 33% higher risk of becoming unemployed.

In Italy the evolution of unemployment is definitely alarming: among the EU countries only Spain has a higher rate of unemployment. As shown in Table 1, the Italian rate of unemployment in the 1960s was approximately 5%, which was more than double the average rate of the 15 EU members. Since the 1970s, following the first oil shock, the rate of unemployment rose steadily and reached a peak of more than 12.5% in 1997. Despite some recent improvements, the rate of unemployment still runs over 10%, with almost three million unemployed persons. Moreover, labor force participation rate is only 57.8 % for persons aged 15-64, approximately 10% lower than in the EU. In Italy total employment decreased by an average 0.3% per year in the decade 1986-96 (OECD, 1999), one of the worst performances in the EU (only Finland with −1.3% and Sweden with −0.8% had a lower employment trend, but these two countries had a much higher employment rate to begin with). Geographical difference is significantly higher than in most European countries: in the North the rate of unemployment is below the European average (and the Northeast has almost reached a full-employment situation), in the Center it is set at the European level, while in the South it is much higher.

Turning to demographic composition, unemployment rates tend to be particularly high among the youngsters and women. Unemployment rate reaches more than 30% for people aged 15–24. One of the most serious problems in Italy is long-term unemployment, its incidence being the highest in the EU. In 1998, 66.7% of the Italian unemployed had been out of work for more than 12 months (Table 3).

Female unemployment in Italy and in the European union: General features

The female labor market shows contradictory aspects. Women's participation has increased in the last thirty years despite the Italian employment crisis. Let us consider, for example, the decade 1987–97, in which the employment performance was really unsatisfactory: the rate of unemployment grew fast and total employment decreased. Nevertheless, female employment increased. The employment crisis has not turned women out of the labor market as in the past.

The improvement in the position of women in the labor market is confirmed by other figures (ISTAT, *Indagine sulle forze di lavoro*, various years).

TABLE 2. Activity rates and unemployment rates for persons aged 15–64 years by sex (1998)

	Activity rate			Unemployment rate		
	Women	Men	Both sexes	Women	Men	Both sexes
Austria	62.5	80.2	71.3	5.6	5.4	5.5
Belgium	53.8	72.5	63.2	11.7	7.6	9.4
Denmark	75.0	83.5	79.3	6.4	3..9	5.1
Finland	69.7	76.6	73.2	12.1	10.9	11.5
France	60.8	74.1	67.4	13.9	10.3	11.9
Germany	60.9	79.2	70.1	8.7	8.5	8.6
Greece	48.2	77.2	62.4	17.8	8.1	11.9
Ireland	52.1	77.8	65.0	7.5	8.2	7.9
Italy	43.9	72.0	57.8	16.4	9.5	12.2
Luxembourg	47.6	76.0	61.9	4.2	1.9	2.8
Netherlands	62.9	82.8	72.9	5.5	3.5	4.3
Portugal	61.9	79.0	70.2	6.0	4.0	4.9
Spain	48.7	77.7	63.1	26.7	13.7	18.8
Sweden	75.5	80.7	78.1	8.0	8.8	8.4
United Kingdom	67.8	83.9	75.9	5.3	6.9	6.2
EU	58.0	77.8	67.9	11.5	8.7	9.9
USA	70.7	84.2	77.4	4.7	4.5	4.5
Total OECD	58.7	81.2	69.8	7.4	6.3	6.8

Source: OECD Employment outlook (1999)

For example:

- between July 1998 and July 1999, women employment increased by 2.5%, while men employment grew only by a small 0.5%;
- 85% of new employed people in 1999 are women.

Despite the recent improvements, the gender gap in Italy is still higher than in most European countries both in unemployment and in participation (Table 2). Female activity rate for persons aged 15–64 years is only 60% of the male activity rate, while unemployment is approximately 70% higher. Women's activity rate is the lowest in Europe. It is lower than in Spain, where till the early 1990's there was an even worse situation. It is more than 30 percentage points lower than in Sweden and Denmark and more than 14 percentage points lower than the average EU activity rate in 1998, with a gap between men and women of 28.1 percentage points against 19.8 in EU.

As far as women unemployment rate is concerned, Italy shows the third worst performance (after Spain and Greece).

As we can see in Table 3, in the 1990's total unemployment in Italy has been higher than in the EU. However, while male unemployment reaches a maximum 1.3% higher than the average European rate, in 1998, the female labor market shows a much poorer performance. In the decade 1988–1998 the female rate of unemployment in Italy varied from 15.8% to 16.8% while in the EU it reached a maximum level of 13% in 1994 and then decreased to 11.5% in 1998, when the gap between Italy and EU rose to almost five percentage points. In 1998 the gender gap in unemployment rate amounted to 6.9 percentage points, while it was just 3.3 points in the European Union. Only Spain has a larger gap between males and females.

TABLE 3. Activity rates and unemployment rates for persons aged 15–64 years by sex in Italy and EU

	Activity rate						Unemployment rate					
	1990	1994	1995	1996	1997	1998	1990	1994	1995	1996	1997	1998
Italy												
women	43.2	42.2	42.5	43.3	43.6	43.9	15.8	15.7	16.3	16.6	16.8	16.4
men	77.0	73.1	72.4	72.3	72.2	72.0	6.5	9.0	9.3	9.7	9.8	9.5
both sexes	59.8	57.5	57.3	57.7	57.7	57.8	9.9	11.5	11.9	12.3	12.5	12.2
European Union												
women	49.0	49.1	49.8	50.2	50.7	51.3	10.5	13.0	12.5	12.5	12.4	11.5
men	81.0	78.0	77.9	77.8	77.6	77.7	6.5	10.1	9.2	9.2	8.9	8.2
both sexes	67.5	67.3	67.4	67.6	67.8	67.9	8.1	11.4	10.8	10.9	10.8	9.9

Source: OECD Employment outlook (1999)

TABLE 4. Incidence of long-term unemployment by sex in Italy and EU as a percentage of total employment

	1990*		1995		1996		1997		1998	
	6 mos. and over	12 mos. and over	6 mos. and over	12 mos. and over	6 mos. and over	12 mos. and over	6 mos. and over	12 mos. and over	6 mos. and over	12 mos. and over
Italy										
men	84.1	68.6	78.9	62.7	78.7	64.1	81.2	66.5	80.5	66.4
women	86.0	70.7	81.5	64.4	82.8	67.1	82.5	66.2	82.5	67.0
total	85.2	69.8	80.2	63.6	80.8	65.6	81.8	66.3	81.6	66.7
EU										
men	63.5	47.0	66.9	49.2	65.4	47.6	66.4	48.5	65.2	48.7
women	66.9	50.1	69.7	51.2	69.6	51.2	70.1	51.8	68.9	51.5
total	65.3	48.6	68.3	50.2	67.4	49.3	68.2	50.1	67.1	50.1

Source: OECD Employment outlook (June 1999)
* indicates a break in the series

It is remarkable that in Sweden and United Kingdom, the unemployment rate is higher for men than for women, while in the United States the gender gap is only 0.2 percentage points.

As we have seen, one of the more troublesome aspects of Italian unemployment is the share of long-term unemployed, which is the highest in Europe. Table 4 shows the incidence of long-term unemployment both for women and men. The situation is really dramatic: about two thirds of the labor force job seekers are not likely to find one within 12 months, and there are no signs that the situation may improve. Yet as far as long-term unemployment is concerned, the gender gap is lower than in the EU.

What is changing?

Let us consider now the main transformations in the Italian female labor market in the period 1993-1998 (Table 5). During this period the number of unemployed increased and total employment decreased, while the labor force grew slightly. Analyzing the situation by gender, one can see a 3.2% increase of women employed against a 3.7% decrease of men employed, raising the male/female ratio from 53.5 to 57.4% (255,000 more women unemployed, or almost half the corresponding figure for men—523,000).

Turning to job distribution, we can find an increasing number of women in managerial, intellectual, and specialized jobs. During the period 1993-98 the share of women entrepreneurs increases from 15.0% to 21.2%. In the hired jobs, women employed in medium to high positions increased from

TABLE 5. Labor market indicators by gender in Italy 1993–1998

	1993	1998
Employed both sexes	20,466	20,197
women	7,135	7,364
men	13,331	12,833
Unemployed both sexes	2,314	2,837
women	1,236	1,491
men	1,078	1,346
Labor force both sexes	22,780	23,034
women	8,371	8,855
men	14,409	14,179

Source: ISTAT Indagine sulle forze di lavoro (1993–1998)

26.8% to 31.5%. The same trend is observable for intellectual, scientific, and highly specialized jobs. In 1998 a 9.2% of the employed women had such jobs compared to a 7.7% in 1993. Also the number of women employees increased by 8.1% while the number of workers decreased by 2.3%.

Altogether, women have been favored more than men by the growth of nonmanual jobs both in highly specialized and in low-skilled areas, while women decreased at the same rate as men in the manual jobs.

Looking at the data, what appears to be emerging is that female participation in labor market is rapidly increasing and the old model "housewife-wife-mother" is declining everywhere in Italy, also in the South. Women start their working experience before leaving the parental house and the majority of them keep on working after the marriage. Between 1993 and 1998 the share of unemployed women that had got married climbed from 50% to 56%, while the share of housewives declined from 39% to 32%. The new model "worker-wife-mother" is more widespread among highly educated women.

Women's status in the labor market has certainly improved, but discrimination is still remarkable. The latter is particularly evident where permanent jobs are concerned. Research on job opportunities for young people (Istat 1997) shows the difficulty of access for young women to nontemporary jobs. Young males have a 50% better chance than young women to find a permanent job. In the last years women's employment has increased, thanks to part-time, temporary jobs, and self-employment. One open question is whether temporary work may be regarded as a step towards more stable types of jobs, or whether it is just a form of discrimination that confines most women in a marginal position.

Evidence for discrimination can be found also as far as top positions are concerned: a strong barrier to upward mobility, the so-called "glass ceiling," still exists. Fornengo and Guadagnini (1999) show that in 1991 in the public service area no women were employed at top levels and only 14.1% of managers were women. Only 16.4% among legislators, managers, and entrepreneurs were women.

Geographical distribution

Turning now to the distribution according to age, duration of unemployment period, and geographical composition, Table 6 highlights the main features of labor market in April 2000, as compared to April 1999.

TABLE 6. Labor market indicators by gender and geographical area, April 1999 / April 2000 (in %)

| | Activity rate | | Unemployment rates | | | | Youth rates | | | |
| | (age 15–64) | | Total | | of which: long term rate | | Activity rate | | Unemployment rate | |
Geographical area	April 1999	April 2000	April 1999	April 2000	April 1999	April 2000	April 1999	April 2000	April 1999	April 2000
Men										
North	74.8	75.0	3.4	3.2	1.4	1.2	47.1	46.0	11.1	11.7
Northwest	74.5	74.6	4.0	3.5	2.0	1.6	47.2	45.6	13.6	14.0
Northeast	75.3	75.5	2.7	2.7	0.7	0.8	47.0	46.7	7.6	8.4
Center	73.0	73.1	7.3	6.6	4.3	3.9	36.8	36.9	26.4	21.7
South	70.9	71.0	17.0	16.2	11.2	10.8	36.4	37.4	50.0	49.3
Italy	73.1	73.2	8.8	8.3	5.4	5.1	40.6	40.7	28.6	28.4
Women										
North	52.6	53.3	8.8	7.6	3.8	3.0	42.7	42.6	19.6	16.8
Northwest	51.7	52.2	9.5	8.5	4.9	4.0	41.5	41.8	22.4	20.4
Northeast	53.9	55.0	7.7	6.3	2.2	1.6	44.3	43.8	15.9	12.0
Center	48.3	49.2	14.1	12.0	8.4	7.7	31.3	31.6	37.4	33.1
South	35.4	35.7	31.6	30.5	21.5	21.2	26.8	27.2	65.6	62.0
Italy	45.6	46.2	16.3	14.9	9.7	9.0	33.8	34.0	38.3	35.3
Both sexes										
North	63.8	64.2	5.6	5.0	2.4	2.0	44.9	44.4	15.1	14.1
Northwest	63.2	63.5	6.2	5.5	3.2	2.6	44.4	43.7	17.6	17.0
Northeast	64.7	65.3	4.8	4.2	1.3	1.1	45.6	45.3	11.6	10.1
Center	60.6	61.1	10.0	8.8	6.0	5.4	34.1	34.3	31.4	26.9
South	53.0	53.3	21.9	21.0	14.7	14.3	31.7	32.4	56.5	54.6
Italy	59.3	59.7	11.7	10.8	7.0	6.6	37.3	37.4	32.9	31.5

Source: ISTAT, *Rilevazione trimestrale sulle forze di lavoro* (April 2000)

On comparing the year 2000 to the previous year, all indicators show that women did perform better than men in the labor market. Nevertheless the data depict a critical situation in which gender is still a strong element of discrimination with regards to access to the labor market, especially in the South. In the North, indicators of the female labor market show a good performance, particularly in the Northeast, at least better than in the EU. In 1998 the female rate of unemployment was below 10% in most regions of the North (4.6% in Trentino Alto Adige, 6.6% in Val d'Aosta, 8.3% in Veneto, 8.4% in Emilia Romagna, 9.1% in Lombardia, and 9.9% in Friuli Venezia Giulia), while the employment rate was over 50% (Table 7). In the North, serious problems of female unemployment

TABLE 7. Participation rate and unemployment rates by regions—1998

	Participation rate			Unemployment rate		
Regions	Women	Men	Both sexes	Women	Men	Both sexes
			Total	Total	Total	Total
Piemonte	39.7	59.8	49.4	13.6	5.3	8.8
Valle d'Aosta	44.2	62.7	52.4	8.7	3.1	5.6
Lombardia	40.4	63.6	51.5	9.1	3.5	5.8
Trentino-Alto Adige	42.6	66.3	54.1	4.8	2.4	3.4
Veneto	39.1	64.1	51.2	8.3	3.1	5.2
Friuli-Venezia Giulia	37.2	59.6	47.9	9.9	3.1	5.8
Liguria	33.9	57.0	44.7	14.9	8.2	10.8
Emilia-Romagna	42.7	61.2	51.7	8.4	3.6	5.7
Toscana	38.0	58.4	47.7	12.8	5.0	8.2
Umbria	36.0	55.8	45.5	14.2	5.2	8.9
Marche	36.8	58.2	48.2	10.4	4.0	6.7
Lazio	34.2	61.5	47.3	16.4	9.9	12.4
Abruzzo	32.8	57.9	45.0	13.3	7.4	9.6
Molise	34.0	59.1	46.0	22.9	12.8	17.5
Campania	29.1	61.0	44.5	33.7	20.5	24.9
Puglia	27.4	61.0	43.6	29.8	16.5	20.9
Basilicata	30.0	56.0	43.0	28.9	13.3	18.4
Calabria	30.0	57.4	43.3	38.5	20.4	26.8
Sicilia	26.0	60.8	42.7	35.4	20.5	25.2
Sardegna	32.1	60.6	46.0	31.1	16.1	21.5
Italy	35.3	61.0	47.5	16.8	9.5	12.3
Northwest	39.5	61.7	50.2	10.9	4.5	7.1
Northeast	40.6	62.7	51.2	8.2	3.3	5.3
Center	36.2	59.6	47.4	14.1	7.2	10.0
South	28.7	60.2	43.9	31.8	18.2	22.8

Source: CNEL, *Terzo rapporto sulla condizione giovanile* (Third Report on the Status of Youth) (Roma 2000)

are restricted to metropolitan areas and to those zones which are undergoing structural industrial transformations (particularly Piemonte and Liguria). In Central Italy, the average situation is very similar to the average EU situation, but there are significant differences among the various regions of the area. In Tuscana and the Marche, the female labor market resembles, on the whole, the one in the North; in the Lazio region, on the other hand, the participation rate of women is at the same level as in the South, and the rate of women's unemployment is higher than in the other Central regions.

The situation in the Southern regions is really severe: the female rate of unemployment is over 30%, reaching 60% in the case of young women (15 to 24 years),—that is, about two young women out of three are unemployed. The worst situation is in Calabria, where in 1998 the female unemployment rate was 39.0% and the participation rate only 30%. Sicilia, Campania, and Puglia follow with a participation rate respectively of 26.0, 29.1 and 27.4%. The unemployment rate in the three regions is therefore, respectively, of 35.4, 33.7 and 29.8%.

Indeed the issue of female unemployment is mainly a Southern one, since the South is the less developed and less industrialized part of the country. The female unemployment rate is approximately four times higher than in the North, while the employment rate is very low (35%), and long-term unemployment, already high for men, shows values well above the average. Efforts spent by governments over decades to raise the area from economic depression have been by and large unsuccessful. The social distress thus suffered by women in the South is very deep, as they are most likely to hold jobs in the hidden labor market, without the protection of contracts and benefits, often at very low salaries.

Unemployment and education

Let us consider now the relationship between unemployment and the level of education. It is important to notice that women invest more than men in education: the percentage of women entering secondary schools and university is higher than men. There are fewer dropouts among girls than among males and females achieve better results. In 1998, 83.8% of women in the age group 14–18 were attending a secondary school, as compared to 80% of men; 47.5% of women in the group 19–23 were enrolled at the university, as compared to 38.5% of men.

* * *

Still the higher levels of education of young women today compared to women in the past do not result in advantages to be gained on the labor market; the rate of unemployment is overall significantly higher for women than it is for men in the case of all age groups and at all levels of education. The gap in the unemployment rate between males and females at all levels of education is definitely higher than the European average (Table 8). The unemployment rate of women with a low level of education is in fact slightly lower than the European average, but one has to consider that in Italy the overall female participation rate is rather low. At a higher level of education, the participation rate comes closer to the European average, but the rate of unemployment is much higher than the European one. Women with a university degree have many more difficulties than men in entering the labor market, although the situation varies highly according to geographical area (Table 9). Despite a relatively low participation rate, in the South 42% of women in the age group 25-34 holding a university degree are unemployed, while the Northwest offers the best opportunities for women with a high level of education. As the Northwest is the area with the oldest industrial tradi-

TABLE 8. Unemployment, activity rates by education level and educational attainment for individuals age 25-64: Italy and the European Union, 1996 (percentage values)

	Italy		European Union	
	Rate of unemployment	Activity rate	Rate of unemployment	Activity Rate
Women				
Less than upper secondary school	13.8	33.5	14.7	44.9
Upper secondary school	11.2	60.6	9.8	70.4
Tertiary level education	10.1	81.3	7.1	83.2
Men				
Less than upper secondary school	7.3	76.1	11.3	77.8
Upper secondary school	6.0	80.0	7.5	86.5
Tertiary level education	5.2	92.0	5.2	91.8
Both sexes				
Less than upper secondary school	9.4	54.0	12.7	59.7
Upper secondary school	8.2	70.5	8.5	78.8
Tertiary level education	7.3	87.1	6.0	88.0

Source: OECD. Employment outlook (1999)

TABLE 9. Activity rate and rate of unemployment for individuals with university degree age 25-34

	Participation rate			Rate of unemployment		
	Men	Women	Total	Men	Women	Total
Northwest	90.6	87.6	89.0	8.0	10.7	9.4
Northeast	89.0	86.9	87.9	8.7	15.9	12.3
Center	86.9	80.6	83.4	14.6	20.3	17.6
South	84.2	75.7	79.7	27.8	42.0	34.8
Islands	83.2	82.3	82.7	24.8	30.0	27.6
Italy	87.6	83.0	85.1	14.8	21.4	18.1

Source: ISTAT

tion—and now the most developed in the service sector of the economy—women, especially women with a high level of education, are likely to be less discriminated in the job market.

Generally speaking, the relatively high rate of unemployment for women with an upper secondary school diploma or a university degree can be explained by the fact that women traditionally choose fields of study for which there is not much demand on the job market, such as literary studies (32.5%) and law (18.7%). This range of choices, however, is rapidly changing and it is to be hoped that this change could lead to changes in the labor market.

Youth unemployment

Approximately one third of the unemployed people belong to the age group 15-24. Considering the period between April 1999 and April 2000, the situation of women in the age group 15-24 has considerably improved, thus confirming the trend of the previous year. The unemployment rate decreased from 38.3 to 35.3%, while the economic activity rate slightly grew. Male unemployment and participation was stable, so the gender gap decreased (see Table 6). The positive trend in employment for young female has characterized all the macroregions in Italy. Again, it is important to notice the uneven distribution of unemployment between North and South. In the North, as of April 2000, the young female rate of unemployment was 16.8% and the activity rate was 42.6%, while in the South they were, respectively, 62% and 27.2%. The large imbalances in the labor market among regions and the difficulties encountered by young people in finding a job are more evident if one considers regional differences with respect to ages 15 to 29 years (see Table 10).

TABLE 10. Youth unemployment and activity rates (15–29 years) by region (1998)

Regions	Participation rate			Rate of unemployment		
	Women	Men	Both sexes	Women	Men	Both sexes
Piemonte	54.1	61.8	58.0	25.5	13.1	18.8
Valle d'Aosta	58.3	61.5	60.0	14.3	12.5	6.7
Lombardia	55.5	60.9	58.2	15.4	7.7	11.2
Trentino-Alto Adige	58.4	66.7	63.1	6.8	4.3	6.2
Veneto	58.0	64.3	61.2	12.3	6.1	9.0
Friuli-Venezia Giulia	53.0	60.0	56.1	16.1	6.9	12.0
Liguria	49.7	55.1	52.8	30.7	24.4	27.2
Emilia-Romagna	57.1	63.9	60.7	15.7	8.7	11.7
Toscana	50.3	57.3	53.9	23.7	12.8	17.8
Umbria	43.2	52.4	47.9	28.6	13.6	20.3
Marche	50.3	55.7	52.7	19.2	9.6	14.8
Lazio	36.3	46.2	41.3	37.6	29.2	32.8
Abruzzo	35.0	47.5	41.3	27.1	18.2	22.8
Molise	37.1	51.4	44.3	46.2	33.3	38.7
Campania	32.7	48.4	40.5	61.0	47.3	52.9
Puglia	32.5	53.7	43.2	51.8	34.5	41.0
Basilicata	30.0	45.1	38.3	57.1	31.3	38.9
Calabria	32.5	44.7	38.7	67.1	50.5	56.9
Sicilia	30.3	53.0	41.7	61.5	44.2	50.4
Sardegna	36.3	50.2	43.2	54.1	36.5	43.8
Italy	44.0	55.4	49.8	30.9	22.3	26.1
Northwest	54.6	60.6	57.7	19.5	10.6	14.7
Northeast	57.1	64.1	60.7	13.4	7.1	10.0
Center	42.7	51.2	47.0	29.5	20.0	24.2
South	32.6	50.3	41.4	56.7	41.0	47.3

Source: CNEL, *Terzo rapporto sulla condizione giovanile* (Third Report on the Status of Youth) (Roma 2000)

Conclusions

On the basis of the above considerations, one may conclude that women find remarkable obstacles in access to the labor market in Europe and particularly in Italy. Though measures intended to guarantee a formal parity between men and women have an old tradition in Italy, equal opportunity and antidiscriminatory policies have not had an easy life. As a consequence, even if women and men are now equal before the law, they are not equal in everyday life. Wage differentials by gender are still remarkable, and women face great obstacles in achieving top positions. As we have seen, female unemployment rates are much higher than male rates. Unemployment is just one aspect of a more general problem concerning women and work, as proven by the very low female participation rate, a feature not to be treated as an exogenous variable.

Though the change is ongoing, there are social and historical causes which account for this state of things. At any rate, the conventional economists' explanation—that is, the inverse relationship existing between women's participation in the work force and fertility—does not appear to apply to the Italian case, which holds in fact the record of low fertility and of low participation. Bettio and Villa (1998) argue that in Italy, and generally in the Mediterranean countries, the low female participation rate is favored by a family-centered welfare system. Women in Italy traditionally perform a social role related to the tasks of caring, since families are still responsible for most of the care services (other than strictly medical ones) for non-self-sufficient people, such as the elderly, the disabled and handicapped people, and so on, and families still provide care for the very young. The welfare system performs mostly a complementary role, while the family is entrusted with the crucial one (Mingione 1995). The implications for women are obvious: the lack of free care service severely limits women's participation in the labor market. An efficient welfare system would be an incentive to increase women's participation in the job market. This is the case of some northern European countries, like Sweden and Denmark, where on account of a well-functioning welfare system the participation rate for both, women and men, is high, the gender gap is minimum, and gender-based wage differentials are lower than in any other European country.

Moreover, when the opportunity of finding a job is higher, the participation rate increases. On the contrary, in a context such as the Italian one, where the percentage of long-term unemployment is very high, many women give up the search for a job and become part of the hidden unemployment army. Protective legislation, such as laws and regulations existing in Italy, may also have a negative impact on female employment. Two instances of the latter are the ban on women working on nightshifts and parental leave restricted to women, both of which were only recently lifted. Tax deductions for a non-working wife may also have encouraged inactivity, or given incentive to early retirement and/or to hold jobs in the "informal" labor market. If protective measures are to improve, rather than discourage, women's performance in the job market, they should be accompanied by projects aiming at establishing equal working conditions and opportunities for women. In some way, the low presence of women in the work force, especially of women with a low level of education, can be the combined result of too much and too little welfare state: too much in terms of tax benefits, too little in terms of care services. These forces work together, but they affect two different age groups: tax benefits discourage older women's employment, while a lack of care services keeps younger women out of the labor market (Addis 1997).

Another obstacle, particularly for older women, can be a low education and qualification level, given that, in the past, women's level of education was much lower than men's. Though that situation has now changed, gender differences still exist with regard to educational and professional training. Even when women have the same qualifications as men, they still encounter more difficulties in securing jobs and in making a career. On the basis of these considerations, the Equal Opportunities Commission and the Ministry of Labor have promoted actions intended to overcome and remove all obstacles that prevent women from entering the labor market. The Italian Council of Ministers voted on 1998 the "Piano d'Azione per l'Occupazione" (Action Plan to Increase Employment), focussing on the following points intended to reduce the gender gap in the employment rate:

- measures fostering new employment opportunities through female entrepreneurship;
- incentives to self-employment;
- measures enabling women to benefit positively from all flexible forms of work (job sharing, reversible part-time, telework, temporary work, etc.) which may take family needs into account;
- incentives, such as part-time measures and training, which may help middle-age women to get back into the job market (the NOW EU Program is funding training courses for such purposes).

Measures such as the ones outlined above are aimed at the removal of inequalities stemming from disadvantages in matter of education and professional training, thus widening the options open to women, and at the elimination of working conditions that generate-sex based discriminations on the job, thus increasing the number of women employed in sectors where they are still a minority. One of government's goals is to make the labor market more flexible: while, on one hand, flexibility tends to favor women's employment, on the other, where the so-called atypical jobs are concerned, flexibility tends to confine women to precarious positions, where there is no possibility of career and where gender-based wage differentials are more common.

In Italy, in addition to specific measures targeting women's employment, a more general policy should be that of favoring women's participation in the labor market through the passing of welfare measures—day care and afterschool activities for children, assistance for the elders, to mention some of the most significant—as is the case in some northern European countries. Specific policies, on the other hand, are needed to deal with unemployment in the South of Italy. Despite decades-long government policies intended to tackle the economic problems in the South, the gap between North and South is still there, and from this viewpoint, female unemployment is only an aspect of a larger economic and social issue. As a consequence, rather than specific measures targeting women's unemployment, what is needed is a more general action intended to favor the economic and social development of the entire area.

Note

1. Explanation of this phenomenon can be found in Blanchard e Summers (1986), Linbeck and Snower (1986), Soskice and Carlin (1989).

References

Addis E., "Economia e differenze di genere", *Clueb*, Bologna 1997.
Bettio F., Villa P., "A Mediterranean perspective on breakdown of the relationship between participation and fertility", *Cambridge Journal of Economics*, 1998, 22, 137-171.
Blanchard O. J., Summers L., "Hysteresis and the European Unemployment Problem", *NBER Macroeconomics Annual*, 1986.
CNEL, *Terzo rapporto sulla condizione giovanile* (Third Report on the Status of Youth) (Roma 2000).
Fornengo G., Guadagnini M., *Un soffitto di cristallo? Le donne nelle posizioni decisionali in Europa*, Fondazione Adriano Olivetti, 1999.
Istat, *Indagine sulle forze di lavoro*, various years.
Istat, "La situazione italiana del paese nel 1996", *Rapporto annuale*, Roma, 1997.
Mingione, E, "Labour market segmentation and informal work in Southern Europe", *Urban and Regional Studies*, 1995, vol. 2, 2.
Lindbeck A., D. Snower D., "Wage Setting, Unemployment and Insider/Outsider Relations", *American Economic Review*, 1986, 76.
OECD, *Employment Outlook*, Paris, June 1999.
Soskice D., Carlin W., "Medium Run Keynesianism: Hysteresis and Capital Scrapping." In P. Davidson and J. Kregel (eds.), *Macroeconomic Problems and Policies of Income Distribution*, Edward Elgar, Aldershot, 1989.

RENATA LIVRAGHI

CHAPTER 7

ECONOMIC ASPECTS OF FAMILIES AND GENERATIONAL EMPLOYMENT PATTERNS IN ITALY

A number of different studies have been recently conducted in Italy focussing on the connection existing between composition and economic status of families and the decisions made by individual family members to enter the labor market and to actively look for work. Findings resulting from such research have given way to somewhat contrasting interpretations. According to some, families play a compensatory role which results in discouraging married women and youngsters from actively looking for work, thus contributing to maintain high rates of female and youth unemployment. Other interpretations, mostly based on empirical evidence, note that in Italy chances for young people to find a job—and a relatively well paid one—and, above all, to avoid remaining unemployed for a long time, depend to a good extent on a satisfactory level of family income. The author, by putting together the conclusions of these two "schools of thought," argues that policies attempting to reduce the compensatory role played by the family by cutting down salaries earned by adult males and entitlement income as perceived by elderly family members, though these attempts may at times prove successful as an incentive for individual members of low-income families to actively look for jobs, in the long run would not significantly reduce youth and female unemployment rates and would prove especially ineffective at increasing married women's access to the labor market. According to the author, both these goals—the reduction of youth unemployment and the increase of women's employment rates—can better be attained by devising structural economic policies and by encouraging a wider use of flexible work schedules.

Introduction

In Italy a lively debate is taking place at present, focussing on the family's "compensating role" for the lack of labor-related income resulting from unemployment. Such a "compensating role", according to some, may help to maintain the existing high rates of both male and female youth unemployment, as well as women's unemployment, especially women with children who are cut off from the labor market.

Along this line, some experts suggest that, in order to face the staggering high rate of youth unemployment, deep changes would be necessary in the internal structure of Italian families, allowing women to occupy "more *dominant* and less *protected* positions" in the economic system, as well as fostering a more explicit discussion on the conflict of interest existing between the young and the adult and older segments of the population (see Padoa Schioppa Kostoris 1997).

In order to devise an adequate approach to such employment problems, which in turn may allow designing social policies addressing family needs, one should analyze in the first place some assumptions concerning trends of *labor supply and demand*. The following assumptions, in a more or less implicit fashion, appear to be the rationale for the approach taken so far:

1) other components of family income may adequately "compensate" for the lack of a single family member's labor-related income;
2) this compensating role of other family incomes—for example, labor-related incomes from adult males and/or transfer incomes from the elders—would not encourage women and youth to look for work and therefore, rather than enhancing the labor supply of both, they would contribute to maintain high rates of youth unemployment;
3) lower labor-related income flows from adult male workers—the fathers—as well as lower transfer incomes from elderly people—the grandparents—to the family, would spur youth and female labor supply and, as a consequence, they would lead to a lower youth unemployment rate.

There has been considerable research in the last years aiming at collecting all possible information from available sources, in particular from ISTAT (*National Statistics Institute*) and the surveys periodically conducted by the Bank of Italy. It is necessary, however, in order to draw an exhaustive picture, that the body of information available in Italy be enriched and better organized by taking into account the data collected by international centers—by EUROSTAT, for instance, to mention one especially significant—so that the information may be harmonized and made comparable on an international basis.

Besides summarizing the main findings from past and current research and highlighting their implications, the purpose of the present study is to identify, on the basis of such an analysis, how the Italian data bank and system may be enriched and harmonized. This would allow for easier comparative evaluations of Italian data against those of other countries.

Implications from findings of past and current research

Assumption 1, that other components of family income may adequately "compensate" for the lack of a single family member's labor-related income, is widely supported by data from Italian surveys on consumption and income distribution as carried out by ISTAT and the Bank of Italy (see Livraghi 1998a). Furthermore, the information supplied by official Italian sources support the argument made by OECD experts, according to whom high non-employment rates of both young people and middle-age women in Italy, Greece, Ireland and Spain, " are probably sustainable because of the lower impact on the household economy, as many unemployed and inactive individuals share a dwelling with others who hold jobs ... *Where extended families tend to live together, the family/household can play a crucial role in providing protection for all its members against adverse overall economic and labor market conditions*"(see OECD, 1998, 8).

On this subject, research by some Italian sociologists on young people living with their parents in the 1990s, by combining the Italian data with those of other European countries and by comparing findings with those of earlier years (see Table 1), explore thoroughly the significance and the limits of the "protective" role played by the "extended" family in regards to young people's performance in the labor market (see, for example, G. Rossi 1998; Carrà 1998).

Assumption 2, that this compensating role of other family incomes would not enhance labour supply on the part of young people and adult women, thus fostering long-term youth and female unemployment, has

TABLE 1. Ratio of young people living with parent(s) in some European countries by sex, years 1986 and 1994 (percentages on the total of any age group)

Countries	15–19 years		20–24 years		25–29 years	
	1986	1994	1986	1994	1986	1994
Males						
Central Europe	94.4	94.6	59.9	61.2	23.1	24.7
France	94.8	94.8	56.9	61.6	19.3	22.5
Germany	94.8	95.4	64.8	64.6	27.4	28.8
United Kingdom	93.6	93.2	57.2	56.8	21.9	20.8
Southern Europe	96.5	96.4	87.1	90.9	51.3	65.3
Spain	95.6	95.6	88.1	91.5	53.2	64.8
Greece	94.6	95.2	76.5	79.3	53.8	62.6
Italy	97.4	97.3	87.8	92.2	49.6	66.0
Females						
Central Europe	89.9	90.9	37.9	41.3	9.4	11.4
France	89.8	90.9	36.4	41.6	8.4	10.3
Germany	92.0	93.2	42.6	44.6	11.0	12.7
United Kingdom	87.8	88.2	33.8	37.0	8.6	10.8
Southern Europe	94.4	94.7	71.1	81.3	28.8	44.3
Spain	93.9	94.6	76.1	84.3	35.3	47.6
Greece	89.2	92.5	52.3	62.3	23.8	32.1
Italy	95.7	95.3	70.4	82.4	25.5	44.1

Source: Data from Eurostat, published by J. A. Cordon, quoted by: G. Rossi, 1998, 72

not been empirically tested in Italy. A few attempts (see Attanasio and Padoa Schioppa Kostoris 1991; Brunello 1992) have been made however by relating statistics information on consumption and on labor gathered by Istat in order to provide some explanation for youth unemployment in Italy. The research focuses on the role played by family income in supporting habits of personal consumption on the part of unemployed youth, though the extent may vary according to the scale of income distribution.

The above assumptions, when empirically tested, lead to the considerations which follow. First, research relating income distribution to youth unemployment in Italy, whose findings were presented by the Seminar of the Siena Group in 1995 in Oslo (see Frey, Ghignoni, and Livraghi 1995), provides probit estimations to the effect that:

- in Italy young people's chances of finding employment is positively affected by the level of family income;
- youth in high income families are more likely to hold wellpaid jobs;

- the lower the family income, the more likely it is for young people to remain unemployed for as long as three years, consequently falling under the category of the *long-term unemployed.*

Additional research (Ghignoni 1997), by employing the results of labor force surveys by ISTAT (October 1995) and applying a simple econometric model, pointed to the impact of different variables on the reservation wage level—that is, the lowest wage which may be considered acceptable by unemployed workers looking for work in Italy. The analysis of separate data in relation to the North and the South of Italy, show the *reservation wage* of unemployed workers to be significantly higher in the case of breadwinners as compared to those of their sons or of other family members—especially women (this is particularly the case in southern Italy). Indeed, a wider investigation on the possible relationship between *reservation wages* and family ties, through a significance analysis of information available through labor force surveys, has highlighted some differences (especially remarkable in the Southern regions—see Table 2) regarding the *reservation wage* differential between "breadwinners" and "partner/s." The wage of a job-holding breadwinner is considerably higher than the one of his/her partner in the same situation.

By conducting a thorough examination of statistical calculations, the research stresses the significant role played by the family structure, in regards to the number of family members (i.e. potential consumers) and of income recipients, on determining the trend of labor supply, which would explain the existence in Italy of territorial differentials of *reservation wages.*

It was further emphasized that, according to an "equivalence scale" based on family member units (Carbonaro 1985), a household consisting of 4 members (which is the modal value of distribution by families per member unit in southern Italy) needs to receive an income of 1,220,000

TABLE 2. Statistical significance of differences between average reservation wages in different areas for "breadwinners" and "partners" (Alpin-Welch Test)

Area	Individual Characteristics	Average monthly reservation wage (Italian Lira)	A-W Test	Signif.*
South	"Breadwinner"	1,818,655	2.27	0.024
	"Partners"	1,570,803		
North	"Breadwinner"	1,242,283	0.54	0.590
	"Partners"	1,267,207		

Source: Elaboration on Istat data

* The results of this column point out the probability of error in the event the null hypothesis is rejected

lire each month to achieve an equivalent level of well-being as compared to a family composed of 3 members (representing the term of maximum frequency in the distribution per member unit in families in northern Italy) receiving an income of 1,000,000 lire each month.

Accordingly, we may assume that the number of dependants of a job-holding worker may carry a positive correlation to his/her *reservation wage* level. Thus, family components belonging to a large family group with fewer labor-income recipients would be paradoxically induced to obtain higher *reservation wages*. Such a conclusion would be a paradox in the light of the job-searching theory according to which breadwinners with more dependents are at a disadvantage in finding a job, because they are under a higher pressure, hence their *reservation wages* should be lower. The ultimate outcome of this research emphasizes the significance of *reservation wages* as possible income source, useful to meet personal and family requirements as a whole.

A research of the nature outlined above undoubtedly throws light on the critical quality of unemployment in the South as it affects breadwinners, a group whose earnings are traditionally intended to support consumption habits as well as the living standard in general of family members. At the same time, findings do not provide backing to the assumption that other income flows in the family have a discouraging effect on labor supply on the part of partners and children.

On the other hand, the research proves that ISTAT surveys at the present time do not provide a sufficient basis for the reconstruction of the family structure. Consequently, it is not possible (a) to determine if the presence of an employed "breadwinner" induces high *reservation wages* on the part of other family members, nor (b) to adequately combine labor market data with data on income distribution.

Surveys on the family conducted by the Research Branch of the Bank of Italy may help to overcome at least some of these limitations. Along this line, a study based on the results of the 1995 surveys by the Bank of Italy (see Ghignoni 1999) suggested, through a standard logistic function, that active job-searching is less likely to be unsuccessful in the case of:

- members of higher income families;
- members of families where the ratio between income recipients and family member units is higher;
- elderly relatives members of the family;
- female family members;

- sons and partners of breadwinners, as compared to the breadwinner himself;
- first-time job-seekers as compared to unemployed people who were previously employed.

If we combine available evidence with the results of previous research exploring the probability of being employed and, for the young, of being long-term unemployed, there are no supporting elements in favor of the above-mentioned assumption 2 (see above). What is clear is that a high ratio between income recipients and members of a family (of course, an extended family group) could hamper the growth of labor supply from those unemployed individuals.

The above is, however, a result which should more likely apply to the assumption we shall label 3, relating to the incentive effect of youth and female labor supply as a consequence of lower labor-income flows from adult males (i.e., fathers) and lower transfers deriving from entitlements of retired workers (i.e., pension incomes from grandparent/s).

The weak aspect of that third assumption does not lie in the impact which might eventually be envisaged with regards to labor supply, but rather with regards to employment and hence, finally, to non-employment, especially where the youth and the female segments are concerned.

Even if we assume that a change in the structure of the "extended" family—and therefore of the ratio between income recipients and family members (all of them maintaining their specific requirements)—should lead to a significant growth of youth and female labor supply in Italy, these higher supply flows would still not produce a proportionate growth in labor demand. As a result, unemployment would increase rather than diminish.

The research being conducted in Italy on the subject of employment (for an extended bibliography, see Frey 1996a, 1996b, and 1997; see also Ciocca 1997) emphasizes that labor demand depends on economic factors (output dynamics, changes in the productive system, different components in the dynamics of demand for products, relative prices of production factors, basic features of the process of capital accumulation, etc.), on innovative factors in the production technology and in the distribution process and, finally, on socio-institutional factors. Among the latter, the dynamics of labor supply, with special regards to employment in output/services for families, plays a role, although a limited one.

Taken to its extreme, the research conducted in Italy may be said to portray an inverse relationship between demand and supply, meaning that the research appears to emphasize the effect of labor demand on the supply, both in the short and in the long run.

Considering past trends and future perspectives of female labor supply in Italy, once we take into account the change in the population structure according to the education level and the effects of such modification on the economic and social system (also in terms of income distribution), an especially significant factor appears, i.e., the trend of female labor demand, particularly with regards to the service sector (see Frey and Livraghi 1996). Other research carried out on the issue of youth employment emphasizes the crucial role of labor demand, again with particular regard to the service sector, in determining the youth unemployment rate and the "explicit" labor supply, as they appear in official data. (see Frey 1993)

A recent analysis of data supplied in labor force surveys (see Frey 1998) shows that, should a growth of the youth employment rate occur in Italy, rather than causing a reduction in adult male employment (presumably, the fathers'), it would impact negatively—and in a rather remarkable way—on employment rates of middle age groups. Thus, data on unemployment rates supplied by European and Italian sources and referring to the mid-1990s (see Tables 3 and 4) allow the following remarks in reference to Italy:

1) the rate of unemployment for males in the age groups 25 to 34 appears to be higher than in other European Union countries (including the Netherlands and Germany), while it is somewhat close to the rates in France and in the United Kingdom;
2) again, looking at males in the age groups 35 to 40, the unemployment rate matches, on the average, that of several other countries, yet it is higher when specifically compared to Greece, Denmark and Austria, and clearly lower only when compared to Spain, Finland, Ireland, Sweden, and the United Kingdom;
3) where females are concerned, in the age group 25 to 40 the unemployment rate is fairly high in Italy, coming close to that of France and Finland, yet even higher when compared to several other countries, such as Germany, the Netherlands, Ireland, and the United Kingdom, and lower only to Spain;
4) for males aged 50 and over, the unemployment rate in Italy, though not excessively high, is still higher than the Danish and the Dutch one, while for women in the same age group the rate in Italy is higher as compared to that of the United Kingdom;
5) looking at adult workers, the unemployment rates on the whole appear clearly higher than in other European countries, apart from Spain. It is definitely so when Italy's southern regions are considered separately from the rest of the country.

TABLE 3. Unemployment rates in the UE Countries, by sex in 1995 (percentages)

Countries	15–24 years	25–29 years	30–34 years	35–39 years	40–44 years	45–49 years	50 years and more	Tot. 15 years and more
Males								
Austria	5.7	4.4	3.6	2.9	3.0	3.2	4.1	3.9
Belgium	19.7	9.0	6.2	5.0	6.6	5.0	4.3	7.3
Denmark	7.8	6.5	4.3	3.9	4.8	5.0	5.8	5.6
Finland	41.3	18.1	15.8	12.7	14.3	14.1	13.4	17.8
France	23.7	12.8	8.2	7.8	8.1	7.4	7.2	10.0
Germany	8.7	6.8	6.4	6.1	6.2	6.0	8.2	7.1
Greece	19.4	10.6	5.5	3.7	3.8	3.3	3.2	6.2
Italy	29.0	14.3	8.0	4.7	3.7	4.2	3.9	9.2
Ireland	20.3	12.7	11.5	10.5	11.0	9.7	7.7	11.9
Luxembourg	6.7	—	—	—	—	—	—	2.1
Netherlands	11.5	7.8	6.2	4.6	4.7	4.1	3.7	6.1
Portugal	15.1	7.4	6.5	4.7	4.2	4.6	4.1	6.5
United Kingdom	17.9	11.7	8.7	7.8	7.3	6.9	8.7	10.1
Spain	36.4	24.7	17.4	12.7	11.4	11.5	11.6	18.0
Sweden	20.2	8.9	9.2	8.7	6.6	6.8	5.9	8.8
EU	20.0	11.9	8.4	6.9	6.7	6.5	7.2	9.4
Females								
Austria	6.2	4.8	4.5	5.7	3.6	3.9	4.8	4.9
Belgium	23.7	14.3	10.8	10.8	11.3	7.6	7.2	12.2
Denmark	12.3	11.7	8.6	5.0	6.7	7.1	7.8	8.6
Finland	41.1	18.7	13.9	13.4	13.6	11.5	9.0	16.2
France	30.7	17.6	14.8	11.9	10.8	8.8	8.1	14.1
Germany	8.2	8.9	9.4	9.5	8.3	9.8	11.9	9.6
Greece	37.7	19.2	11.2	9.4	7.2	7.8	3.9	13.8
Italy	37.6	22.5	15.4	10.7	8.4	6.4	4.7	16.2
Ireland	17.3	10.6	9.2	10.8	13.0	11.0	9.1	12.1
Luxembourg	7.8	—	—	—	—	—	—	4.4
Netherlands	12.7	7.1	8.0	9.9	8.2	6.7	5.5	8.7
Portugal	17.1	9.7	9.8	5.8	6.3	5.5	3.0	7.8
United Kingdom	12.5	8.2	6.8	6.1	5.7	4.5	4.2	6.9
Spain	48.1	36.6	30.0	26.4	23.2	20.6	13.4	30.3
Sweden	17.8	8.2	9.2	6.4	3.4	3.6	5.7	7.4
EU	22.5	15.2	12.4	10.7	9.3	8.2	7.9	12.4

Source: Eurostat, Labour Force Survey—Results 1995, Luxembourg (1996), 34

TABLE 4. Unemployment rates in Italy by age, sex and large area, average 1996 (percentages)

Age	Italy	Northern Italy	Central Italy	Continental Southern and Islands of Italy
Males				
15–19 years	30.2	16.4	33.3	48.8
20–24 years	29.1	13.4	30.1	50.1
25–29 years	15.4	6.2	14.2	29.0
30–34 years	8.8	3.2	6.4	17.2
35–39 years	5.6	2.2	3.6	11.3
40–44 years	3.8	1.7	2.6	7.6
45–49 years	3.3	1.5	2.6	6.7
50 years and more	3.5	1.9	2.5	6.1
total 15 years and more	9.4	4.2	7.4	17.5
Females				
15–19 years	43.8	32.1	44.9	62.5
20–24 years	38.0	22.5	39.3	66.0
25–29 years	22.3	11.5	22.8	44.9
30–34 years	16.2	8.3	15.5	32.2
35–39 years	11.9	6.8	10.6	22.6
40–44 years	8.1	5.8	6.4	14.1
45–49 years	6.4	5.3	5.3	9.6
50 years and more	4.6	4.1	3.4	7.4
total 15 years and more	16.6	10.1	14.8	30.2
Males and females				
15–19 years	36.0	23.4	33.7	54.3
20–24 years	33.1	18.1	34.6	56.6
25–29 years	18.3	8.6	17.9	34.6
30–34 years	11.7	5.4	10.0	22.3
35–39 years	8.0	4.2	6.6	15.0
40–44 years	5.4	3.3	4.1	9.6
45–49 years	4.4	2.9	3.4	7.6
50 years and more	3.9	2.6	2.7	6.5
total 15 years and more	12.1	6.6	10.3	21.7

Source: Our elaboration. Istat, Forze di lavoro —Media 1996, Annuari, Roma (1997)

In this regard, available data from the Istat labor force survey for 1996 (see Table 4), which shows for the south of Italy an average trend by which youth unemployment rates for both sexes are definitely higher than the average Spanish ones, give an indication of how severe the problem is in that part of Italy. At the same time, the unemployment rates for males in the age group 30 to 45 in the south of Italy are above the EU average and definitely higher than in most countries, excluding Spain, Finland, France and Ireland. Also in the case of women of mature age in the South, the unemployment rates are remarkably higher as compared to most European countries, again with the exception of Spain.

Also, in central Italy, women's unemployment rates in all age groups up to the age of 40 are higher than the EU average, and definitely higher than in Germany, the Netherlands, Portugal, Switzerland, United Kingdom, Denmark, and Austria. Similar rates are also to be observed when looking at the North of Italy, where on the other hand the rates for males over 30 appear to be definitely lower than the EU average and specifically lower than the average rate of France, Germany, United Kingdom, and the Netherlands, as well than the average minimum of Austria and Greece.

On the basis of a comparative analysis it is possible to state that, while adult unemployment is considered in Italy as in most European countries as an economic and a social problem, the suggested remedy of reducing youth unemployment—the rates of which are usually higher than those of adults—at the expense of adult employment is not a realistic one. Such a strategy appears to be an inadequate measure to reduce unemployment in central and northern Italy, but especially when it comes to the southern regions. Even a replacement of middle age and elderly female workers by younger people in the north of Italy (an occurrence that is not entirely unlikely) will not be without consequences.

Plenty of data emerging from surveys conducted in Italy (see Table 5 for the 1995 Bank of Italy survey) converge to show that, among a series of considerable negative effects linked to unemployment for all age groups, a trend like the one described above could also bring about a negative attitude on the part of middle age or elderly workers (particularly males and in the south) vis-à-vis the young, on account of a loss of self-confidence and of their own role within the family.

In conclusion, the following strong arguments could be made against policies intended to lower youth unemployment at the expense of adult employment:

1) as far as the average adult unemployment rate is concerned, the situation in Italy shows no considerable differences when compared to the rest of Europe;
2) in the South of Italy, where unemployment is largely concentrated, adult unemployment, though still lower than youth non-employment, affects both men and women, though mostly the latter;
3) unemployment of older workers appears to be more contained in Italy than in other leading European countries. Older workers, however, are more likely to be replaced by younger workers and—

TABLE 5. Social consequences of unemployment according to the 1995 results of the Bank of Italy households surveys (Points in a scale of ten)

Age	Role in the household	Health	Relationship with other people	Level of self-confidence	Leisure	Total evaluation
Age						
up to 30 years	5.3	5.8	5.7	5.1	6.3	4.6
31-40 years	4.9	5.6	5.5	4.9	6.2	4.3
41-50 years	5.0	5.6	5.5	4.9	6.4	4.0
51-65 years	5.1	5.2	5.4	5.1	5.8	3.9
more 65 years	4.6	5.1	5.2	4.3	5.4	3.7
Educational level						
no education	4.8	4.6	4.8	6.5	7.7	4.1
Elementary level	4.9	5.4	5.3	5.0	6.2	4.6
Lower secondary school	5.0	5.5	5.5	4.6	6.2	3.9
Upper secondary school	5.3	6.1	5.8	5.0	5.9	4.2
University degree	4.7	6.2	6.1	4.8	6.0	4.1
Area						
North	5.2	5.6	5.4	4.8	5.9	4.3
Center	5.3	5.9	6.0	5.3	6.2	4.5
South	4.6	5.2	5.4	4.9	6.3	3.8
Sex						
males	4.8	5.3	5.3	4.8	6.1	3.8
females	5.3	5.8	5.7	5.1	6.1	4.7
Total males and females	5.0	5.5	5.5	4.9	6.1	4.2

Source: Banca d'Italia, *I bilanci delle famiglie italiane nell'anno 1995*, Supplemento al Bollettino Statistico, Anno VII, 14, 20 marzo 1997, 47

due to their qualitative characteristics—to be then permanently cut off from the labor market; as a consequence, they are likely to create a burden on the welfare system;

4) an increasing unemployment rate of adult males may bring about negative consequences in terms of social marginalization of the individuals involved and therefore have a negative impact on the communities as well. Such a scenario appears therefore undesirable in view of a rationally reformed welfare system based on the concept of an extended well-being.

While the theory of replacing youth unemployment with adult unemployment has not gained wide support, especially considering the territorial concentration of youth unemployment in Italy, it is clearly evident that the existence of conflicts of interests among different generations (also, in some cases, inside the family) does not help to contain a growing youth unemployment rate. According to the experience of several countries in the past and also in the present, many indicators suggest that youth unemployment may be more effectively contained on a long-term basis with the help of structural policies in the field of employment and labor. Such policies include introducing a higher flexibility in working schedules and, especially, targeting a steady-pace employment growth in the service sector, so as to lead to increasingly significant employment rates and to slowly bring about a reduction, in the middle or long-term, of male and female unemployment in all age groups, particularly in regards to those regions where unemployment is not specific to any one age group.

One should, however, exclude from structural policies in the field of employment and labor any measure attempting to limit or discourage the "compensating" role of the family, as some Italian experts in the field have at one point suggested. The first reason for this is that the family income is necessary to ensure "acceptable" living standards to the unemployed young, both males and females, at least until employment and labor policies are not able to guarantee "regular" labor-related incomes from dependent and self-employment work to the large part of job-searching individuals, regardless of their gender and age, and especially to people in the South. The second reason is that the family does not only play a "compensating" role for the lack of labor-related income, but it also functions as a productive unit and a provider of basic services to its members, both young and old.

All available data show that indeed the family, as producer/provider of essential services to its members of all age groups, contributes considerably to their well-being. In addition, several widely recognized multipurpose surveys carried out in Italy in the last ten years (for comments on the methodology, see Zuliani, 1994) have gathered some helpful information on the structural characteristics of the individuals involved (see Table 6).

These surveys provide a confirmation that the rate of young males and females still living in the family in Italy is indeed quite high. Table 6 shows that a good 80% of young people in the age group 14 to 24 lived with their parents in 1993-94 (the percentage is slightly higher where the Northeast and Southern regions are concerned), and on the average a good 10% where families with a single parent are concerned. It is to be noted, however, that the higher rates refer mainly to younger students who are likely to hold the mixed status of student/worker while searching for a stable job on the basis of their educational qualifications (university degree or at least upper secondary education). Furthermore, there is no

TABLE 6. Youth and adult till 44 years old living in the household with the position of sons, daughters, by age, sex, professional status and area (percentages)

Characteristics	Males—age group			Females—age group		
	14–24	25–34	35–44	14–24	25–34	35–44
Living in families with both parents						
Italy -total	82.9	33.1	4.2	77.4	18.5	2.3
North—Western	80.9	32.9	3.9	78.2	18.1	2.1
North—Eastern	84.0	35.0	5.7	78.5	18.9	2.6
Central	80.2	34.1	4.5	75.7	20.5	1.3
Continental Southern	85.8	33.9	3.2	78.7	17.6	3.0
Islands	82.8	27.0	4.0	73.6	17.5	2.5
Employment	74.9	27.5	3.5	66.1	19.9	2.6
Unemployment	80.9	51.7	12.0	79.9	39.7	9.6
Housewives	—	—	—	37.0	3.3	0.8
Students	88.5	75.5	27.0	88.2	63.4	10.0
Retired	66.0	20.2	4.0	100.0	5.6	—
Other status	79.3	55.8	14.8	76.5	35.5	21.8
University degree	74.3	48.9	6.1	65.6	32.0	3.1
Upper secondary school level	83.8	38.1	3.8	78.9	24.5	2.4
Lower secondary school level	83.5	28.5	4.0	77.6	12.9	2.3
Lesser level	70.2	19.8	4.0	58.2	7.8	1.9
Living in families with only one parent						
Italy -total	10.1	9.4	4.1	9.6	5.4	2.1
North—Western	12.4	9.8	5.7	11.1	6.1	1.7
North—Eastern	10.1	9.9	4.8	9.5	5.3	2.3
Central	10.3	9.1	2.8	12.3	5.2	1.5
Continental Southern	8.9	9.2	3.3	7.8	5.3	2.4
Islands	8.5	8.8	2.8	7.2	4.8	3.4
Employment	11.2	8.2	3.6	11.5	5.8	2.6
Unemployment	11.2	14.5	9.6	10.9	12.5	8.3
Housewives	—	—	—	5.8	1.1	0.9
Students	8.8	13.7	6.6	9.1	14.7	3.0
Retired	—	10.1	1.5	—	—	—
Other status	13.7	18.9	15.6	16.8	12.7	11.7
University degree	25.4	9.2	3.8	8.6	8.8	2.8
Upper secondary school level	9.7	9.1	3.1	10.2	6.5	2.5
Lower secondary school level	9.9	9.4	4.4	9.3	4.0	2.0
Lesser level	15.9	11.9	5.5	8.6	5.4	1.7

Source: Istat, *Famiglia, abitazione, servizi di pubblica utilità*, Indagini multiscopo sulle famiglie 1993-94, Argomenti, 6 (1996), 126

striking difference between the number of unemployed young people who are living with their families as compared to those employed in the same situation. Finally, it is also worth mentioning that:

1) there is a very high percentage of young people older than 25 still holding the student status who are living in families with both parents or a single parent;
2) among the unemployed there is a considerable percentage of young people nearly 30 years of age or older—especially males, with a relatively high education level—still living with their parents.

One should recall the third theory mentioned above (see page 130), which maintains that a reduction of income flows deriving to the family from transfers from elderly members (grandparents), due to increasing youth and female labor supply, would lead to lower youth unemployment or underemployment.

If we analyze the relationship between labor supply and demand and the corresponding effects on youth employment problems, we cannot but justify the soundness of the previously stated arguments on behalf of the fundamental independence of trends of labor demand from labour supply. However, when considering the effects on youth and female labor supply of lower income flows from transfers, we have a confirmation from much of the current research that it is appropriate, when looking at the families, to take into consideration their structural peculiar features and the incidence of transfer incomes on overall family incomes.

The Bank of Italy survey shows, first of all, that by the mid-1990s the incidence of transfer incomes on overall family incomes in Italy was rather high in the case of the first 10% of the families in the lower income deciles, while it was clearly lower in families in the middle income deciles and even lower in the case of higher incomes families (see Table 7). Moreover, families in the lower income deciles receive only limited amounts of income from labor-related sources in the case of both wage workers and the self-employed. Hence, in the light of such information, we are drawn to assume that a reduced flow of transfer incomes would negatively impact on the family income to an extent which could hardly be compensated by a growing labor supply.

An adequate analysis of the information supplied by the Bank of Italy surveys (see Livraghi 1998b; Rossi N.1998) allows us to further examine the relation between income distribution per family and their specific structure according to type and number of recipients. As it can be further

TABLE 7. Structure of household income by tenth of Italian households, 1995

Tenth of households	Income from dependent work	Income from self-employment	Income from transfers	Income from capital	Household Income
'000 of lire					
0-1 decile	1,300	629	6,143	1,880	9,952
1-2 decile	3,760	1,428	9,431	2,955	17,574
2-3 decile	7,155	1,759	9,840	4,202	22,956
3-4 decile	9,883	2,566	10,054	5,396	27,899
4-5 decile	13,224	2,516	10,465	6,805	33,010
5-6 decile	16,704	4,210	10,351	7,755	39,020
6-7 decile	22,408	4,569	10,301	9,096	46,374
7-8 decile	27,462	5,715	11,644	10,864	55,685
8-9 decile	33,062	7,962	12,769	15,249	69,042
more than 9 decile	40,664	22,997	18,540	34,045	116,2467
Average	17,560	5,434	10,953	9,823	43,770
Percentages					
0-1 decile	13.1	6.3	61.7	18.9	100.0
1-2 decile	21.4	8.1	53.7	16.8	100.0
2-3 decile	31.1	7.7	42.9	18.3	100.0
3-4 decile	35.4	9.2	36.1	19.3	100.0
4-5 decile	40.1	7.6	31.7	20.6	100.0
5-6 decile	42.8	10.8	26.5	19.9	100.0
6-7 decile	48.3	9.9	22.2	19.6	100.0
7-8 decile	49.3	10.3	20.9	19.5	100.0
8-9 decile	47.9	11.5	18.5	22.1	100.0
more than 9 decile	35.0	19.8	15.9	29.3	100.0
Average	40.1	12.4	25.0	22.5	100.0

Source: Our elaboration on Bank of Italy data

remarked (see Table 8), in the case of a retired breadwinner the amount of labor-related income of families in the lower income deciles is indeed extremely low. When the breadwinner is a dependent worker, however, the situation is remarkably different (see Table 9): while the transfer incomes are rather low (also in the case of families in the lower income deciles), the incidence of labor-related income is high. Thus, we may be led to conclude that a possible reduction in transfer incomes would not lead to a growth of labor supply on the part of all unemployed family members (presumably young people and middle-age women).

An attempt has recently been made to compare data supplied through the Bank of Italy surveys with data on income distribution referring to other OECD countries (see OECD 1998a), as to the family's place in the

TABLE 8. Composition of net equivalent, 1995 household income by income deciles: head of the family = retired worker (percentages)

		Income from work and capital				
		Income from work		Income from capital		
Income deciles	Average income by each decile	Dependent work	Self employment	Real assets	Financial assets	Total
First	12,240	2.0	0.2	9.7	3.8	15.6
Second	17,666	5.6	0.6	11.2	4.9	22.3
Third	21,106	5.6	1.4	13.9	8.6	29.6
Fourth	26,244	10.1	1.6	15.5	8.8	36.0
Fifth	31,500	9.5	2.1	17.2	11.7	40.5
Sixth	38,913	17.7	4.5	16.8	10.9	49.9
Seventh	44,200	24.4	3.9	15.9	12.7	57.0
Eighth	54,520	27.6	4.0	15.7	14.5	61.8
Nineth	66,098	28.5	9.8	16.2	16.1	70.6
Tenth	111,546	20.6	17.8	17.9	29.3	85.6
Total	42,424	19.5	7.9	16.1	16.5	60.1
Average '000 of lire		8,271	3,352	6,845	7,026	25,494

	Transfers		Fiscal drawings		
	Pensions	Other transfers	Social contribution	Taxes	Net transfers
First	75.5	11.7	0.2	2.6	84.4
Second	75.9	7.2	0.7	4.8	77.7
Third	74.1	4.8	0.9	7.6	70.4
Fourth	72.5	3.8	1.5	10.8	64.0
Fifth	71.3	2.5	1.6	12.7	59.5
Sixth	63.8	3.5	2.7	14.5	50.1
Seventh	60.5	2.1	3.3	16.2	43.0
Eighth	57.3	2.3	3.6	17.8	38.2
Nineth	50.8	2.0	4.5	18.9	29.4
Tenth	42.1	1.1	5.4	23.4	14.4
Total	57.3	2.7	3.5	16.7	39.9
Average '000 of lire	24,324	1,161	1,475	7,080	16,930

Source: Battaglia P., Birindelli A., D'Alessio G., De Carli R., Fabbri F., Iorio F., and Rizzi D.(1998), 124

scale of income distribution, considered on the basis of an *equivalence scale elasticity* equal to 0.5, according to a) the breadwinner's age (see Table 11) and, b) to the existence inside the family of no workers, one worker, or two contributing labor-related incomes (see Tables 10 and 12).

For the year 1993, where the presence of labor-related income recipients in a family is concerned, of all the countries whose differentials have

TABLE 9. Composition of net equivalent, 1995 household income by income deciles: head of the family = dependent worker (percentages)

		Income from work and capital				
		Income from work		Income from capital		
Income deciles	Average income by each decile	Dependent work	Self employment	Real assets	Financial assets	Total
First	21,470	88.8	0.0	7.8	−0.6	96.0
Second	30,263	99.3	0.7	9.8	1.3	111.1
Third	35,001	103.9	2.6	12.2	1.4	118.1
Fourth	41,824	103.4	2.6	13.1	2.3	121.3
Fifth	46,245	104.9	2.5	13.3	3.3	124.1
Sixth	53,137	107.0	3.5	12.7	2.6	124.9
Seventh	59,336	107.7	5.6	14.3	2.0	127.5
Eighth	67,428	101.8	5.1	16.6	4.3	128.3
Nineth	77,057	103.3	12.3	16.0	6.8	131.3
Tenth	114,006	92.1	5.1	20.4	10.9	135.7
Total	54,598	101.0	2,795	15.1	4.8	126.1
Average '000 of lire		55,139		8,257	2,640	68,831

	Transfers		Fiscal drawings		
	Pensions	Other transfers	Social contribution	Taxes	Net transfers
First	0.0	18.0	8.4	6.2	3.5
Second	0.0	10.9	9.9	12.5	−11.5
Third	0.0	6.6	10.5	16.1	−20.1
Fourth	0.0	4.5	10.7	17.3	−23.6
Fifth	0.0	2.4	11.0	20.0	−28.7
Sixth	0.0	2.0	11.2	20.9	−30.1
Seventh	0.0	1.3	12.1	24.3	−35.2
Eighth	0.0	1.7	11.2	23.4	−32.9
Nineth	0.0	1.4	11.2	25.5	−35.3
Tenth	0.0	1.6	10.7	28.9	−38.0
Total	0.0	3.4	10.9	22.2	−29.7
Average '000 of lire	0.0	1,718	5,564	11,291	−15,137

Source: Rossi N., ed. (1998), 120

TABLE 10. Relative disposable income, by degree of work attachment of households. Equivalence scale elasticity = 0.5. Population in households with a working-age head

		Worker		
		No	One	Two
Australia	Level 93–94	45.4	79.9	121.3
	% change 75/76–93/94	8.2	3.0	−1.8
	Percentage point change	3.4	2.4	−2.2
Belgium	Level 1995	—	—	—
	% change 1983–1994	—	—	—
	Percentage point change	—	—	—
Denmark	Level 1994	67.0	84.38	111.9
	% change 1983–1994	2.9	1.4	−0.7
	Percentage point change	1.9	1.2	−0.8
Finland	Level 1995	58.4	82.7	106.7
	% change 1983–1995	−6.2	2.5	−0.4
	Percentage point change	−3.8	2.0	−0.5
France	Level 1990	74.8	92.0	116.0
	% change 1979–1990	−0.3	0.5	−0.6
	Percentage point change	−0.2	0.5	−0.7
Germany	Level 1994	55.9	89.3	122.3
	% change 1984–1994	−14.5	−1.3	3.0
	Percentage point change	−9.5	−1.2	3.6
Italy	Level 1993	51.0	77.4	131.2
	% change 1984–1993	−2.5	−6.6	5.1
	Percentage point change	−1.3	−5.5	6.3
Japan	Level 1994	62.7	88.7	110.0
	% change 1984–1994	9.2	−5.3	3.5
	Percentage point change	5.3	−5.0	3.8
Holland	Level 1994	62.0	89.7	119.3
	% change 1977–1994	−15.0	0.1	1.5
	Percentage point change	−10.2	0.1	1.7
Norway	Level 1995	49.4	85.7	115.4
	% change 1986–1995	5.2	−0.2	−0.1
	Percentage point change	2.4	−0.2	−0.1
Sweden	Level 1995	58.2	80.8	115.1
	% change 1975–1995	20.6	−7.2	−0.1
	Percentage point change	9.9	−6.3	−0.1
USA	Level 1995	39.6	82.2	116.7
	% change 1974–1995	3.3	−5.7	2.7
	Percentage point change	1.3	−5.0	3.1

Source: OECD 1998, 116,7

TABLE 11. Relative disposable income, by age of household head. Equivalence scale elasticity = 0,5

		Households			
		Young	Prime age	Older age	Retired
Australia	Level 93–94	101.1	104.4	110.9	68.2
	% change 75/76–93/94	–4.2	1.4	2.9	–7.7
	Percentage point change	–4.4	1.4	3.1	–5.7
Belgium	Level 1995	—	—	—	—
	% change 1983–1994	—	—	—	—
	Percentage point change	—	—	—	—
Denmark	Level 1994	89.6	105.9	117.3	73.4
	% change 1983–1994	–10.8	–1.4	10.0	6.8
	Percentage point change	–10.9	–1.5	10.7	4.7
Finland	Level 1995	80.3	106.8	114.5	78.1
	% change 1983–1995	–8.7	0.3	6.0	1.4
	Percentage point change	–7.6	0.3	6.4	1.1
France	Level 1990	78.7	101.7	110.1	95.0
	% change 1979–1990	–10.2	0.8	2.1	0.8
	Percentage point change	–8.9	0.8	2.3	0.8
Germany	Level 1994	78.5	100.9	113.0	89.3
	% change 1984–1994	–2.4	–1.5	0.5	5.1
	Percentage point change	–1.9	–1.5	0.6	4.3
Italy	Level 1993	92.1	98.1	109.9	84.7
	% change 1984–1993	–5.0	1.6	–2.4	3.5
	Percentage point change	–4.8	1.5	–2.7	2.9
Japan	Level 1994	75.9	94.2	120.7	93.1
	% change 1984–1994	–7.4	–0.9	3.1	–0.9
	Percentage point change	–6.0	–0.9	3.6	–0.8
Holland	Level 1994	85.2	100.8	114.0	87.5
	% change 1977–1994	–6.4	5.2	–1.9	–9.2
	Percentage point change	–5.9	5.0	–2.2	–8.9
Norway	Level 1995	78.0	107.3	117.3	73.7
	% change 1986–1995	–12.8	0.5	4.1	5.7
	Percentage point change	–11.5	0.6	4.6	4.0
Sweden	Level 1995	73.3	104.2	125.8	89.3
	% change 1975–1995	–17.7	–4.8	10.7	22.7
	Percentage point change	–15.8	–5.3	12.2	16.5
USA	Level 1995	75.0	101.5	120.0	91.9
	% change 1974–1995	–11.2	0.9	1.5	7.5
	Percentage point change	–9.5	0.9	1.8	6.4

Source: OECD 1998

TABLE 12. Relative disposable income, by family type. Equivalence scale elasticity = 0.5

		Family type			
		Single adult with children	Single adult no child	Two adult with children	Two adult no child
Australia	Level 93–94	58.5	78.6	95.7	119.8
	% change 75/76–93/94	–12.0	–0.7	0.4	–0.1
	Percentage point change	–8.0	–0.6	0.4	–0.1
Belgium	Level 1995	73.7	74.2	115.3	107.8
	% change 1983–1994	—	—	—	—
	Percentage point change	—	—	—	—
Denmark	Level 1994	61.9	71.1	104.4	108.6
	% change 1983–1994	–4.2	0.4	–2.1	–1.0
	Percentage point change	–2.7	0.3	–2.2	–1.0
Finland	Level 1995	77.9	71.5	103.1	108.0
	% change 1983–1995	1.5	–0.7	0.7	–1.9
	Percentage point change	1.2	–0.5	0.7	–2.1
France	Level 1990	70.3	84.4	101.2	110.3
	% change 1979–1990	–10.1	–1.5	1.5	0.0
	Percentage point change	–7.9	–1.3	1.5	0.0
Germany	Level 1994	58.9	85.0	97.4	112.7
	% change 1984–1994	4.7	3.2	–0.9	0.1
	Percentage point change	2.7	2.7	–0.9	0.1
Italy	Level 1993	54.1	71.1	93.6	121.5
	% change 1984–1993	–7.9	–5.6	0.3	2.2
	Percentage point change	–4.6	–4.3	0.3	2.6
Japan	Level 1994	57.4	82.4	94.2	118.1
	% change 1984–1994	–2.1	–5.7	–0.6	1.1
	Percentage point change	–1.2	–5.0	–0.5	1.3
Holland	Level 1994	58.6	80.0	95.0	111.5
	% change 1977–1994	–5.7	–11.5	0.8	0.9
	Percentage point change	–3.5	–10.4	0.8	1.0
Norway	Level 1995	69.9	69.3	103.8	121.7
	% change 1986–1995	1.7	–3.8	0.0	0.9
	Percentage point change	1.1	–2.7	0.0	1.0
Sweden	Level 1995	73.9	74.5	103.7	121.7
	% change 1975–1995	13.5	–1.7	–2.5	7.0
	Percentage point change	–11.6	–1.3	–2.7	8.0
USA	Level 1995	49.9	88.4	94.9	122.4
	% change 1974–1995	12.6	8.5	–0.9	–0.7
	Percentage point change	5.6	7.0	–0.9	–0.9

Source: OECD 1998

increased in the period 1984–1993, Italy shows the most striking differences in available incomes in families where the number of workers is high. Where the breadwinner's age is concerned, this does not appear to have any remarkable impact on family income differences—or at any rate it is less than in other industrialized countries. It must be noted, however, that in families where the breadwinner is middle age or older, better income equivalent conditions emerge if compared to those occurring in families where the breadwinner is younger (in the latter significant distribution problems are encountered if there are also dependent children). Data of this nature would suggest that a strong incentive to secure labor-related income might be found in the lack of employed family members—or at least in the insufficient presence of same—along with the presence of dependent children per breadwinner, rather than in the presence of transfer income. Since the existing information, however, is not by its nature in direct reference to attitudes of young members and/or adult women in the family who might be benefiting from transfer incomes from older members, we are not provided with sufficient evidence in support of or against the assumption that a reduced flow of transfer incomes (especially elderly pension income) would favor the growth of youth and female labor supply.

In order to gather information on attitudes and behavior, not only examined by *ex-ante* intentions but also by *ex-post* outcomes, *longitudinal modules* would have to be made available through their routine inclusion in income distribution surveys. Finally, one has to consider that a reduced flow of pension-income transfers, besides the obvious impact on the income of those families where grandparents live together with individuals of different ages, would also affect the income of families whose breadwinner is a retired worker and whom we have seen to be placed mostly at the bottom end of the income decile scale. Hence, the possible outcome of such a strategy in terms of equitable income distribution—that is, the economic well-being of the individuals who would be involved.

Research on the economic and social well-being of elderly people (see L. Frey and R. Livraghi 1995) increasingly shows that an eventual flow reduction (or postponed fruition) of pension income would likely foster labor supply on the part of elderly people—already considerably and increasingly dissatisfied with their available family income to an extent that is causing a growing black labor market. It is reasonable to assume, therefore, that a flow reduction of pension income transfers may cause a growing labor supply on the part of older individuals rather than of young people and middle-age women. Again, one should therefore conclude that in order to test the assumptions which have been here under discussion against real situations, it would be necessary for the income distribution surveys to systematically include appropriate *longitudinal modules* regarding attitudes and behaviour towards labor—in this case of older people.

References

Attanasio O.P. and Padoa Schioppa Kostoris F., 1991, "Regional Inequalities Migration and Mismatch in Jtaly, 1960-1986", Padoa Schioppa Kostoris F., ed., *Mismatch and Labour Mobilitv*, Cambridge University Press, Cambridge, Mass.

Banca d'Italia, 1997, *Bilanci delle famiglie italiane nell'anno 1995*, Supplemento al Bollettino Statistico, anno VII, 14.

Battaglia P., Birindelli A., D'Alessio G., De Carli R., Fabbri F., Iorio F. and Rizzi D., " La distribuzione personale e familiare delle risorse, " Rossi N., ed., "*Il lavoro e la sovranità sociale, 1996-1997*", Fourth CNEL Report on Income Distribution in Italy, Il Mulino, 1998.

Brunello G., 1992, Un modello generazionale del mercato del lavoro italiano, *Politica Economica*, 1.

Carbonaro G., 1985, "Nota sulle scale di equivalenza", *Commissione di indagine sulla poverta'. La poverta' in Italia*, Istituto Poligrafico dello Stato, Roma, 153-159.

Carrà E., 1998, ed., *Una famiglia, tre famiglie*, Unicopli, Milano.

Caselli L., ed., *Ripensare il lavoro*, Edizioni Dehoniane, Bologna.

Ciocca P., 1997, ed., *Disoccupazione di fine secolo*, Bollati Boringhieri, Torino, 1997.

Eurostat, *Labour Force Survey—Results 1995*, Luxembourg 1996

Frey L., 1993, *Condizioni strutturali in atto e problematica dell'occupazione giovanile*, Università degli Studi di Roma "La Sapienza", Opening Conference for the Academic Year 1993/94, Roma, 17 novembre 1993.

Frey L., 1994, "Dalla comparabilità all' integrabilita' delle informazioni sul lavoro", Frey L., ed., *Lavoro e benessere. La costruzione di indicatori sociali*, Quaderni di Economia del Lavoro, 49-50, Angeli, Milano.

Frey L., 1996a, *La problematica occupazionale in Europa. Il punto di vista degli economisti*, Quaderni di Economia del Lavoro, 54, Angeli, Milano.

Frey L., 1996b, *Le politiche dell'occupazione e del lavoro in Europa*, Quaderni di Economia del Lavoro, 55, Angeli, Milano.

Frey L., 1997, *Il lavoro nei servizi verso il secolo XXI*, Quaderni di Economia del Lavoro, 57, Angeli, Milano.

Frey L., 1998, *Famiglia e disoccupazione*, Tutela, 1-2, Jan-June 1998, p. 53-70.

Frey L., Ghignoni E. and Livraghi R., 1995, *Youth Unemployment and Household Support*, Oslo, The Siena Group Seminar, June 8-9, 1995.

Frey L., Livraghi, R., 1995, *Il reddito e la ricchezza degli anziani in Italia*, Il benessere degli anziani, Ceres, Rome, I, 3-4, maggio-giugno 1995.

Frey L. and Livraghi R., 1996, *Occupazione nei servizi, istruzione e condizioni socioeconomiche delle donne in Italia*, Rivista Italiana degli Economisti, dicembre 1996, p. 399-422.

Ghignoni E., 1997, *I differenziali territoriali nei salari minimi di accettazione in Italia*, Quaderni di Economia del Lavoro, 59, Angeli, Milano.

Ghignoni E., 1999, *Famiglia e ricerca attiva del lavoro in Italia a metà degli anni '90*, Quaderni di Economia del Lavoro, 64, Angeli Milano.

Istat, *Famiglia, abitazione, servizi di pubblica utilita'*, Indagini multiscopo sulle famiglie 1993-94, Argomenti, 6 (1996), 126.

Istat 1995, *Rilevazione delle forze di lavoro*, Annuari, Roma.

Istat 1997, *Rilevazione sui consumi delle famiglie italiane 1996*, Annuari, Roma.

Istat 1998a, *Rilevazione de/le forze di lavoro. Media 1997*, Annuari, Roma.

Istat 1998b, *La distribuzione quantitativa del reddito in Italia nelle indagini sui bilanci di famiglia. Anno 1996*, Informazioni, 62, Roma.

Livraghi R., 1998a, "Il ruolo del lavoro e della famiglia nel processo di formazione del benessere", Caselli L., ed., *Ripensare il lavoro*, Edizioni Dehoniane, Bologna, p. 113-146.

Livraghi R., 1998b, "Ineguaglianza nella distribuzione dei redditi delle famiglie in Italia," *Tutela*, 1-2, p. 36-52.

OECD, 1998a, *Income Distribution and Poverty in Selected OECD Countries*, Economic Department Working Papers, No. 189, Paris.

OECD, 1998b, *Employment Outlook*—June, Paris.

Padoa Schioppa Kostoris P., 1997, *Giovani e occupazione, vecchi e pensionamento: il nostro welfare state a confronto con quello europeo*, Working Paper, 67/97, Ispe, Roma.

Rossi G., 1998, *Giovani in famiglia: autonomia e dipendenza*, Tutela, 1-2, pp. 71-85.

Rossi N., ed., "Il lavoro e la sovranità sociale, 1996-1997," *Fourth CNEL Report on Income Distribution in Italy*, Il Mulino, 1998.

Zuliani A., 1994, "L' indagine multiscopo," Frey L., ed., *Lavoro e benessere. La costruzione di indicatori sociali*, Quaderni di Economia del Lavoro, 49-50, Angeli, Milano.

ANDREA BRANDOLINI

GIOVANNI D'ALESSIO

CHAPTER 8

HOUSEHOLD STRUCTURE AND INCOME INEQUALITY IN ITALY

A Comparative European Perspective

This paper examines the effects of demographic structure on the evolution of income inequality in Italy from 1977 to 1995, and on its inequality ranking relative to 11 of the other 14 European Union countries in the mid-1990s. The composition of Italian households was substantially different in 1995 both from that observed in the two preceding decades and from that recorded in other EU countries. The distance between mean equivalent disposable household incomes in various demographic groups varied significantly over time and between countries. Nevertheless, demographic effects on inequality appear on the whole to be secondary. The following results hold, irrespective of the correction for demographic differences: (a) inequality in the distribution of equivalent disposable incomes between persons showed considerable fluctuations but no particular medium-term tendency in Italy; (b) in the mid-1990s Italy was, together with the United Kingdom, the EU country with the highest inequality, a result which is only partly explained by the regional dualism of the Italian economy.

We should like to thank Salvatore Chiri, Marco Magnani, and Luigi Federico Signorini for their comments on earlier versions of the paper. The core files of the Historical

Introduction

There is a close link between the demographic characteristics of a population and the distribution of income among its members. The age structure matters because the size and composition of personal incomes (from work, property, and transfer) vary during the life cycle, and also because individual experiences reflect the different historical periods in which people live. Employment opportunities tend to vary between individuals born during a baby boom and those belonging to smaller cohorts. The potential income and career opportunities of newly hired people depend on the macroeconomic and institutional conditions prevailing when they enter into the labor market; their pensions are affected by the conditions of the moment when they leave the market. Likewise, distribution of household income depends on the size and composition of the households and is influenced by the way in which decisions are made to leave the family of origin, to set up new families, and to procreate. On the other hand, the causal relationship is not unidirectional, since the resources available to people are themselves a determining factor behind these decisions.

The diversity of demographic structures may contribute as much to lessen as to amplify the differences observed in comparisons of economic inequalities across time or regions. The aim of this paper is to measure the influence of demographic variables on the distribution of income in Italy, based on its historical progression in the period 1977-1995, and on international comparisons with other countries in the European Union in the mid-1990s. The term *demographic variables* will be used to indicate the age and sex of the head of the household, and the size of the household unit, variables already examined by Simon Kuznets (1976,1) in one of the first systematic studies on the subject:

Archive of the Bank of Italy's Survey of Households' Income and Wealth, from which the microdata for Italy have been taken, were initially created by Luigi Cannari and Giovanni D'Alessio, and have subsequently been revised and supplemented by Giovanni D'Alessio and Massimo Gallo. The archive which has derived from them was created by Giovanni D'Alessio and Ivan Faiella. Microdata of the Luxembourg Income Study for the United Kingdom are taken from the Family Expenditure Survey for 1995 and are Crown Copyright; they were made available by the United Kingdom Office for National Statistics through the ESRC Data Archive and their use has been authorized. Neither the Office for National Statistics nor the ESRC Data Archive are responsible for the analysis or interpretation of the data given here. Lastly, the views expressed here are solely those of the authors and do not necessarily reflect those of the Bank of Italy.

These characteristics of size and age of the family or household unit, changing in a systematic way through the lifetime span of the unit, are what we mean by the demographic aspects of the size distribution of income. They bear partly on the problem of the recipient unit (size) and partly on the time span over which income and its inequalities are to be considered (age of head, or age phases in general).

The first part of the paper examines the relationship between demographic structure and income inequality, and describes the methodology used to break down the latter into a component caused by the distance *between* homogeneous groups of the population, into one explained by dispersion *within* the groups, and into one ascribed to the *relative weight* of the groups. The second part provides documentary evidence of demographic and distribution trends in Italy over the years 1977-1995, on the basis of microdata from the Historical Archive (HA) of the Bank of Italy's Survey of Households' Income and Wealth (SHIW). In the third part, the level of income inequality in Italy is compared with those in 11 of the other 14 EU countries, using microdata from the Luxembourg Income Study (LIS), an international project for the collection and dissemination of information on the distribution of income.

The analysis conducted in this paper establishes two basic facts. Firstly, the inequality of "equivalent" (i.e. corrected for the household size) household incomes, net of interest and dividends, exhibited large fluctuations in Italy between 1977 and 1995, but no particular medium-term tendency. Secondly, in the early 1990s Italy was, together with the United Kingdom, the EU country in which total equivalent incomes were distributed in the most unequal manner.

Do these results depend on different demographic structure? The composition of Italian households in 1995 was indeed substantially different from that observed in the two previous decades and in other EU countries. Moreover, the distance between mean equivalent household incomes in various demographic groups varied significantly over time and between countries. For example, the situation for heads of household below the age of 40 worsened between 1977 and 1995, while it improved for heads aged over 65; and in no other EU country was the equivalent income of households of old people so high in relative terms. Yet, demographic differences played only a secondary role–both among the factors which caused the evolution of inequality in Italy, and among those factors that explain the deviations from the levels recorded in the other EU countries.

Demography and economic inequality

The relationship between demographic structure and economic inequality

The relationship between demographic structure and economic inequality can be examined from various points of view. The first level of analysis involves an assessment of the distance between homogeneous demographic groups: to what degree men have, on average, higher levels of income than women, or older persons than young. A classic example is the analysis of gender pay differences, in order to determine whether there is discrimination in the labor market. Another example is the study of cohort effects. Typically, the income of an individual is hump-shaped over his or her life cycle: it tends to grow from the moment of entry into the labor market up to the age of about 60, later dropping when employment income is replaced by pension income. The exact form of the curve is, however, not fixed, for the interaction of market forces and economic policies affects the redistribution between generations differently over time, or across countries.[1]

The average gap between demographic groups adds to the dispersion within these groups: the degree of inequality measured for the distribution as a whole reflects the average differences between people in different stages of their lives as much as it does the variability between people who belong to the same cohort. The second level of analysis aims to separate these two components, evaluating the portion of the overall inequality which can be attributed to the gap between the average income of the demographic classes. All other conditions being equal, greater distance between the groups tends to increase the overall inequality,[2] but to a degree that depends on their relative weight: the greater the weight of groups with particularly eccentric (high or low) average values, the greater the overall inequality will be.

Coming back to the example of the cohorts, even if average incomes are supposed to develop at the same rate and to maintain relative gaps unaltered, the evolution of the population age structure is by itself sufficient to impart a specific long-term tendency to the distribution. On the theoretical level, von Weizsäcker (1989, 1994) has shown that the direct effect of the ageing of the population is, *ceteris paribus*, that of augmenting income inequality; the final outcome may be the opposite, once the indirect effects of the budget constraint of the government are taken into account.[3] Other sociodemographic mechanisms can lead to similar results. For example, Rivlin (1975,5) suggested that a drive towards a more unequal distribution was caused in the United States after the Second World War by the growing fragmentation of families: "Young people move out of the parental household sooner than they used to, old people are less likely to live with their children, and women—especially black women—are more likely to be family heads than they were a couple of decades ago."

The third level of analysis attempts to identify the effect that different demographic composition has on the comparison of inequality between two or more societies. The exercise necessarily refers to hypothetical situations, responding to questions such as "How would inequality have evolved in Italy if the population had not aged?" or "What would the concentration of income be in Germany if the demographic structure of the country were the same as in Italy?" As in any counterfactual analysis, this too is not without its drawbacks; in particular, reconstructing the level of inequality in a country on the basis of the demographic composition of another means assuming, among other things, that the average incomes of the groups are not dependent on their number. In spite of its mechanical nature, the exercise is still useful for making an initial estimate of the extent to which differences in demographic structures matter in distribution comparisons.

The decomposition of inequality

As seen above, our analysis of the impact of demography on inequality has three main objectives: (a) to assess the divergence in the mean incomes of homogeneous groups of households; (b) to measure how much of the overall inequality can be attributed to the distance between these groups rather than to inequalities within them; (c) to show how comparisons are influenced by differences in the underlying demographic structure. To achieve these objectives, we resort to an *exactly decomposable* measure of inequality that separates the effect of the *relative weight* of each group both from the distance *between* the groups, and from the inequality *within* the groups. The measure used in this paper is the *mean logarithmic deviation*,[4]

(1) $$L = -\tfrac{1}{n} \sum_{i=1}^{n} \log\left(\tfrac{y_i}{\mu}\right),$$

where y_i indicates the income of unit i, μ the average income and n the total number of units. If the units are partitioned into K groups according to some demographic characteristic, the overall inequality as measured by (1) can be exactly decomposed into within-groups, L^W, and between-groups, L^B, as follows:

$$(2) \quad L = L^W + L^B = \sum_{k=1}^{K} w_k L_k - \sum_{k=1}^{K} w_k \log(\tfrac{\mu_k}{\mu}),$$

where w_k, μ_k and L_k are the share in population, the average income, and the mean logarithmic deviation of each group k, respectively. Since in spatial and temporal comparisons, all three of them may vary, it is worth rewriting (2) as

$$(3) \quad L = L^{\bar{W}} + L^{\bar{B}} + L^P = \sum_{k=1}^{K} \bar{w}_k L_k - \sum_{k=1}^{K} \bar{w}_k \log(\tfrac{\mu_k}{\bar{\mu}}) + L^P,$$

where the weights $\bar{w}_k$ are those of the reference population and the total mean is duly recalculated at fixed weights—that is, $\bar{\mu} = \Sigma_k \bar{w}_k \mu_k$.[5] In (3) the within-groups and between-groups components are corrected for differences in the weight of each population group, and the effect of the demographic structure is taken up in the residual term L^P. In this paper, the reference situation coincides with the year 1995 in the historical analysis, and with Italy in the international comparison.[6]

The hypotheses behind the measurement of inequality

Demographic variables such as the size of the household and the characteristics of its components have a direct influence on the statistical measurement of inequality. To interpret the results correctly, it is thus necessary to focus on the definitional hypotheses below, ensuring they are as consistent as possible in their temporal and geographical contexts.

- The *economic unit of aggregation*, that is, the basic unit for sharing of resources, is the household. This is defined as a group of persons living together who, independently of their kinship, share their income wholly or in part. Generally speaking, all databases used in this paper conform to this definition, but for minor discrepancies. The only important exception concerns the Swedish data, which refer to a particularly restricted concept of the family, including only parents (as a couple or single) and children under the age of 18.[7]
- In order to take into consideration the economies of scale generated by cohabitation, aggregate incomes for each unit have been corrected with the *equivalence scale* used, among others, by

Atkinson, Rainwater and Smeeding (1995).[8] More precisely, equivalent incomes have been obtained by dividing household incomes by the number of equivalent persons $N^{0.5}$, where N is the number of members of the household and 0.5 is a value that accounts for economies of scale.

- It is assumed that *intrahousehold distribution* is egalitarian—that is, that household incomes are placed together and shared equally among all members of the household. This assumption is unrealistic, but it is made for lack of better information.[9]

- The *welfare unit*, that is, the elementary unit for which the welfare is assessed using the equivalent income as *proxy*, is the person (e.g. Danziger and Taussig 1979; Ebert 1997). Distribution is thus measured among individuals, attributing to each person the equivalent income of the household to which he or she belongs. This means counting the equivalent income of each household as many times as it has members.

- Since the mean logarithmic deviation is sensitive to extreme values, which are more likely to contain measurement errors (Cowell and Victoria-Feser 1996), and it is not defined for nonpositive incomes, equivalent incomes below the 3rd percentile and above the 97th have been recoded to equal the value of the corresponding percentile (*bottom-top coding*).

Effects of demographic evolution on inequality from 1977 to 1995 in Italy

Data: The historical archive of the survey of households' income and wealth

The Bank of Italy has been surveying the budgets of Italian households since 1965, but only recently, in conjunction with much greater recourse to microeconomic data, have they become an important source for studying the behaviour of Italian households (see Brandolini 1999 for a historical description and an overall assessment). In this paper we rely on data from the historical archive of the survey (version 1.1, released in October 2000; see Banca d'Italia 2000), which includes information collected as from 1977, since individual data for previous surveys are no longer available.

The archive contains the historical series of elementary variables recorded on an ongoing and homogeneous basis, and the series of variables derived from them, such as household income and wealth, obtained using standardized methodologies. Two series of household incomes are used in this paper: the first, and longer, includes income from work (as employees or self-employed), pensions, public transfers, income from real properties, and the imputed rental income from owner-occupied dwellings; the second series also includes interest on financial assets, net of interest paid on mortgages, but only as from 1987.

The archive also contains two types of weights. The first type only takes into consideration the different probability of extraction of the households, and generates marginal distributions for the principal sociodemographic characteristics which present excessive variation compared with the values from various official sources, impairing the comparability of data from different surveys.[10] The second type of weights is obtained by post-stratifying the samples: the marginal distributions of components by sex, age group, type of job, geographical area, and demographic size of the municipality of residence, as registered in population and labor force statistics, are reestablished by using iterative raking techniques. In order to provide greater stability to our estimates, in this paper we use the latter weights, in the version rescaled so that their sums add up to the total Italian population.

Household structure

The Italian population rose between 1977 and 1995 by over 2 per cent, from 56 to 57.3 million.[11] The increase was concentrated almost entirely in the South (inclusive of Sicily and Sardinia; from 19.7 to 20.9 millions), while the population in the Center was essentially stable (10.7 to 11 millions), and in the North it declined slightly (from 25.7 to 25.4 millions). The number of households, as defined by the SHIW, grew by about 16 per cent, from 17.4 to 20.2 million; contrary to what was observed in the population, the increase was greater in the North than in the Center and the South. From 1977 to 1995, the population resident in the South grew in proportion to the total in terms of people, but declined in terms of households.[12]

The proportion of households consisting of a single person almost doubled over the same period (from 10 to 18 per cent), while that of households with five or more members declined from 16 to 10 per cent. Households consisting of two persons were the modal value in 1995. The average household size fell from 3.2 to 2.8 members. This drop was more noticeable in the North (from 3.1 to 2.6) than in the Center (from 3.3 to 3.0) and in the South (from 3.4 to 3.1).

As concerns the characteristics of the head of the household,[13] between

1977 and 1995 households with a female head rose considerably (from 12 to 28 per cent of the total), with a similar trend in all geographical areas of the country. The process of ageing, which has involved the population as a whole, shows up in the rise in the share of heads over the age of 65 (from 23 to 29 per cent), which has become the modal group. Correspondingly—perhaps partly due to the greater difficulty encountered by the young in entering the jobs market—the number of household heads below the age of 30 drops from 8 to 5 per cent.

These trends can be summarized by classifying households in categories which combine various demographic characteristics, such as the sex and age of the head and the presence of the spouse, and of adult or younger children and other members. The increase in the share of people living alone mentioned earlier concerns older women almost exclusively: in 1995 they account for one tenth of all Italian households. The increase for men is modest and almost nil for women under the age of 65. The weights of couples with no children or with one or two children remain fairly stable throughout the period, accounting for about three-fifths of the total. The proportion of households consisting of a single parent and one or more children exhibits an increase from 5 to 7 per cent of the total; the increase is almost entirely due to households with one adult child, while the share of those with a minor remains stable at a very low level (around 0.5 per cent). Lastly, the decline in large households can be seen in the reduction of the proportion of couples with three or more children (from 11 to 8 per cent of the total) and of the "other households"—that is, those including other relatives or members in no way related to the household head (from 13 to 9 per cent).

The evolution of the overall inequality of incomes

Table 1 shows the values for the mean logarithmic deviation and the Gini index, calculated on incomes net of interest on financial assets for the years 1977–1995, and on total incomes for 1987–1995. Their trends from 1977 to 1995 are similar, and the relative coefficient of simple correlation is equal to 0.99 (Figure 1).

The two indices of inequality show some growth between 1977 and 1979, a sharp drop in the following three years and another rise between 1982 and 1987. In 1989 and 1991, they fall to the lowest levels of 1982 and then, in 1993 and 1995, return to the levels of 1977. The indices calculated on the total income confirm the growth of inequality between 1991 and 1993. The frequency of data, initially annual and then biennial as

TABLE 1. Inequality of equivalent disposable incomes in Italy, 1977–1995

	Incomes net of interest on financial assets			Total income		
Year	Mean equivalent income (thousand lire)	Mean logarithmic deviation	Gini index	Mean equivalent income (thousand lire)	Mean logarithmic deviation	Gini index
1977	3,649	0.156	0.307			
1978	4,288	0.149	0.299			
1979	5,264	0.166	0.315			
1980	6,517	0.134	0.287			
1981	7,362	0.126	0.279			
1982	9,122	0.116	0.269			
1983	10,470	0.121	0.274			
1984	12,004	0.130	0.283			
1986	13,170	0.128	0.280			
1987	15,088	0.145	0.297	15,618	0.153	0.305
1989	18,577	0.116	0.269	19,288	0.124	0.278
1991	21,309	0.111	0.262	21,956	0.118	0.269
1993	22,592	0.156	0.301	23,428	0.168	0.313
1995	24,695	0.158	0.302	25,430	0.167	0.312

Sources and notes: authors' calculations on data from the SHIW-HA (Version 1.1, October 2000). Measures calculated for the distribution of equivalent disposable incomes between persons; bottom- and top-coded incomes; equivalence coefficients equal to No.5, where N is the number of household members.

from the late 1980s, makes it difficult to pinpoint the link with the business cycle, but qualitatively the relationship seems to have been positive at least until the early 1990s: the dispersion of incomes tended to increase in periods of economic expansion and decrease during recessions. Without considering fluctuations from one year to the next, there would appear to be no particular medium-term trend.

Inequality between demographic groups

The mean values of equivalent incomes (net of interest on financial assets) vary significantly from one demographic group to another.[14] One-person households have the lowest mean values, even though the gap narrowed slightly between 1977 and 1995. In particular, there has been a clear improvement, in relative terms, in the condition of older people who live alone: in 1977, women in this condition obtained 53 per cent of the average income, and men 71 per cent. Just short of 20 years later, the figures had risen to 71 and 82 per cent, respectively. In contrast, the situation of larger households has gradually worsened: their equivalent incomes

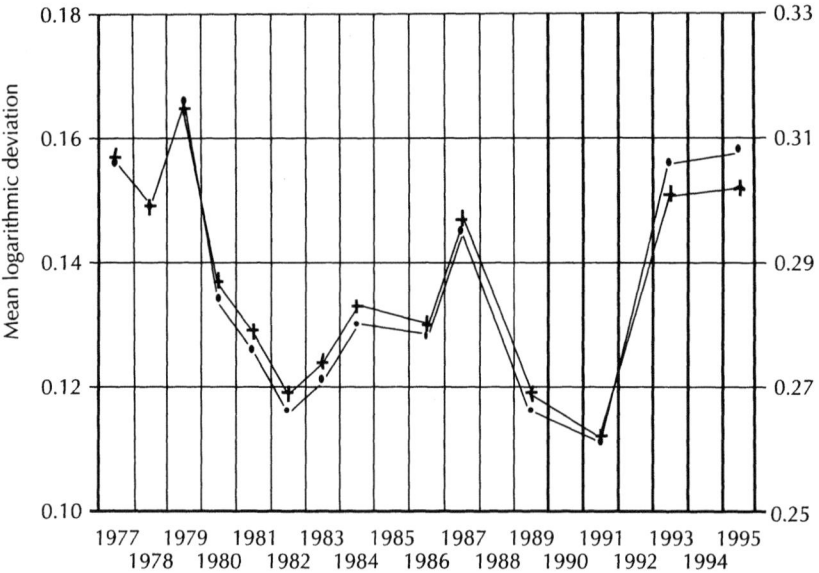

FIGURE 1. Income Inequality in Italy, 1977–1995. *Sources and notes: authors' calculations on data from the SHIW-HA (Version 1.1, October 2000). Measures calculated for the distribution of equivalent disposable incomes between persons, where incomes are net of interest on financial assets; bottom- and top-coded incomes; equivalence coefficients equal to No.5, where N is the number of household members.*

have declined from values that were close to the average in the early 1980s to about one tenth below average in the 1990s. As concerns gender differences, male heads of household receive equivalent incomes between 10 and 20 per cent higher than those of female heads. The gap does not show any precise trend, and at the end of the period it was virtually the same as at the beginning.

Mean equivalent incomes (net of financial earnings) of households classified by the age of their head show a typical hump-shaped curve in 1995: they rise up from the young to the intermediate groups and reach of a maximum in the 51–65 year segment, before declining for the older age group (Figure 2). This profile of incomes by age underwent important variations between 1977 and 1995: the situation for household heads below the age of 40 worsened considerably, while for those aged over 65 it improved. The gradual development of a more generous welfare system may have influenced this result as much as a growing concentration of unemployment in the younger sectors of the population. An inversion of the

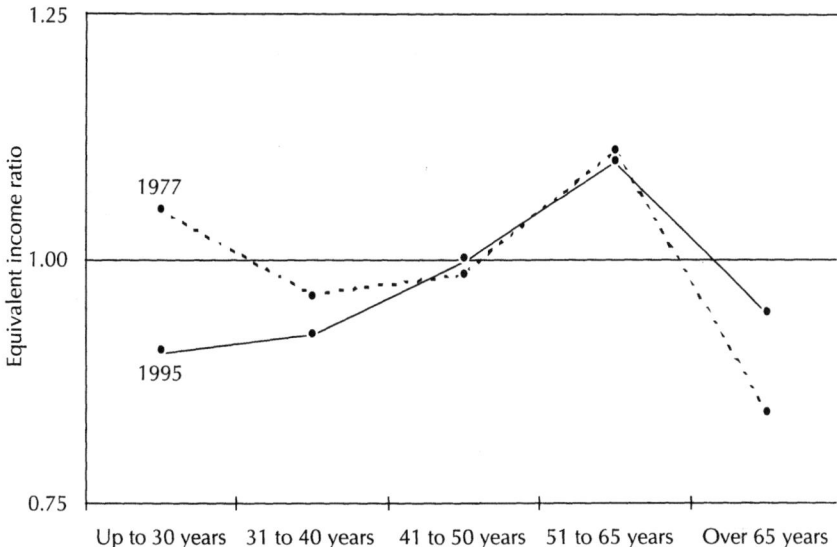

FIGURE 2 Age Profile of Incomes in Italy, 1977 And 1995. *Sources and notes: authors' calculations on data from the SHIW-HA (Version 1.1, October 2000). Ratio to the overall mean of the mean equivalent disposable incomes (net of interest on financial assets) of households with heads in the age group indicated; bottom- and top-coded incomes; equivalence coefficients equal to $N^{0.5}$, where N is the number of household members; households counted as many times as there are members.*

(average) position of households of older people in relation to young people points to the existence of important mechanisms for redistribution among generations. It would be inappropriate to exclude them from an assessment of economic inequality as proposed by Paglin (1975).

Demographic composition and inequality of incomes

The breakdown of the mean logarithmic deviation into homogeneous demographic groups makes it possible to measure how much of the total inequality can be attributed to the distances between the groups of households rather than to inequality within them.[15] On the basis of the results of the breakdown, demographic characteristics explain the total inequality only to a very small extent (Table 2). With the mean logarithmic deviation of total equivalent income in 1995 set at 100, cancellation of the differences in the average incomes would lead to a modest reduction of the index: from 0.6 per cent for the groups defined on the basis of the sex of the household head, to 3.3 per cent for those based on household type. The degree of inequality which can be attributed to the between-group component tends to be higher in the previous years, but the effect is still modest. The largest effect is obtained with the division by household type, which includes a number of demographic characteristics: if the various groups had had the same mean equivalent incomes, the mean logarithmic deviation would have been lower, especially at the end of the 1970s, but its trend over time would have remained substantially the same (Figure 3).

Moving on to the impact of changes in the demographic structure on the evolution of inequality, the calculation of the mean logarithmic deviation with the weights of the demographic groups in 1995 brings about limited change in the index. The greatest change occurs in the classifica-

TABLE 2. Decomposition of the mean logarithmic deviation in Italy, 1977–1995

	Household size						Sex of the household head					
	Within-groups at fixed weights		Between-groups at fixed weights		Demographic effect		Within-groups at fixed weights		Between-groups at fixed weights		Demographic effect	
Year	value	share	value	share	value	share	value	share	value	share	value	share
Income net of interest on financial assets												
1977	0.153	98.5	0.005	3.3	−0.003	−1.7	0.160	102.7	0.001	0.6	−0.005	−3.3
1978	0.141	95.1	0.007	5.0	−0.000	−0.0	0.152	102.5	0.003	2.3	−0.007	−4.8
1979	0.161	96.8	0.003	2.1	0.002	1.1	0.167	100.6	0.004	2.1	−0.004	−2.7
1980	0.129	96.3	0.003	2.3	0.002	1.4	0.140	104.9	0.001	0.6	−0.007	−5.5
1981	0.121	96.1	0.004	3.6	0.000	0.4	0.128	101.5	0.002	1.2	−0.003	−2.8
1982	0.113	97.9	0.004	3.4	−0.002	−1.3	0.118	102.3	0.001	1.2	−0.004	−3.4
1983	0.117	96.7	0.004	3.5	−0.000	−0.2	0.122	100.4	0.003	2.5	−0.004	−2.9
1984	0.127	97.9	0.003	2.3	−0.000	−0.2	0.129	99.2	0.004	3.0	−0.003	−2.2
1986	0.125	97.2	0.003	2.1	0.001	0.7	0.127	99.3	0.002	1.9	−0.002	−1.2
1987	0.139	96.4	0.004	2.8	0.001	0.8	0.142	98.3	0.004	2.5	−0.001	−0.8
1989	0.113	97.3	0.003	2.7	−0.000	−0.1	0.115	98.9	0.002	1.4	−0.000	−0.3
1991	0.109	97.7	0.002	2.1	0.000	0.1	0.113	101.0	0.001	0.7	−0.002	−1.7
1993	0.151	97.0	0.004	2.6	0.001	0.4	0.154	98.6	0.002	1.4	−0.000	−0.0
1995	0.155	98.3	0.003	1.7	—	—	0.157	99.4	0.001	0.6	—	—
Total income												
1987	0.147	96.5	0.004	2.7	0.001	0.8	0.150	98.1	0.004	2.5	−0.001	−0.6
1989	0.121	97.3	0.003	2.7	−0.000	−0.1	0.123	98.9	0.002	1.3	−0.000	−0.2
1991	0.116	97.9	0.002	2.0	0.000	0.2	0.119	100.9	0.001	0.7	−0.002	−1.6
1993	0.163	97.2	0.004	2.5	0.001	0.3	0.166	98.6	0.002	1.4	−0.000	−0.0
1995	0.164	98.3	0.003	1.7	—	—	0.166	99.4	0.001	0.6	—	—

Sources and notes: authors' calculations on data from the SHIW-HA (Version 1.1, October 2000). Measures calculated for the distribution of equivalent disposable incomes between persons; bottom- and top-coded incomes; equivalence coefficients equal to $N^{0.5}$, where N is the number of household members. "Value" refers

tion by the sex of the household head. If the composition of the household heads had been the same in 1977 as it was in 1995, overall inequality would have been 3.3 per cent higher, mainly due to the greater weight attributed to women, among whom dispersion of incomes was higher. In the following years, there was some convergence both in average incomes and in the variability within the two types of household. The impact of the composition by the sex of the head also gradually attenuated. Decompositions by the other demographic characteristics are less informative. The drop in the number of members per household, the ageing of the population, and the evolution of household types do not appear to have influenced trends in inequality to any significant extent.

Age class of the household head						Household type						
Within-groups at fixed weights		Between-groups at fixed weights		Demographic effect		Within-groups at fixed weights		Between-groups at fixed weights		Demographic effect		
value	share	value	share	value	share	value	share	value	share	value	share	Total
0.151	97.4	0.005	2.9	−0.001	−0.3	0.144	92.5	0.015	9.7	−0.003	−2.2	0.156
0.146	98.5	0.003	2.3	−0.001	−0.7	0.138	92.6	0.014	9.5	−0.003	−2.1	0.149
0.160	96.3	0.007	4.1	−0.001	−0.4	0.154	93.1	0.011	6.8	0.000	0.2	0.166
0.129	96.5	0.005	3.6	−0.000	−0.2	0.124	93.0	0.010	7.3	−0.000	−0.3	0.134
0.123	98.0	0.003	2.4	−0.001	−0.4	0.118	93.5	0.010	7.7	−0.001	−1.1	0.126
0.114	98.6	0.003	2.4	−0.001	−1.1	0.109	94.3	0.009	7.7	−0.002	−2.0	0.116
0.118	96.9	0.004	3.4	−0.000	−0.3	0.113	93.3	0.009	7.4	−0.001	−0.7	0.121
0.125	96.7	0.004	3.0	0.000	0.3	0.121	93.3	0.010	7.9	−0.002	−1.2	0.130
0.125	97.5	0.003	2.5	−0.000	−0.1	0.121	94.6	0.007	5.3	0.000	0.1	0.128
0.141	97.8	0.003	1.8	0.001	0.4	0.134	93.0	0.009	6.4	0.001	0.5	0.145
0.113	97.3	0.003	2.6	0.000	0.1	0.107	92.6	0.009	7.6	−0.000	−0.2	0.116
0.110	98.2	0.002	2.1	−0.000	−0.3	0.105	94.1	0.007	6.3	−0.000	−0.4	0.111
0.153	98.0	0.003	1.8	0.000	0.2	0.146	93.8	0.009	5.9	0.000	0.3	0.156
0.155	98.3	0.003	1.7	—	—	0.152	96.5	0.006	3.5	—	—	0.158
0.149	97.8	0.003	1.9	0.001	0.3	0.142	93.2	0.010	6.3	0.001	0.5	0.153
0.121	97.6	0.003	2.4	−0.000	−0.0	0.115	92.9	0.009	7.2	−0.000	−0.2	0.124
0.116	98.1	0.003	2.1	−0.000	−0.3	0.112	94.6	0.007	5.8	−0.000	−0.4	0.118
0.165	97.9	0.003	1.9	0.000	0.2	0.158	94.2	0.009	5.6	0.000	0.3	0.168
0.164	98.1	0.003	1.9	—	—	0.161	96.7	0.006	3.3	—	—	0.167

to the absolute contribution of the component to the total index; "share" refers to the percentage impact of the same contribution on the total index.

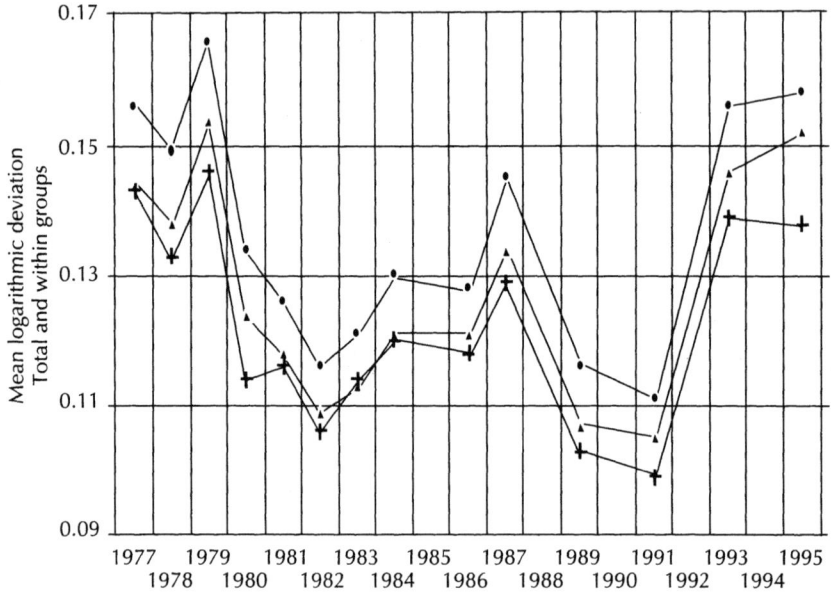

+   Mean logarithmic deviation
•   Within-groups component, by household type
▲   Within-groups component, by geographical area of residence

FIGURE 3 Total and Within-Group Inequality in Italy, 1977–1995. *Sources and notes: authors' calculations on data from the SHIW-HA (Version 1.1, October 2000). Measures calculated for the distribution of equivalent disposable incomes between persons, where incomes are net of interest on financial assets; bottom- and top-coded incomes; equivalence coefficients equal to No.5, where N is the number of household members.*

As a term of comparison and for the importance it has in the Italian context, the mean logarithmic deviation has been decomposed also by geographical area of residence of the households (Table 3). The gap between mean incomes in the main three areas of the country (North, Center and South) explains a significant part of the overall inequality, about 12 per cent in 1995; this gap has tended to widen since the mid-1980s. If no geographical differences had existed, the inequality measures in the years being examined would have shown fluctuations similar to those of the total index, but with a slightly declining overall trend (Figure 3). On the other hand, in spite of the different growth rate of the population in the various areas, changes in the relative weights did not influence the profile of the index over time. Lastly, the degree of inequality proved to be generally higher in the South than the substantially similar levels reached in the central and northern regions. This difference increased slightly in the period 1977–1995.

TABLE 3. Decomposition of the mean logarithmic deviation in Italy by area of residence, 1977–1995

Year	Within-groups at fixed weights		Between-groups at fixed weights		Demographic effect		Total
	value	share	value	share	value	share	
Income net of interest on financial assets							
1977	0.143	92.0	0.013	8.2	–0.000	–0.2	0.156
1978	0.133	89.5	0.016	10.7	–0.000	–0.2	0.149
1979	0.146	87.8	0.021	12.6	–0.001	–0.4	0.166
1980	0.114	85.0	0.020	15.3	–0.000	–0.3	0.134
1981	0.116	91.8	0.011	8.4	–0.000	–0.2	0.126
1982	0.106	92.0	0.009	8.1	–0.000	–0.1	0.116
1983	0.114	93.8	0.008	6.3	–0.000	–0.1	0.121
1984	0.120	92.5	0.010	7.6	–0.000	–0.1	0.130
1986	0.118	92.4	0.010	7.6	–0.000	–0.0	0.128
1987	0.129	89.2	0.016	10.8	0.000	0.0	0.145
1989	0.103	88.6	0.013	11.4	0.000	0.1	0.116
1991	0.099	89.2	0.012	10.9	–0.000	–0.1	0.111
1993	0.139	89.1	0.017	11.0	–0.000	–0.1	0.156
1995	0.138	87.7	0.019	12.3	0.000	0.0	0.158
Total income							
1987	0.135	88.3	0.018	11.7	0.000	0.0	0.153
1989	0.109	87.9	0.015	12.0	0.000	0.1	0.124
1991	0.105	88.3	0.014	11.8	–0.000	–0.1	0.118
1993	0.149	88.5	0.019	11.6	–0.000	–0.1	0.168
1995	0.145	87.1	0.022	12.9	0.000	0.0	0.167

Sources and notes: authors' calculations on data from the SHIW-HA (Version 1.1, October 2000). Measures calculated for the distribution of equivalent disposable incomes between persons; bottom- and top-coded incomes; equivalence coefficients equal to $N^{0.5}$, where N is the number of household members. "Value" refers to the absolute contribution of the component to the total index; "share" refers to the percentage impact of the same contribution on the total index. The three areas underlying the decomposition are defined as follows: "North" includes Valle d'Aosta, Piedmont, Lombardy, Veneto, Trentino-Alto Adige, Friuli-Venezia Giulia, Liguria, and Emilia-Romagna; "Center" includes Tuscany, Umbria, Marche and Lazio; "South" includes Abruzzo, Molise, Campania, Puglia, Basilicata, Calabria, Sicily and Sardinia.

Inequality and demographic structures in selected EU countries

Data: The Luxembourg Income Study

The Luxembourg Income Study is an international project for the dissemination of information about the distribution of income. It was launched in 1983 under the joint sponsorship of the government of Luxembourg and the Center for Population, Poverty, and Policy Studies. The LIS is based in Luxembourg and is funded on a continuing basis by national research councils and by other institutions of the member countries. The project has led to the creation of a database in which the economic microdata from national surveys are reclassified according to standardized criteria and are completed with full and detailed illustrative documentation. Since harmonization is effected at a later stage, and not when drawing up the samples and drafting the questionnaires (as is the case, for example, for the European Community Household Panel), some national peculiarities remain. Despite the enormous progress made, they still make comparability of data between countries only partial.[16] At the end of February 2001, the LIS database contained over 90 surveys covering 25 countries, from which the most recent for 12 EU countries were chosen.[17] The data for Italy included in the LIS are those of the SHIW for 1995.[18] All the LIS estimates discussed in this paper were computed on 24 February 2001.

As already pointed out, the definition of "household" is basically the same as that of the SHIW in all the surveys used, except for the one in Sweden, in which a particularly restricted notion is adopted (parents, together or singly, and children under 18). Compared with the original sources (including the SHIW), one important modification introduced during standardization of the data, is the recoding of the declared household head whenever it is a woman and her male husband or partner is present. This reclassification has significant effects on the estimate of income differentials according to the sex of the household head. As concerns income, we used the "disposable income" variable (*DPI*) contained in the LIS archive, which includes the entire household's monetary income, net of tax and social security contributions. The definition of *DPI* differs from that used in the previous historical analysis in that it excludes in-kind labor earnings and imputed rental income from owner-occupied dwellings.[19]

Household structure

Household structure varies considerably from one European country to another. Households are more extended in Ireland and Spain, where the average size is about 3.5 persons per unit. They are smallest in Scandinavian countries, although the particularly low figure for Sweden also reflects the different definition of the household. In Germany, the Netherlands, the United Kingdom, France, and Belgium, the average number of members is between 2.3 and 2.5, while Luxembourg and Italy exhibit a somewhat higher household size. The same differences can be seen in the percentage composition: while in Ireland and Spain households with five or more members account for 31 and 22 per cent of the total respectively, in Denmark and Finland they are no more than 6 per cent; conversely, there are half as many one-person units in the first two countries as there are in the other two. Modal values are represented by households with five or more members in Ireland, and with four members in Spain; with a single member in Denmark, Finland, Germany, and Sweden; and with two members in the other countries.

Differences by sex and age of household head are also considerable. The highest proportion of female household heads is to be found in northern European countries (between 27 and 31 per cent in Finland, Germany, Denmark and Sweden); while at the other extreme we have Ireland and Spain, with levels below 20 per cent; in Italy, the incidence of female heads is equal to 22 per cent.[20] In composition by age, Italy is at an extreme: it has the highest proportion of heads aged over 65 (28 per cent, more than 4 percentage points higher than the average in other countries), but it has the lowest number of heads aged under 30 (5 per cent). Except in Spain (7.5 per cent), the incidence of young household heads is markedly below the levels in other countries (from 12 to 17 per cent, up to 22 in Denmark and 25 in Sweden).

The various household types tend to be distributed differently in the various countries. In Italy, the most common types are couples with one or two children (each accounting for about a fifth of the total); in Denmark, the most frequent are males living alone aged under 65 and couples without children with a non-elderly household head (17–18 per cent); in France, Germany, and the United Kingdom, the most common type is the couple without children, even though couples with one or two children are also frequent. Spain comes closest to the Italian profile even though with some characteristics accentuated: couples with two children are far more numerous than those with a single child, and couples with three or more children are also much more common (14 per cent).

There are important differences in single-parent households: incidence tends to vary between 5 and 7 per cent of the total, but it reaches 10 per cent in the United Kingdom. Single parents with one child under the age of 18 account for between 2 and 3 per cent in Germany, Scandinavian countries, and the United Kingdom, while they are almost non-existent in Italy and Spain. On the contrary, Italy is the country with the greatest proportion (almost 4 per cent) of units consisting of a single parent and an adult child. Households consisting of a single parent and more than one child generally constitute between 2 and 3 per cent of the total, except in the United Kingdom where they account for 5 per cent.

"Other households," which include relatives other than children, or unrelated persons, account for about 15 per cent of the total in Spain, between 7 and 10 per cent in Finland, Luxembourg, and Italy, and less than 5 per cent in the other countries. In Denmark and the Netherlands the figure is below 1 per cent.

Comparison of overall inequality of incomes

The LIS is currently the best database for comparing the degree of inequality in the distribution of income in industrialized countries. However, the comparability of data remains imperfect and the results must be interpreted with caution. Another reason for caution comes from the fact that the comparison was carried out for a single year in each country and is thus affected by their individual economic conditions. This diversity is probably amplified by the fact that the latest surveys available for EU countries cover a period of a decade, from 1987 for Ireland to 1996 for Belgium, though in 9 out of 12 cases they refer to the years 1994-96.

Both the mean logarithmic deviation and the Gini index indicate the presence of a group of countries with lower levels of inequality (the Scandinavian countries and Luxembourg) and another group in which levels of inequality are decidedly higher (the United Kingdom and Italy). The remaining countries are in an intermediate position, with nations in central Europe somewhat closer to the Nordic ones (Table 4; Figure 4).

Thus, as in previous studies based on the same source (e.g. Atkinson, Rainwater and Smeeding, 1995; Gottschalk and Smeeding, 1997), the equivalent disposable household incomes appear more equally distributed in Scandinavia and in the Benelux countries. However, a radical change in the ranking concerns Italy, which has joined the United Kingdom in having the most unequal income distribution among EU countries. This result—brought about by the sharp rise in inequality experienced in the early 1990s—depends only partly on the territorial dualism of the Italian economy: correcting for the gap in average incomes between the Center-North and the South, the mean logarithmic deviation of household incomes would be lowered to that of Ireland (the third country in the ranking), below the level registered in the United Kingdom, but still well above those observed in the other continental economies.

Inequality between demographic groups

In all countries there are higher average values of equivalent income for male heads than for women. The most unfavorable differentials for

TABLE 4. Inequality of equivalent disposable incomes in selected EU countries

Country	Year	Survey	Sample size	Mean logarithmic deviation	Gini index
Belgium	1996	Panel Survey of the Centre for Social Policy	4,632	0.103	0.247
Denmark	1992	Income Tax Survey	12,895	0.080	0.216
Finland	1995	Income Distribution Survey	9,262	0.068	0.206
France	1994	Family Budget Survey	11,294	0.112	0.265
Germany	1994	German Social Economic Panel Study (GSOEP)[a]	6,045	0.114	0.259
Ireland	1987	ESRI Survey of Income Distribution, Poverty and Usage of State Services	3,294	0.148	0.300
Italy	1995	Survey of Households' Income and Wealth	8,135	0.176	0.316
Luxembourg	1994	The Luxembourg Social Economic Panel Study (Liewen zu Letzebuerg)	1,813	0.077	0.222
Netherlands	1994	Socio-Economic Panel (SEP)	5,187	0.120	0.248
Spain	1990	Expenditure and Income Survey	21,153	0.133	0.284
Sweden	1995	Income Distribution Survey (Inkomstfördelningsundersökningen)	16,260	0.077	0.203
United Kingdom	1995	The Family Expenditure Survey[b]	6,797	0.165	0.315

Sources and notes: authors' calculations on data from the LIS (24 February 2001). Measures calculated for the distribution of equivalent disposable incomes between persons; bottom- and top-coded incomes; equivalence coefficients equal to $N0.5$, where N is the number of household members.

a. 208 observations were ignored because some components of income were missing.

b. Crown Copyright 1995. Source: Office for National Statistics.

women are found in the United Kingdom and in Denmark, while the opposite is true of Ireland, Luxembourg, and Spain. Italy lies between these two groups.[21] This ordering stems from the fact that only a minority of women, presumably those with higher levels of income, are independent in Ireland and Spain. As concerns household size, lone persons, and, in most cases, large households obtain lower mean incomes than the national average. The best-off household types are generally non-elderly couples without children, or couples with one child; diminishing income levels are seen in couples with two or three children. The least privileged are old people living alone, especially women, and single parents with children under 18 (particularly in Germany and the United Kingdom). The situation of single-parent households with one or more children appears to be critical in the United Kingdom where, unlike in Italy, they are relatively common.

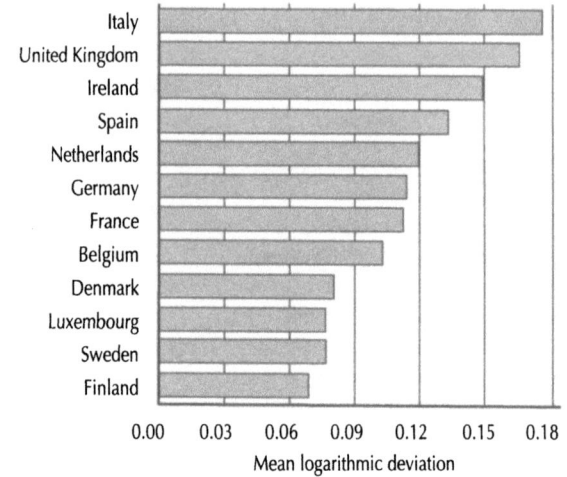

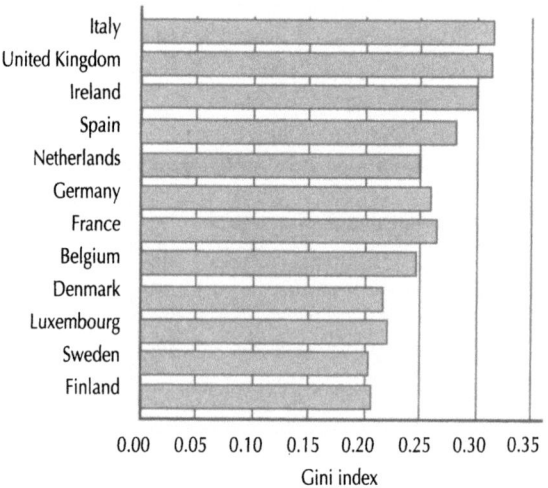

FIGURE 4 Income Inequality in Selected EU Countries.
Sources and notes: authors' calculations on data from the LIS (24 February 2001). Measures calculated for the distribution of equivalent disposable incomes between persons; bottom- and top-coded incomes; equivalence coefficients equal to $N^{0.5}$, where N is the number of household members. Countries listed in descending order, from top to the bottom, according to the value of the mean logarithmic deviation.

When compared with other countries, the profile of equivalent household incomes by age group in Italy is notable for the lower values in the central age groups, especially in the 31-to-40-year range, and for the near-average value of household heads aged over 65 (Figure 5).[22] In no other EU country is the equivalent household income of old people so high in

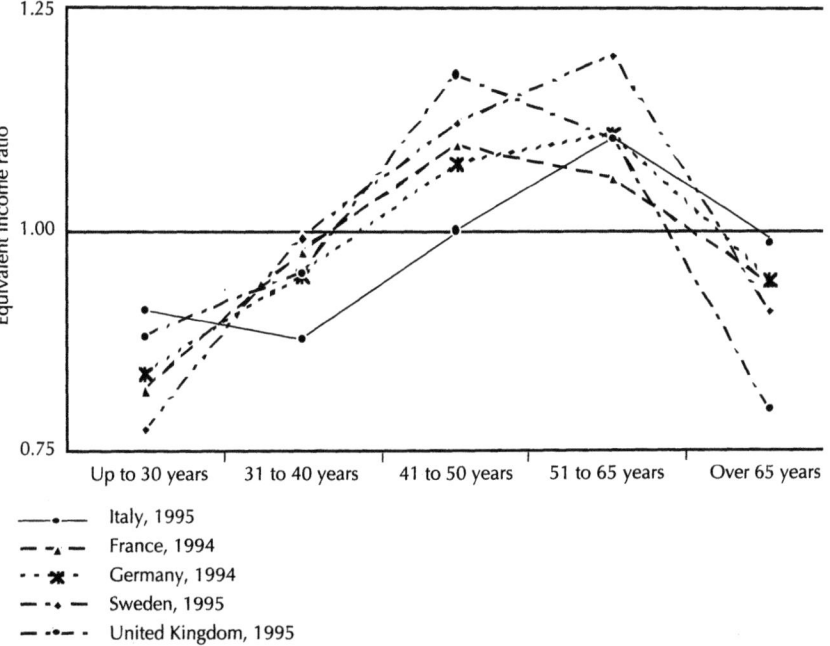

FIGURE 5 Age Profile of Incomes in Selected EU Countries. *Sources and notes: authors' calculations on data from the LIS (24 February 2001). Ratio to the overall mean of the mean equivalent disposable incomes of households with heads in the age group indicated; bottom- and top-coded incomes; equivalence coefficients equal to $N^{0.5}$, where N is the number of household members; households counted as many times as there are members.*

relative terms. The German profile is the closest to the Italian one, even though characterized by a less favorable situation for younger heads of household. In France and in the United Kingdom, the pattern is different from that of other countries since the highest average income is in the 41 to 50 year age group, rather than in the 51 to 65 group. Sweden and Denmark are at the other end of the spectrum from Italy and show a much more arched profile by age group.

Demographic composition and inequality of incomes

When the groups are identified on the basis of household size, between 10 and 31 per cent of the mean logarithmic deviation measured for Finland, Denmark, and Sweden can be attributed to the different composition of the population as compared with Italy (Table 5). This figure goes down to 8 per cent in Belgium and 5 in the Netherlands, and is no higher than 4

TABLE 5. Decomposition of the mean logarithmic deviation in selected EU countries

Country	Household size						Sex of the household head					
	Within-groups at fixed weights		Between-groups at fixed weights		Demographic effect		Within-groups at fixed weights		Between-groups at fixed weights		Demographic effect	
	value	share	value	share	value	share	value	share	value	share	value	share
Belgium	0.091	88.4	0.003	3.3	0.009	8.3	0.098	95.5	0.004	4.3	0.000	0.2
Denmark	0.059	74.4	0.005	6.2	0.016	19.5	0.069	86.9	0.008	9.8	0.003	3.4
Finland	0.058	85.2	0.003	4.5	0.007	10.4	0.062	91.6	0.005	6.8	0.001	1.6
France	0.106	94.1	0.002	2.0	0.004	3.9	0.108	95.9	0.004	3.5	0.001	0.6
Germany	0.108	94.7	0.002	1.7	0.004	3.6	0.109	95.4	0.004	3.2	0.002	1.4
Ireland	0.151	102.2	0.005	3.3	–0.008	–5.5	0.149	100.6	0.000	0.0	–0.001	–0.6
Italy	0.172	98.2	0.003	1.8	—	—	0.174	98.9	0.002	1.1	—	—
Luxembourg	0.075	97.6	0.001	1.0	0.001	1.4	0.076	98.7	0.001	0.7	0.000	0.6
Netherlands	0.111	92.7	0.003	2.2	0.006	5.1	0.116	96.5	0.004	3.5	0.000	0.0
Spain	0.133	99.8	0.002	1.8	–0.002	–1.6	0.134	100.6	0.001	0.4	–0.001	–1.0
Sweden	0.049	63.8	0.004	5.3	0.024	30.8	0.070	90.4	0.005	5.9	0.003	3.7
United Kingdom	0.158	96.1	0.004	2.3	0.003	1.6	0.152	92.6	0.010	5.9	0.003	1.5

Sources and notes: authors' calculations on data from the LIS (24 February 2001). Measures calculated for the distribution of equivalent disposable incomes between persons; bottom- and top-coded incomes; equivalence coefficients equal to No.5, where N is the number of household members. "Value" refers to the absolute

per cent in the other countries in which the average household size is lower than in Italy. Negative values suggest that, *ceteris paribus*, inequality would rise in Spain and Ireland (by 2 and 6 per cent, respectively) if the distributions of households by size were the same as that observed in Italy. The effects due to the different structure of the population are similar, even though more limited, for the other demographic variables. In most cases, alignment with the distribution in Italy would tend to widen the gap between Italy and the other countries. Significant corrections in the opposite direction would occur in the case of Ireland, by aligning household size, and, to a lesser extent, in the case of the Netherlands, Belgium, and France, by aligning the age groups of the heads (Figure 6).

Once the differences in demographic structures are removed, comparisons with other European countries show that in Italy inequalities within groups tend to be greater than between groups. The difference is particularly great when the comparison is made with Scandinavian countries, where the groups are both more uniform internally, and more differentiated one from the other. In particular, the very arched age-group profile found in Finland, Denmark, and, Sweden is reflected in the high contribution of between-group inequality to the overall index at fixed weights— between 9 and 17 per cent, against 2 per cent in Italy.

Age class of the household head						Household type						
Within-groups at fixed weights		Between-groups at fixed weights		Demographic effect		Within-groups at fixed weights		Between-groups at fixed weights		Demographic effect		
value	share	value	share	value	share	value	share	value	share	value	share	Total
0.099	96.0	0.007	6.8	-0.003	-2.8	0.088	85.3	0.008	7.5	0.007	7.2	0.103
0.063	79.0	0.013	16.3	0.004	4.7	0.056	69.8	0.013	16.1	0.011	14.0	0.080
0.062	91.5	0.006	9.1	–0.000	-0.6	0.054	80.1	0.006	9.6	0.007	10.4	0.068
0.112	99.6	0.003	2.4	-0.002	-2.0	0.102	90.5	0.006	5.4	0.005	4.1	0.112
0.110	96.6	0.003	3.0	0.000	0.4	0.102	89.7	0.005	4.8	0.006	5.5	0.114
0.142	96.1	0.004	3.0	0.001	0.9	—	—	—	—	—	—	0.148
0.172	98.0	0.004	2.0	—	—	0.170	96.9	0.005	3.1	—	—	0.176
0.075	97.5	0.002	3.0	–0.000	–0.5	0.072	93.3	0.003	4.2	0.002	2.5	0.077
0.120	99.4	0.003	2.7	–0.003	–2.1	0.104	86.9	0.006	5.4	0.009	7.7	0.120
0.131	98.6	0.002	1.6	–0.000	–0.2	0.129	96.9	0.006	4.7	–0.002	–1.6	0.133
0.057	74.0	0.007	9.6	0.013	16.4	—	—	—	—	—	—	0.077
0.150	91.0	0.010	6.0	0.005	3.0	0.140	85.1	0.016	9.7	0.009	5.2	0.165

contribution of the component to the total index; "share" refers to the percentage impact of the same contribution on the total index.

The differences between Italian households and those of other European countries (particularly in terms of their size and the age of the head of the household) are very conspicuous in many cases. However, they are of little help to explain why inequality is greater in Italy: all other factors being equal, when the same demographic structure is imposed, the distribution of incomes in other countries is generally corrected in the direction of less inequality, including the case of the United Kingdom. The reasons for the higher level of inequality in Italy should thus be sought in the differences within demographic groups, which can only superficially be considered homogeneous.

Conclusions

Between 1977 and 1995, the average size of Italian households fell; the share of both female and elderly household heads increased, whereas that of young household heads declined; the number of lone persons and single-parent households with children rose, while the number of households with other relatives or unrelated members fell. At the end of this process, the demographic structure of Italy was different from the prevailing

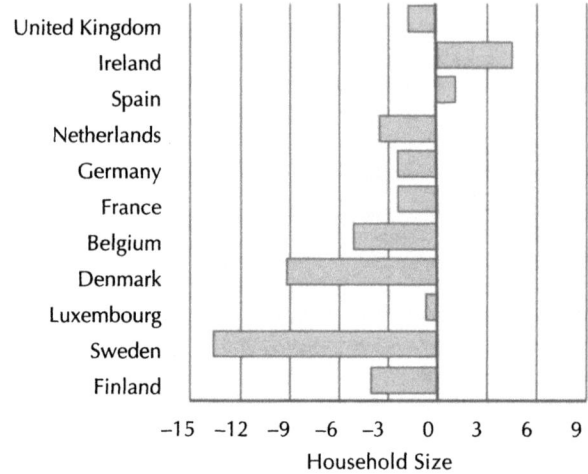

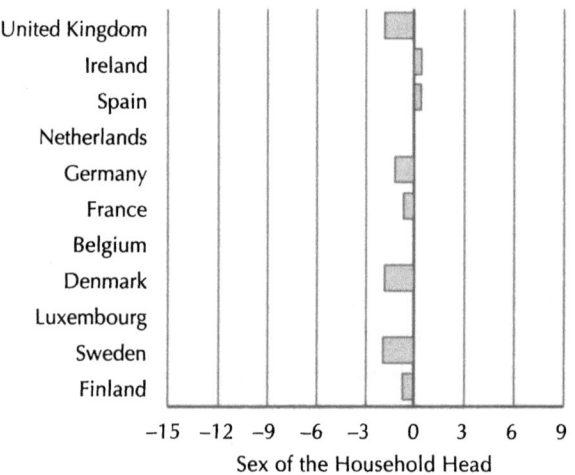

Figure 6 Demographic Effects on Inequality in Selected EU Countries. *Sources and notes: authors' calculations on data from the LIS (24 February 2001). Percentage variations in the mean logarithmic deviation obtained by imposing the demographic structure of Italy, expressed as a percentage of the mean logarithmic deviation of Italy. Measures calculated for the distribu-*

one in the rest of the EU, and the differences between Italy and Nordic countries were even greater. Along with Ireland and Spain, Italy was distinguished by its larger households and lower proportion of female heads. Italy at the end of the age spectrum, with a much higher proportion of older household heads than young.

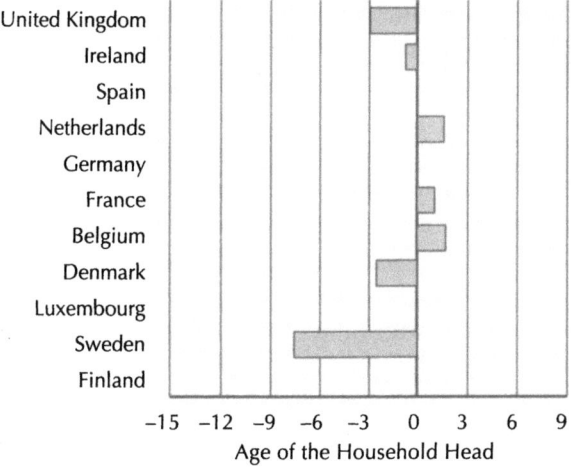

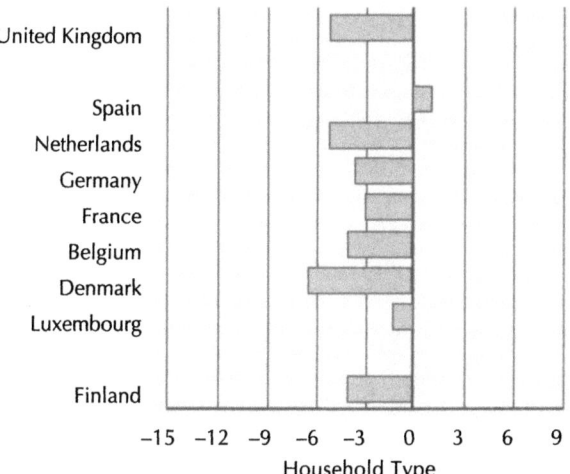

tion of equivalent disposable incomes between persons; bottom- and top-coded incomes; equivalence coefficients equal to No.5, where N is the number of household members. Countries listed in descending order, from top to the bottom, according to the value of the mean logarithmic deviation.

What are the effects of these demographic differences on comparisons of economic inequality over time or across countries? This paper has attempted to respond to this question by decomposing the overall inequality—as measured by the mean logarithmic deviation—into three component parts: the dispersion of incomes within groups defined on the basis of a particular demographic characteristic; the distance between the average incomes of these groups; and the effect that can be attributed to their weight. The decomposition exercise was carried out using Italian data from the SHIW-HA for 1977–1995, together with European data taken from the LIS for the early 1990s.

From 1977 to 1995, there were significant fluctuations in inequality in Italy, but no particular medium-term trend. The frequency of data, initially annual and then biannual, makes it difficult to pinpoint a link with the business cycle, but qualitatively the relationship seems to have been positive, at least until the early 1990s: distribution tended to widen during periods of economic expansion and to narrow during recessions. In the same period, the trend of mean equivalent incomes by demographic group led to an improvement, in relative terms, for households with a single member and for older heads of household, and to a gradual worsening for young heads and larger households. Gender differentials did not show any precise trend, and equivalent incomes of male heads of household remained between 10 and 20 per cent above those of female heads. The effect of demographic changes on distributive trends was almost negligible, except for a slight bias towards greater inequality imparted by the increase in the share of female heads of household.

During the 1990s, the dispersion of equivalent incomes between persons in Italy was the same as in the United Kingdom and higher than in other European nations, of which Nordic countries proved to be the most egalitarian; this result was only partly, although significantly, influenced by the territorial dualism of the Italian economy. In all countries, mean equivalent incomes were higher for non-elderly couples (without children or with a single child) and for male heads of household, while they were lower for large households or for those with a single member, and for aged female heads of household. These differentials varied from country to country: the gaps between the sexes were greater in the United Kingdom and in Denmark, and least pronounced in Ireland, Luxembourg, and Spain, with Italy in an intermediate position. Italy was notable for the particular age profile of mean equivalent disposable household incomes: it was less arched than in other nations, and the relative disadvantage for households of old people was distinctly smaller. When compared with other countries, it does not seem that differences in the levels of inequality can be attributed to any great extent to the different demographic structures. Nor would the inequality ranking of the various countries be substantially changed if all of them had the same household composition as in Italy. Bearing in mind its demographic diversity, Italy appears to be the country with the most unequal distribution, in many cases with gaps that would be even greater than those observed.

To sum up, neither the changes in inequality experienced by Italy from 1977 to 1995 nor its position in relation to other countries appear to depend on the composition of its population. The secondary role played by demographic variables confirms the results obtained by other studies using similar methodologies (e.g. Danziger and Plotnick, 1977; Mookherjee and Shorrocks, 1982; Cowell, 1984; Tsakloglou, 1993; Goodman, Johnson and Webb, 1994; Jenkins, 1995; Asher and Defina, 1995; Rainwater and Smeeding, 1998). Even so, it is necessary to state the limits within which this conclusion is true.

First of all, the decomposition exercise tends to provide a mechanical view of demographic factors, which are artificially isolated from those of a different nature. On one side, demographic changes are not exogenous, but they respond to socioeconomic circumstances: the growth in the number of old women who live alone in Italy, for instance, certainly reflects a lengthening of the average lifespan, but it is also caused by a modification of the parent-child relations, as well as by improved economic conditions and, in particular, improved social security. On the other side, demographic effects are identified under the assumption, admittedly unrealistic, that the distribution of incomes within and between groups is independent of the group size.

Secondly, the lesser influence of demographic variables registered in Italy may depend on a more composite household structure—where a number of generations and various sources of income often coexist—which makes the classification based on the simple variables used here that much less significant than in other countries. In any case, even in countries in which these classifications describe more or less homogeneous situations, the ability of demographic factors to provide explanations is limited, meaning that research into other causes of economic inequalities remains to be done.

Appendix. Statistical tables

TABLE C1. Distribution of households and household members by geographical area of residence in Italy, 1977-1995

	Household members					Households				
	Percentage share					Percentage share				
Year	North	Center	South and Islands	Total	Total number (thousands)	North	Center	South and Islands	Total	Total number (thousands)
1977	47.5	18.5	34.0	100.0	55,973	47.5	18.5	34.0	100.0	17,380
1978	48.5	17.7	33.8	100.0	56,184	48.5	17.7	33.8	100.0	17,468
1979	49.0	17.3	33.7	100.0	56,344	49.0	17.3	33.7	100.0	17,875
1980	49.5	17.2	33.3	100.0	56,447	49.5	17.2	33.3	100.0	18,007
1981	49.6	19.0	31.5	100.0	56,514	49.6	19.0	31.5	100.0	18,153
1982	48.3	18.5	33.3	100.0	56,524	48.3	18.5	33.3	100.0	17,796
1983	47.7	19.8	32.5	100.0	56,563	47.7	19.8	32.5	100.0	18,209
1984	49.1	19.6	31.2	100.0	56,565	49.1	19.6	31.2	100.0	18,580
1986	48.4	19.3	32.3	100.0	56,598	48.4	19.3	32.3	100.0	18,701
1987	47.0	19.6	33.4	100.0	56,594	47.0	19.6	33.4	100.0	18,724
1989	47.9	19.3	32.9	100.0	56,649	47.9	19.3	32.9	100.0	19,504
1991	47.6	20.1	32.3	100.0	56,744	47.6	20.1	32.3	100.0	19,630
1993	49.1	18.7	32.1	100.0	56,960	49.1	18.7	32.1	100.0	19,675
1995	48.5	18.2	33.2	100.0	57,269	48.5	18.2	33.2	100.0	20,151

Sources and notes: authors' calculations on data from the SHIW-HA (Version 1.1, October 2000). Figures may not add up to 100 because of rounding.

TABLE C2. Distribution of households in Italy by number of members, 1977–1995 (in %)

Year	1 member	2 members	3 members	4 members	5 or more members	Total	Average number of members
1977	9.7	24.8	25.4	24.0	16.1	100.0	3.2
1978	9.8	23.8	26.3	23.8	16.3	100.0	3.2
1979	13.4	23.6	23.4	23.3	16.3	100.0	3.2
1980	11.8	25.4	25.0	21.8	16.0	100.0	3.1
1981	12.8	24.6	24.6	23.3	14.8	100.0	3.1
1982	10.4	25.5	24.2	23.9	16.0	100.0	3.2
1983	12.3	25.0	23.9	24.5	14.3	100.0	3.1
1984	14.3	24.0	25.2	22.9	13.7	100.0	3.0
1986	14.5	24.5	24.0	23.5	13.5	100.0	3.0
1987	14.8	23.8	23.8	25.2	12.5	100.0	3.0
1989	17.3	24.8	23.7	23.1	11.0	100.0	2.9
1991	18.2	23.7	23.9	23.6	10.6	100.0	2.9
1993	17.5	24.6	23.5	23.6	10.7	100.0	2.9
1995	18.3	25.4	23.5	22.9	9.9	100.0	2.8

Sources and notes: authors' calculations on data from the SHIW-HA (Version 1.1, October 2000). Figures may not add up to 100 because of rounding.

TABLE C3. Distribution of heads of household in Italy by sex and age, 1977–1995 (in %)

	Sex		Age					
Year	males	females	up to 30	31 to 40	41 to 50	51 to 65	over 65	Total
1977	88.2	11.8	7.7	17.8	21.3	30.3	22.8	100.0
1978	87.0	13.0	5.5	18.6	20.6	32.7	22.5	100.0
1979	86.3	13.7	6.8	17.7	22.6	30.6	22.3	100.0
1980	85.7	14.3	6.2	16.9	21.3	32.7	22.9	100.0
1981	84.8	15.2	8.2	18.2	20.1	28.5	25.0	100.0
1982	87.8	12.2	7.4	17.0	21.2	31.3	23.1	100.0
1983	85.2	14.8	6.0	17.6	21.7	31.8	22.9	100.0
1984	84.1	15.9	6.4	18.6	21.1	30.8	23.1	100.0
1986	81.8	18.2	6.3	18.9	20.4	30.1	24.3	100.0
1987	81.8	18.2	6.7	17.7	20.7	29.8	25.0	100.0
1989	80.5	19.5	7.4	16.8	21.0	28.6	26.2	100.0
1991	78.8	21.2	6.5	16.3	20.2	29.5	27.6	100.0
1993	71.9	28.1	6.5	18.3	20.0	27.3	27.8	100.0
1995	71.7	28.3	5.4	17.9	19.4	28.2	29.2	100.0

Sources and notes: authors' calculations on data from the SHIW-HA (Version 1.1, October 2000). Figures may not add up to 100 because of rounding.

TABLE C4. Distribution of households by household type in Italy, 1977-1995 (in %)

Year	Singles				Couples		Couples with children			Single parents with children				Other households	Total
	male up to 65	female up to 65	male over 65	female over 65	household head up to 65	household head over 65	1 child	2 children	3 or more children	with child up to 17 years	up to 65 with child over 17	over 65 with child over 17	with 2 or more children		
1977	1.8	2.9	1.4	3.6	10.3	9.7	20.8	20.5	11.3	0.2	0.9	1.0	2.6	13.0	100.0
1978	1.1	2.8	1.6	4.4	10.6	8.7	21.4	20.5	11.1	0.3	0.8	1.2	2.6	13.0	100.0
1979	3.0	3.4	1.8	5.2	10.1	8.8	19.4	19.9	11.1	0.5	1.2	0.7	2.1	12.7	100.0
1980	1.7	3.1	1.7	5.3	10.9	8.6	21.1	19.1	11.0	0.5	1.7	0.8	1.9	12.6	100.0
1981	1.1	3.9	2.4	5.3	9.5	9.6	21.0	20.4	11.1	0.5	1.2	1.6	2.4	9.8	100.0
1982	1.7	2.3	2.1	4.2	10.2	10.0	20.7	20.7	10.8	0.3	1.1	1.1	2.2	12.5	100.0
1983	1.5	3.9	1.7	5.2	10.2	9.4	20.1	21.2	10.5	0.5	1.2	1.0	2.3	11.2	100.0
1984	2.9	3.4	1.9	6.1	9.9	8.8	22.1	20.1	9.5	0.5	1.9	1.3	2.2	9.5	100.0
1986	2.0	3.6	1.7	7.2	10.5	8.8	20.3	21.1	9.8	0.5	1.6	1.0	2.3	9.6	100.0
1987	2.1	3.1	2.5	7.1	9.2	8.3	20.5	22.3	9.2	0.6	1.5	1.6	2.3	9.9	100.0
1989	3.5	3.5	2.2	8.2	10.1	8.9	20.4	20.9	8.0	0.6	1.6	1.5	2.2	8.6	100.0
1991	3.2	3.9	1.9	9.3	9.4	8.9	20.2	21.5	7.5	0.7	1.8	1.4	2.5	8.1	100.0
1993	3.1	3.1	1.7	9.6	8.7	9.4	19.0	21.2	7.9	0.6	1.8	1.6	3.0	9.2	100.0
1995	3.0	3.1	1.9	10.3	9.5	9.2	19.2	20.6	7.5	0.4	2.1	1.6	2.7	9.0	100.0

Sources and notes: authors' calculations on data from the SHIW-HA (Version 1.1, October 2000). Figures may not add up to 100 because of rounding.

TABLE C5. Relative mean incomes in Italy by household characteristic, 1977–1995

Household characteristic	1977	1978	1979	1980	1981	1982	1983	1984	1986	1987	1989	1991	1993	1995
Number of members														
1	0.79	0.65	0.82	0.83	0.75	0.74	0.75	0.84	0.81	0.78	0.84	0.88	0.80	0.83
2	0.91	0.91	0.87	0.89	0.96	0.91	0.90	0.96	0.97	0.96	0.98	0.99	1.00	1.02
3	1.13	1.09	1.05	1.09	1.10	1.05	1.07	1.09	1.08	1.10	1.11	1.10	1.10	1.09
4	1.04	1.05	1.03	0.99	1.04	1.04	1.04	1.04	1.04	1.04	1.01	1.01	1.03	1.01
5 or more	0.92	0.96	1.02	1.02	0.92	0.99	0.99	0.91	0.94	0.91	0.91	0.91	0.89	0.91
Sex of household head														
male	1.01	1.01	1.01	1.01	1.01	1.01	1.01	1.02	1.02	1.02	1.02	1.01	1.03	1.02
female	0.90	0.82	0.82	0.91	0.88	0.88	0.83	0.81	0.85	0.82	0.88	0.91	0.87	0.92
Age of household head														
up to 30	1.05	1.00	0.95	0.92	0.95	0.96	0.87	0.93	0.88	0.86	0.97	0.94	0.92	0.91
from 31 to 40	0.96	0.93	0.96	0.99	1.00	1.00	0.99	0.95	0.97	0.98	0.96	0.93	0.94	0.92
from 41 to 50	0.98	1.04	1.01	1.01	1.01	1.01	1.02	0.98	1.05	1.00	1.04	1.04	1.02	1.00
from 51 to 65	1.11	1.08	1.12	1.09	1.08	1.06	1.08	1.12	1.07	1.09	1.07	1.07	1.10	1.10
over 65	0.84	0.87	0.80	0.82	0.86	0.86	0.84	0.88	0.87	0.91	0.87	0.92	0.91	0.95
Household type														
single male up to 65	1.21	0.93	1.21	1.07	1.07	0.92	1.07	1.30	1.23	1.22	1.17	1.29	1.11	1.15
single female up to 65	0.90	0.79	0.83	0.94	0.89	0.86	0.87	0.87	0.83	0.79	0.93	1.00	0.90	0.95
single male over 65	0.71	0.51	0.79	0.82	0.72	0.75	0.58	0.80	0.79	0.72	0.78	0.89	0.74	0.82
single female over 65	0.53	0.55	0.60	0.69	0.60	0.60	0.61	0.62	0.69	0.68	0.68	0.68	0.67	0.71
couple with household head up to 65	1.09	1.03	1.00	1.01	1.11	1.05	1.02	1.11	1.09	1.11	1.12	1.14	1.19	1.18
couple with household head over 65	0.71	0.71	0.70	0.72	0.81	0.73	0.76	0.77	0.81	0.84	0.79	0.81	0.88	0.90
couple with 1 child	1.13	1.13	1.08	1.10	1.11	1.05	1.06	1.09	1.09	1.10	1.13	1.09	1.12	1.10
couple with 2 children	1.01	1.03	1.00	0.97	1.02	1.03	1.03	1.03	1.01	1.02	1.00	1.00	1.03	1.00

TABLE C5. (continued)

Household characteristic	1977	1978	1979	1980	1981	1982	1983	1984	1986	1987	1989	1991	1993	1995
couple with 3 or more children	0.85	0.89	0.92	0.91	0.88	0.94	0.94	0.84	0.89	0.84	0.85	0.88	0.85	0.89
single parent with child up to 17	0.51	0.94	0.98	1.03	0.72	0.72	0.80	0.84	0.76	0.62	0.85	0.81	0.77	0.99
single parent up to 65 with child over 17	1.03	1.07	0.91	1.06	1.24	1.03	0.92	1.08	0.98	0.90	1.11	1.19	0.95	0.99
single parent over 65 with child over 17	0.90	0.97	0.80	0.60	0.83	1.20	0.87	0.84	0.97	0.83	0.94	0.95	0.82	0.90
single parent with 2 or more children	1.15	0.83	0.88	1.10	1.06	0.98	0.93	1.00	0.96	0.90	0.91	1.07	0.80	0.96
other household	1.12	1.11	1.18	1.15	1.10	1.10	1.14	1.09	1.11	1.14	1.09	1.04	1.08	1.04
Area of residence														
North	1.15	1.14	1.09	1.09	1.09	1.10	1.09	1.09	1.11	1.15	1.13	1.13	1.15	1.16
Center	1.03	1.10	1.26	1.25	1.13	1.10	1.08	1.13	1.09	1.09	1.08	1.07	1.11	1.09
South	0.80	0.77	0.75	0.75	0.81	0.82	0.84	0.82	0.82	0.78	0.79	0.80	0.77	0.75
Total	1.00	1.00	1.00	1.00	1.00	1.00	1.00	1.00	1.00	1.00	1.00	1.00	1.00	1.00

Sources and notes: authors' calculations on data from the SHIW-HA (Version 1.1, October 2000). Measures calculated for the distribution of equivalent disposable incomes between persons, where incomes are net of interest on financial assets; bottom- and top-coded incomes; equivalence coefficients equal to No.5, where N is the number of household members.

TABLE C6. Distribution of households by number of members in selected EU countries

Country	1 member	2 members	3 members	4 members	5 or more members	Total	Average number of members
Belgium	26.7	34.0	17.0	14.7	7.7	100.0	2.5
Denmark	44.0	29.8	12.5	10.5	3.2	100.0	2.0
Finland	36.8	31.5	14.0	11.7	6.0	100.0	2.2
France	28.3	31.9	16.7	14.6	8.4	100.0	2.5
Germany	33.2	31.4	16.4	13.8	5.3	100.0	2.3
Ireland	16.6	18.8	16.2	17.6	30.8	100.0	3.6
Italy	17.2	24.8	23.8	23.8	10.3	100.0	2.9
Luxembourg	23.0	27.8	20.8	19.4	9.0	100.0	2.7
Netherlands	29.9	34.7	13.5	15.1	6.7	100.0	2.4
Spain	10.0	22.3	20.8	25.0	22.0	100.0	3.4
Sweden	53.0	27.6	8.2	7.8	3.4	100.0	1.8
United Kingdom	26.1	35.7	17.0	14.5	6.7	100.0	2.4

Sources and notes: authors' calculations on data from the LIS (24 February 2001). Figures may not add up to 100 because of rounding.

TABLE C7. Distribution of heads of household by sex and age in selected EU countries

County	Sex		Age					Total
	males	females	up to 30	31 to 40	41 to 50	51 to 65	over 65	
Belgium	77.6	22.4	10.9	19.1	20.4	23.6	26.0	100.0
Denmark	71.8	28.2	21.7	17.6	18.4	19.4	23.0	100.0
Finland	72.6	27.4	16.7	19.5	22.1	21.2	20.5	100.0
France	75.2	24.8	13.4	20.2	20.3	21.5	24.6	100.0
Germany	72.0	28.0	13.3	21.4	15.8	24.2	25.4	100.0
Ireland	81.4	18.6	12.1	23.2	17.4	25.6	21.7	100.0
Italy	78.5	21.5	5.0	18.0	20.2	29.1	27.7	100.0
Luxembourg	75.5	24.5	11.8	22.5	18.3	25.2	22.1	100.0
Netherlands	77.3	22.7	17.4	22.2	20.0	21.1	19.3	100.0
Spain	84.8	15.2	7.5	18.7	20.0	30.8	23.0	100.0
Sweden	69.2	30.8	25.0	16.2	16.8	19.4	22.5	100.0
United Kingdom	73.9	26.1	14.8	20.4	19.1	21.9	23.9	100.0

Sources and notes: authors' calculations on data from the LIS (24 February 2001). Figures may not add up to 100 because of rounding.

TABLE C8. Distribution of households by household type in selected EU countries

	Singles				Couples		Couples with children			Single parents with children					
Country	male up to 65	female up to 65	male over 65	female over 65	household head up to 65	household head over 65	1 child	2 children	3 or more children	with child up to 17 years	up to 65 with child over 17	over 65 with child over 17	all ages with 2 or more children	Other households	Total
Belgium	7.9	6.3	2.7	9.7	18.1	10.6	14.3	13.6	7.1	1.3	2.0	0.8	2.6	3.0	100.0
Denmark	17.0	12.3	3.8	10.9	17.7	7.9	10.5	10.1	3.1	2.8	0.9	0.1	2.2	0.7	100.0
Finland	13.0	11.7	2.3	9.8	19.0	6.8	9.5	10.0	4.9	2.2	1.0	0.5	2.1	7.1	100.0
France	8.1	8.6	2.5	9.1	15.9	10.2	14.2	13.7	7.5	1.8	1.3	0.7	2.4	3.9	100.0
Germany	9.6	8.7	1.9	13.0	17.8	8.7	14.3	13.2	4.7	2.2	1.4	0.6	1.9	2.1	100.0
Ireland	—	—	—	—	—	—	—	—	—	—	—	—	—	—	—
Italy	2.8	3.2	1.7	9.5	9.3	8.8	19.5	21.4	7.5	0.4	2.2	1.6	2.8	9.3	100.0
Luxembourg	5.6	5.8	1.4	10.2	16.2	6.7	17.5	17.3	6.0	1.2	1.3	1.1	2.0	7.7	100.0
Netherlands	9.6	9.9	2.2	8.2	24.0	7.6	11.6	14.7	6.5	1.2	1.1	0.4	2.1	0.8	100.0
Spain	1.7	2.2	1.1	5.0	8.1	8.9	16.5	21.3	14.3	0.5	1.0	1.3	2.7	15.4	100.0
Sweden	23.2	16.0	3.7	10.1	15.9	8.7	6.4	7.3	3.3	3.0	—	—	2.4	—	100.0
United Kingdom	7.4	7.0	2.9	8.9	19.5	9.2	12.6	12.6	5.6	3.0	1.0	0.9	4.9	4.6	100.0

Sources and notes: authors' calculations on data from the LIS (24 February 2001). Figures may not add up to 100 because of rounding.

TABLE C9. Relative mean incomes by household characteristic in selected EU countries

Household characteristic	Belgium	Denmark	Finland	France	Germany	Ireland	Italy	Luxembourg	Netherlands	Spain	Sweden	United Kingdom
Number of members												
1	0.77	0.74	0.76	0.86	0.89	0.75	0.81	0.88	0.88	0.83	0.79	0.80
2	0.96	1.04	1.05	1.05	1.08	1.00	1.03	1.04	1.12	0.92	1.16	1.07
3	1.08	1.14	1.09	1.06	1.05	1.15	1.09	1.03	1.02	1.07	1.07	1.04
4	1.08	1.09	1.05	1.03	0.98	1.06	1.00	0.98	0.97	1.03	1.05	1.04
5 or more	1.01	0.98	0.99	0.91	0.92	0.96	0.91	1.00	0.91	0.98	0.94	0.88
Sex of household head												
male	1.04	1.06	1.04	1.04	1.04	1.00	1.02	1.01	1.03	1.01	1.06	1.07
female	0.77	0.71	0.77	0.79	0.80	0.97	0.84	0.92	0.78	0.91	0.78	0.69
Age of household head												
up to 30	0.92	0.86	0.83	0.82	0.84	1.02	0.91	0.92	0.95	0.98	0.77	0.88
from 31 to 40	0.98	1.04	0.99	0.98	0.95	0.91	0.88	0.95	1.00	0.98	0.99	0.95
from 41 to 50	1.10	1.14	1.11	1.10	1.08	0.98	1.00	1.05	1.05	0.99	1.12	1.18
from 51 to 65	1.09	1.14	1.10	1.06	1.11	1.15	1.11	1.09	1.07	1.08	1.20	1.10
over 65	0.80	0.73	0.83	0.94	0.94	0.93	0.98	0.93	0.85	0.89	0.91	0.80
Household type												
single male up to 65	0.88	0.82	0.82	0.95	0.97	(*)	1.07	1.06	0.99	1.21	(*)	1.00
single female up to 65	0.79	0.75	0.79	0.87	0.88		0.89	0.90	0.87	0.90		0.88
single male over 65	0.72	0.66	0.82	0.95	0.97							
couple with household head up to 65	1.10	1.20	1.14	1.15	1.19		1.17	1.13	1.23	1.04		1.27

TABLE C9. (continued)

Household characteristic	Belgium	Denmark	Finland	France	Germany	Ireland	Italy	Luxembourg	Netherlands	Spain	Sweden	United Kingdom
couple with household head over 65	0.80	0.79	0.95	1.02	1.00		0.92	0.90	0.89	0.77		0.84
couple with 1 child	1.11	1.22	1.13	1.10	1.08		1.10	1.03	1.06	1.06		1.17
couple with 2 children	1.09	1.10	1.06	1.04	0.98		1.00	0.96	0.97	1.02		1.07
couple with 3 or more children	1.01	0.98	0.97	0.92	0.91		0.87	1.00	0.91	0.94		0.88
single parent with child up to 17	0.62	0.76	0.78	0.70	0.57		0.90	0.79	0.66	0.77		0.58
single parent up to 65 with child over 17	0.86	1.03	0.97	0.96	0.99		0.99	0.97	0.84	0.98		0.97
single parent over 65 with child over 17	0.94	0.84	0.84	0.88	1.04		0.94	1.17	0.98	0.85		0.84
single parent with 2 or more children	0.82	0.73	0.86	0.71	0.70		0.93	0.83	0.68	0.95		0.58
other household	1.05	1.04	1.04	0.93	1.04		1.07	1.07	0.95	1.09		1.06
Total	1.00	1.00	1.00	1.00	1.00	1.00	1.00	1.00	1.00	1.00	1.00	1.00

Sources and notes: authors' calculations on data from the LIS (24 February 2001). Measures calculated for the distribution of equivalent disposable incomes between persons; bottom- and top-coded incomes; equivalence coefficients equal to No.5, where N is the number of household members.

(*) Data not available in original sources

Notes

1. In 1975 Paglin advanced the view that perfect equality is defined as "equal incomes for all families at the same stage of their life cycle, but not necessarily equal incomes between different age groups" (1975, 602). In practice, Paglin suggested that measures of inequality be cleansed of the part which could be attributed to differences between the average incomes of the cohorts. Recalculating "corrected" Gini indices for the distribution of household income in the United States, Paglin found that the "true" degree of inequality had been overestimated by more than one-third, and that there had actually been a significant decline between 1947 and 1972, in contrast with the then prevalent opinion of basic stability. In the debate sparked off by Paglin's paper, critics questioned the normative foundations (is it right to ignore differences between cohorts when judging the equity of distribution?), the *cardinal* interpretation of the inequality index (considered as nonsense by Mookherjee and Shorrocks, 1982, 899) and the particular methodological solution (the inequality attributed by Paglin to variations in income throughout the life cycle depends on the arbitrary choice of age groups; the Gini index does not lend itself to an exact decomposition into *between* and *within* inequality, but it gives rise to a residual term which is difficult to interpret unambiguously). See the comments by Danziger, Haveman, and Smolensky (1977), Johnson (1977), Kurien (1977), Minarik (1977), Nelson (1977) and Wertz (1979) and the responses from Paglin (1977, 1979); subsequently, Formby and Seaks (1980), Mookherjee and Shorrocks (1982), Atkinson (1983, 70–6), Cowell (1984), Formby, Seaks, and Smith (1989) and the reply by Paglin (1989), and Asher and Defina (1995).
2. This statement holds only for exactly decomposable measures of inequality; it is not true for the Gini index.
3. Von Weizsäcker's model describes a population consisting of workers of different ages and of pensioners. The former earn salaries that increase with age; the latter receive pensions proportional to the rights they have accrued, and are paid on the basis of a pay-as-you-go system. The ageing of the population is registered by the increase in the share of pensioners and by the rise in the average age of the workers. For a more detailed model for the labor market alone, see von Weizsäcker (1988).
4. The mean logarithmic deviation was introduced by Theil (1967) and its properties were investigated by Shorrocks (1980) and Cowell (1980). It varies between 0 (absolute equality) and ∞ (maximum inequality). As a term of comparison, we also report figures for the Gini concentration index, which measures the mean distance of each income from all the other incomes, expressed in relation to the mean. It varies, for nonnegative values, between 0 (absolute equality) and 1 (maximum inequality). Unlike the mean logarithmic deviation, it is not exactly decomposable.
5. Unlike other works which have used a similar methodology (Mookherjee and Shorrocks, 1982; Cowell, 1984; Tsakloglou, 1993; Jenkins, 1995) attention focuses here on relative average incomes (μ_k/μ) rather than on absolute ones (μ_k); this requires that the overall mean is recalculated with fixed weights.
6. A shift-share analysis was used by Semple (1975) to evaluate the effect of changes in the composition of households on the evolution of income distribution in the United Kingdom in the period from 1961 to 1973, and by Danziger and Plotnick (1977), using data for the United States in 1965 and in 1974. Both papers focused on the Gini index.

7. The broader the definition of household, the more the measure of inequality tends to decrease, since the dispersion of individual incomes is abated by their aggregation and supposedly egalitarian distribution among all members of the unit. For example, the Gini index was found to fall significantly after replacing the household for the family as aggregation unit by Johnson and Webb (1989) on data for the United Kingdom, and Redmond (1998) on data for Australia.
8. An equivalence scale is a series of deflators which vary according to the type of unit. The many equivalence scales referred to in the literature differ both for the method of derivation and for the number of variables they take into consideration. On the importance of the equivalence scale for income inequality measurement see Buhmann, Rainwater, Schmaus, and Smeeding (1988) and Coulter, Cowell, and Jenkins (1992a, 1992b).
9. As shown by Haddad and Kanbur (1990), this assumption implies that the degree of inequality between persons is underestimated by all the indices generally used. On the redistributive role of the family in Italy, see D'Alessio and Signorini (2000).
10. In the case of surveys carried out after 1984, the original weights have been maintained unchanged. The original weights for previous surveys have been corrected to take into consideration that the samples were then extracted from the electoral lists, entailing a probability of inclusion of a household which was proportional to the number of adult members.
11. Figures on distributions and relative mean incomes by household characteristics are reported in the Appendix for both Italy and other European countries.
12. The increase in the influx of immigrants over the past few years has become particularly significant in Italy. The SHIW can only partially take the phenomenon into account, both because extraction of the sample from population registers excludes foreign households without a residence permit, and because there is no specific demand concerning migratory movements. Using place of birth, registered only as from 1989, as a proxy, the SHIW-HA reports a modest increase between 1989 and 1995, both in the members and in the household heads born abroad (from 1.1 to 1.6 and from 0.9 to 1.3 per cent, respectively).
13. The definition of the household head reflects both statistical conventions and social customs. In the SHIW, the head is he or she who declares to be "responsible for the economic and financial choices of the household." Recently, the Italian Central Statistical Office (ISTAT) has introduced the notion of the "reference person," who is the "nominee on the household certificate in the registry office of the municipality of residence" (ISTAT 1998,7). In the European Community Household Panel the definition of the head changes from one country to another. From the second wave of the panel, Eurostat adopted the notion of the reference person: "Where possible, the reference person was taken to be an economically active person in the following order of priority: the head if economically active, otherwise the head's spouse or partner if economically active; otherwise the oldest economically active person. In a household not containing any economically active person, the head was automatically taken as the reference person" (Eurostat 1996, 19). Calculations based on notions other than the one used by the SHIW, such as the definition of the reference person used by Eurostat or one that considers the head to be the person who has the highest level of income, do not modify our results to any significant degree.

14. Annual fluctuations should be considered with caution, because in several cases they are influenced by the low sample size of demographic groups.
15. The results, which are not given, for other decomposable measures (namely the Theil index and half the squared coefficient of variation) give similar indications about the importance of the demographic effects. Generally speaking, the greater the number of groups into which the population is divided, the greater the weight of the between-group component will be in relation to the within-group. At the extreme, if each household formed a separate group, the latter component would be zero (Tsakloglou 1992).
16. Factors of differentiation include: (a) the nature of the original data which, in some cases, are taken from sample surveys, while in other cases they come partly or entirely from administrative records; (b) the size of the national samples in relation to the population of each country (the relative exiguousness of the German sample, in particular, is cause for some concern); (c) the ability of the original data to provide an accurate picture of the income available to the households. For further discussion, see chapter 3 of Atkinson, Rainwater, and Smeeding (1995), where it is stressed that "complete comparability is impossible" (26).
17. The LIS database does not include data for Greece and Portugal; data from the 1995 survey for Austria have not been used since they exclude incomes from self-employment and property.
18. The LIS figures for Italy reported below need not coincide with the corresponding SHIW-HA figures, because of the different sample weights used.
19. Comparison of mean incomes across countries is made particularly complex by the different representativeness of the sample data with respect to the corresponding aggregates of national accounts, both for the different years they refer to (from 1987 for Ireland to 1996 for Belgium). This problem is compounded by the choice of exchange rate necessary to adapt all the incomes to a common currency unit. For these reasons, and bearing in mind that this work focuses on measuring "relative" inequalities (i.e., independent of the level of income), we have chosen not to comment, nor to give the mean values.
20. This value is almost 7 percentage points below the SHIW-HA figure reported in section 3.2, due to the reclassification of the household head operated by the LIS.
21. The choice of who is the head of the household has important effects on estimates of the income differentials by sex. In Italy, equivalent household incomes of female-headed households are about one tenth lower than those of male-headed in the SHIW-HA data, as opposed to about one sixth in the LIS data.
22. In addition to the reasons mentioned earlier (different weights and reclassification of the household heads), the profile of Italy by age group in Figure 5 is different from the one in Figure 2 also because the definition of income includes interest on financial assets and excludes imputed rental income from owner-occupied dwellings.

References

Asher, M. A. and R. H. Defina (1995), "Age-Adjustment of Income Inequality Trends: A Methodological Critique", *Journal of Economic and Social Measurement*, vol. 21, pp. 33-44.

Atkinson, A. B. (1983), *The Economics of Inequality*, 2nd ed., Oxford, Clarendon Press.

Atkinson, A. B., L. Rainwater, and T. M. Smeeding (1995), *Income Distribution in OECD Countries. Evidence from the Luxembourg Income Study*, Paris, OCSE.

Banca d'Italia (2000), *Indagine sui bilanci delle famiglie italiane*, CD-ROM Versione 1.1, October.

Brandolini, A. (1999), "The Distribution of Personal Income in Postwar Italy: Source Description, Data Quality, and the Time Pattern of Income Inequality", *Giornale degli Economisti e Annali di Economia*, vol. 58, pp. 183-239.

Buhmann, B., L. Rainwater, G. Schmaus and T. M. Smeeding (1988), "Equivalence Scales, Well-Being, Inequality, and Poverty: Sensitivity Estimates Across Ten Countries Using the Luxembourg Income Study (LIS) Database", *Review of Income and Wealth*, vol. 34, pp. 115-142.

Coulter F. A. E., F. A. Cowell and S. P. Jenkins (1992a), "Equivalence Scale Relativities and the Extent of Inequality and Poverty", *Economic Journal*, vol. 102, pp. 1067-1082.

Coulter, F. A. E., F. A. Cowell and S. P. Jenkins (1992b), "Differences in Needs and Assessment of Income Distribution", *Bulletin of Economic Research*, vol. 44, pp. 77-124.

Cowell, F. A. (1980), "On the Structure of Additive Inequality Measures", *Review of Economic Studies*, vol. 47, pp. 521-531.

Cowell, F. A. (1984), "The Structure of American Income Inequality", *Review of Income and Wealth*, vol. 30, pp. 351-375.

Cowell, F. A. and M.-P. Victoria-Feser (1996), "Robustness Properties of Inequality Measures", *Econometrica*, vol. 64, pp. 77-101.

D'Alessio, G. and L. F. Signorini (2000), "Disuguaglianza dei redditi individuali e ruolo della famiglia in Italia", Banca d'Italia, Temi di discussione, No. 390, December.

Danziger, S. and R. Plotnick (1977), "Demographic Change, Government Transfer, and Income Distribution", *Monthly Labor Review*, vol. 100, No. 4, pp. 7-11.

Danziger, S. and M. K. Taussig (1979), "The Income Unit and the Anatomy of Income Distribution", *Review of Income and Wealth*, vol. 25, pp. 365-375.

Danziger, S., R. Haveman and E. Smolensky (1977), "The Measurement and Trend of Inequality: Comment", *American Economic Review*, vol. 67, pp. 502-512.

Ebert, U. (1997), "Social Welfare When Needs Differ: An Axiomatic Approach", *Economica*, vol. 64, pp. 233-244.

Eurostat (1996), *The European Community Household Panel (EHCP): Survey Methodology and Implementation. Volume 1*, Theme 3, Series E, Luxembourg, Office for Official Publications of the European Communities.

Formby, J. P. and T. G. Seaks (1980), "Paglin's Gini Measure of Inequality: A Modification", *American Economic Review*, vol. 70, pp. 479-482.

Formby, J. P., T. G. Seaks and W. J. Smith (1989), "On the Measurement and Trend of Inequality: A Reconsideration", *American Economic Review*, vol. 79, pp. 256-264.

Goodman, A., P. Johnson and S. Webb (1994), "The U.K. Income Distribution 1961-91: The Role of Demographic and Economic Changes", mimeo, London, Institute for Fiscal Studies.

Gottschalk, P. and T. M. Smeeding (1997), "Cross-National Comparisons of Earnings and Income Inequality", *Journal of Economic Literature*, vol. 35, pp. 633-687.

Haddad, L. and R. Kanbur (1990), "How Serious Is the Neglect of Intrahousehold Inequality?", *Economic Journal*, vol. 100, pp. 866-881.

ISTAT(1998), "La distribuzione quantitativa del reddito in Italia nelle indagini sui bilanci di famiglia. Anno 1996", *Informazioni*, No. 62.

Jenkins, S. (1995), "Accounting for Inequality Trends: Decomposition Analyses for the UK, 1971-86", *Economica*, vol. 62, pp. 29-63.

Johnson, P. and S. Webb (1989), "Counting People with Low Incomes: the Impact of Recent Changes in Official Statistics", *Fiscal Studies*, vol. 10, No. 4, pp. 66-82.

Johnson, W. R. (1977), "The Measurement and Trend of Inequality: Comment", *American Economic Review*, vol. 67, pp. 502-504.

Kurien, C. J. (1977), "The Measurement and Trend of Inequality: Comment", *American Economic Review*, vol. 67, pp. 517-519.

Kuznets, S. (1976), "Demographic Aspects of the Size Distribution of Income: An Exploratory Essay", *Economic Development and Cultural Change*, vol. 25, No. 1, pp. 1-94.

Minarik, J. J. (1977), "The Measurement and Trend of Inequality: Comment", *American Economic Review*, vol. 67, pp. 513-516.

Mookherjee, D. and A. F. Shorrocks (1982), "A Decomposition Analysis of the Trend in UK Income Inequality", *Economic Journal*, vol. 92, pp. 886-902.

Nelson, E. R. (1977), "The Measurement and Trend of Inequality: Comment", *American Economic Review*, vol. 67, pp. 497-501.

Paglin, M. (1975), "The Measurement and Trend of Inequality: A Basic Revision", *American Economic Review*, vol. 65, pp. 598-609.

Paglin, M. (1977), "The Measurement and Trend of Inequality: Reply", *American Economic Review*, vol. 67, pp. 520-531.

Paglin, M. (1979), "The Measurement of Inequality: Reply", *American Economic Review*, vol. 69, pp. 673-677.

Paglin, M. (1989), "On the Measurement and Trend of Inequality: Reply", *American Economic Review*, vol. 79, pp. 265-266.

Rainwater, L. and T. M. Smeeding (1998), "Demography and Income Packaging: What Explains the Income Distribution?", in H. P. Galler and G. Wagner (eds.), *Empirische Forschung und wirtschaftspolitische Beratung. Fetschrift für Hans-Jürgen Krupp zum 65. Geburstag*, pp. 99-118, Frankfurt, Campus Verlag.

Redmond, G. (1998), "Households, Families and the Distribution of Income", *Social Policy Research Centre Newsletter*, No. 71, pp. 1, 4-5.

Rivlin, A. M. (1975), "Income Distribution-Can Economists Help?", *American Economic Review Papers and Proceedings*, vol. 65, No. 2, pp. 1-15.

Semple, G. A. (1975), "The Effects of Changes in Household Composition on the Distribution of Income, 1961–73", *Economic Trends*, No. 266, pp. 99–105.

Shorrocks, A. F. (1980), "The Class of Additively Decomposable Inequality Measures", *Econometrica*, vol. 48, pp. 613–625.

Theil, H. (1967), *Economics and Information Theory*, Amsterdam, North Holland.

Tsakloglou, P. (1992), "Multivariate Decomposition of Inequality: Greece 1974, 1982", *Greek Economic Review*, vol. 14, pp. 89–102.

Tsakloglou, P. (1993), "Aspects of Inequality in Greece. Measurement, Decomposition and Intertemporal Change: 1974, 1982", *Journal of Development Economics*, vol. 40, pp. 53–74.

von Weizsäcker, R. K. (1988), "Age Structure and Income Distribution Policy", *Journal of Population Economics*, vol. 1, pp. 33–55.

von Weizsäcker, R. K. (1989), "Demographic Change and Income Distribution", *European Economic Review*, vol. 33, pp. 377–388.

von Weizsäcker, R. K. (1994), "Public Pension Reform, Demographics, and Inequality", Centre for Economic Policy Research, Discussion Paper, No. 978, June.

Wertz, K. L. (1979), "The Measurement of Inequality: Comment", *American Economic Review*, vol. 69, pp. 670–672.

CONTRIBUTORS

Tindara Addabbo is Professor in Economics at the University of Modena and Reggio Emilia (Italy). She holds a Ph.D. in Economics from the European University Institute in Florence and a Master of Science in Economics from the London School of Economics and Political Science. Tindara Addabbo is an associate member of CAPP (Centro Analisi delle Politiche Pubbliche) and of CHILD (Centre for Household Income, Labour and Demographic Economics). She has extensively researched and published on the following topics: labor supply, unpaid work, poverty, income distribution, non-standard employment, evaluation of the effects of public and social policies and economics of performing arts. Among her most recent publications are: "Unpaid work by gender in Italy"; "Extended income estimation and income inequality by gender" (with A. Caiumi); "The gender impact of workfare policies in Italy and the effect of unpaid work" (with M.Baldini), in A. Picchio, ed., *Unpaid Work and the Economy: A Gender Analysis of the Standard of Living* (2003).
e-mail: *addabbo@unimore.it*

Andrea Brandolini is an economist at the Economic Research Department of the Bank of Italy, the Italian central bank. Since 1993 he has been a member of Poverty Commissions established by Italian governments. He is currently a member of the executive board of the Luxembourg Income Study and he serves on the council of the International Association for Research in Income and Wealth. His research interests are: income and wealth distribution, poverty and social exclusion, methods of measurement of economic well-being, the relationship between distributive issues and macroeconomic conditions. Among his recent publications are: "Urban Poverty in Developed Countries" (with P. Cipollone) in *Research*

on *Economic Inequality. Inequality, Welfare and Poverty: Theory and Measurement* (2003); "Earning Dispersion, Low Pay and Household Poverty in Italy, 1977-1998" (with P. Cipollone and P. Sestito) in Cohen, D., Piketty, T., and Saint-Paul, G. (eds.), *The Economics of Rising Inequalities* (2002).
e-mail: *brandolini.andrea@insedia.interbusiness.it*

Giovanni D'Alessio is a statistician at the Economic Research Department of the Bank of Italy, the Italian central bank, where he is the head of the Surveys and Statistical Methods Division. He was a member of the Poverty Commission established by the Italian government in 1992-1993 and a member of the Commission for the definition of means-testing procedures at the Finance Ministry in 1999-2000. His research interests are non-sampling errors, small area estimators, methods of measurement of economic well-being, income and wealth distribution. Among his recent publications are: "Nonresponse Behaviour in the Bank of Italy's Survey of Household Income and Wealth" (with I. Faiella), Banca d'Italia (2002); "Income from Employment and the Return to Schooling in Italy" (with L. Cannari), *Statistica Applicata* (1996).
e-mail: *dalessio.giovanni@insedia.interbusiness.it*

Daniela Del Boca, Ph.D. University of Wisconsin-Madison, is Professor of Economics at the University of Turin. In the last several years she has been an Associate Professor at the Polytechnic of Milan and repeatedly a Visiting Professor at New York University. Daniela Del Boca's work in the area of Labor Economics and of Family Economics has appeared in international journals, among them *The American Economic Review, The Journal of Human Resources, Labour, Structural Change and Economic Dynamics, Review of Income and Wealth*. A member of the Editorial Board of *Labour* and of *The Review of the Economics of the Household and Studies in the European Union*, and a Fellow of the Center for European Studies at NYU, and of IZA (Institute for the Study of Labor, University of Bonn), Daniela Del Boca is the Director of the Centre for Household Income, Labour and Demographics (CHILD), University of Turin.
e-mail:*daniela.delboca@unito.it* .

Lia Fubini teaches Macroeconomics at the Faculty of Political Sciences at the University of Turin. She has widely researched in the field of Economics of Industry and she is currently working on the subject of Labor Market Economics. Her publications include articles and books on topics of labor flexibility, unemployment and employment strategies. Her most recent publications include: "Politiche per il lavoro e flessibilita' in Italia",

Quaderni del dipartimento di Economia dell'Universita' di Pavia (2003); "Il lavoro atipico:tendenze e conseguenze", *Quaderni di rassegna sindacale"* (2001); *Strategie per l'occupazione. Il lavoro tra flessibilita' e tutela* (ed., 2000); e-mail: *lia.fubini@unito.it*

Renata Livraghi is Professor of Economic Policy at the University of Parma. She has published widely in the areas of family and work, income distribution and poverty, human development, human capital, learning and knowledge economics. Her previous books include *L'importanza della riforma universitaria in corso in Italia* (2002); *Sviluppo umano, povertà ed esclusione sociale* (2000); *Gestione del tempo di lavoro e lavoro femminile* (1999); *Distribuzione dei redditi, benessere e lavoro* (1999); *Contratti atipici e tempo di lavoro* (1998).
e-mail: *renatalivraghi@tiscali.it*

Marilena Locatelli holds her Ph.D. from the Polytechnic of Milan and is a Research Fellow at the Department of Economics "C. De Martiis" at the University of Turin. Her research fields are Applied Microeconometrics, Economics of the family and Public Economics. She is a Member of the European Society for Population and a Fellow of the Centre for Household Income, Labour and Demographics (CHILD) at the University of Turin. Among her recent works are: "The impact of childcare characteristics on mothers' employment. Evidence from Italy" (with D. Del Boca and D. Vuri), European Society for Population Economics Conference, New York 2003; "Modelling household choices of dwelling and local public services" (with U. Colombino), CHILD Working Paper 16/2001, European Society for Population Economics Conference, Bilbao 2002; "Employment Decisions of Married Women: Evidence and Explanations" (with D. Del Boca and S. Pasqua), *Labour* (2000).
e-mail: *marilena.locatelli@unito.it*

Silvia Pasqua, Ph.D. in Economics at the University of Pavia and M. Phil. in Economics of Developing Countries at the University of Cambridge (UK), is Assistant Professor of Economics at the University of Turin. She is member of ESPE (European Society for Population Economics) and of the Executive Committee of CHILD (Centre for Household Income, Labour and Demographics). Her research interests are Household Economics, Labour Economics and Development Economics. Her articles appeared in *Labour, Review of Income and Wealth* and in several other volumes of collected essays.
e-mail: *silvia.pasqua@unito.it*

Margherita Repetto-Alaia has been the director of the Italian Cultural Institute in Vancouver (1999-2003) and in Washington, D.C. (1994-1996). A recipient of the Fulbright-Hays Fellowship (1955-1957) and a graduate in Modern European History from the University of Rome, she actively campaigned in Italy in the 1960's and 1970's on behalf of women, for the reform of family laws, equality in the workplace and equal opportunity. A lecturer at Columbia University (1983—1994), she has widely published, first in Italy and later in the US, on the subject of women in modern and contemporary social and political movements. Books: *UDI Union of Italian Women 1944–1978* (with M.Michetti and L. Viviani, 2000, 2nd edition); *The Formation of the Italian Republic/1945-1963* (co-editor with F. Coppa, 1993).
e-mail: *m.repetto@telus.net*

Stefania Rossetti, Ph.D. in Economics from the University of Siena. She works at the Microsimulation Unit of the Italian National Statistics Institute (ISTAT). Her main field of interest is labor economics, with special attention to human capital investment and active labor market policies. Among her recent publications: "Human Capital, Wages and Family Interactions" (with P. Tanda), *Labour* (2000).
e-mail: *strosset@istat.it*

Chiara Saraceno, Professor of Sociology of at the University of Torino, Italy, is the Director of the Interdisciplinary Center on Gender and Women's Studies (CIRSDe) at that university. She has published extensively on gender and the family, on social policies and on poverty and social exclusion. Among her publications: *Mutamenti della famiglia e politiche sociali* (2003); *Social Assistance Dynamics in Europe. National and local welfare regimes* (ed., 2002); "Changing Gender and Family Models: Their Impact on the Social Contract in European Welfare States", in O. Zunz, L. Schoppa and N. Hiwatari (eds.), *Social Contracts under Stress* (2002); *Sociologia della famiglia* (with M. Naldini, 2001); *Separarsi in Italia* (with M. Barbagli, 1998).
e-mail: *chiara.saraceno@unito.it*

Paola Tanda, Ph.D. in Economics from the University of Rome "Tor Vergata". Current position: Senior Researcher at Institute for Studies and Economic Analyses (ISAE) in the Microeconomics Area. Her primary areas of interest are labor economics and social policy analysis, with special interest on family, human capital and education aspects of public policies. Among her publications are: "Human Capital, Wages and Family Interactions" (with S. Rossetti), in *Labour* (2000); "Children and Gender Differentials " (with G. Bottone), in *Labour* (1996).
e-mail: *p.tanda@isae.it*

Edited by: Margherita Reppetto-Alaia

Competing economic interests, political stalemates, internal disparities, and regional economic commonalties cutting across national boundaries are among some of the developments characterizing the difficult process of integrating of the Old Continent and building a united Europe. The monographs in this series intend to explore the practical and institutional aspects of the ongoing process, as well as to elucidate the anthropological, sociological, and cultural issues that pose a challenge to, or on the contrary, may be helping the process of achieving a continental identity. Among the purposes of this series is to make readers aware of the different options that may be available to the people of Europe and to their leaders in defining the borders of the unified continent and in designing its role in the context of global interdependence.

For additional information about this series or for the submission of manuscripts, please contact:
      Margherita Repetto-Alaia
      c/o Peter Lang Publishing, Inc.
      275 Seventh Avenue, 28th Floor
      New York, NY 10001

To order other books in this series, please contact our Customer Service Department:
      (800) 770-LANG (within the U.S.)
      (212) 647-7706 (outside the U.S.)
      (212) 647-7707 FAX

or browse online by series:
      www.peterlangusa.com